D0536905

arms control arrangements for the far east

Hoover Institution Publications

EXPLANATORY NOTE

Beginning on page v is the full and unaltered text of a report, *Arms Control Arrangements for the Far East*, submitted in January 1967 by the Hoover Institution on War, Revolution and Peace to the United States Arms Control and Disarmament Agency in partial fulfillment of the conditions of Contract No. ACDA/IR-53.

The Hoover Institution has prepared this commercial edition of the report as a public service. It is offered for sale at cost. Under terms of the contract cited above, the Institution has requested and received the Agency's permission to distribute the report in this manner. That approval in no way dilutes or modifies the disclaimer found elsewhere in these pages, to the effect that the views expressed in the report are solely those of its authors and do not necessarily represent the views of the Arms Control and Disarmament Agency or any other agency of the United States Government.

arms control arrangements for the far east

The Hoover Institution on War, Revolution and Peace
Stanford University 1967

The Hoover Institution on War, Revolution and Peace, founded at Stanford University in 1919 by the late President Herbert Hoover, is a center for advanced study and research on public and international affairs in the twentieth century. The views expressed in its publications are entirely those of the authors and do not necessarily reflect the views of the Hoover Institution.

This report was prepared under a contract with the United States Arms Control and Disarmament Agency. The judgments expressed in this report are those of the authors and do not necessarily reflect the views of the United States Arms Control and Disarmament Agency or of any other department or agency of the United States Government.

Library of Congress Catalog Card Number: 67-20822
Printed in the United States of America

PREFACE

This report, undertaken on behalf of the Arms Control and Disarmament Agency, outlines steps that could be taken to relax tension and enhance the peaceful resolution of actual and potential conflicts in the Far East. An attempt has been made to determine both what is feasible and what will best serve the interests of the United States.

Work on the project began in June 1964, and research was completed in the main in the Spring of 1966. However, where possible and practical, an attempt was made to take into account major developments through the Summer of 1966 and to benefit from some of the findings up to that time of related research on Communist China. During the entire period, many scholars contributed to the study. Thus, the report that has emerged in the end is a team effort. It is almost impossible to attribute authorship of individual chapters exclusively to any one person; first drafts of chapters, often based on the research findings of several persons, have been prepared by one or two individuals. They have been subjected to team discussion and, not infrequently, fundamental alteration. While this method has its inherent dangers, we believe that the final product embodies the research experience and expert knowledge of all participants wihtout suffering from incoherence and disunity. A remarkably free give-and-take attitude and esprit de corps has been maintained throughout by the entire research team.

With this in mind, one may attribute specific sections of the report to the following researchers as persons primarily responsible for the initial drafts.

In Part I, Chapter 1, "The Conceptual Framework," Yuan-li Wu with the advice of Claude A. Buss, Dennis J. Doolin, Robert C. North, and Anthony E. Sokol;

Chapter 2, "Principal ACD Measures Since World War II and Their Relevance to the Far East," Dennis J. Doolin with the assistance of Jeanne T. Friedman and Somsak Rakwijit;

In Part II, Chapter 1, "General Characteristics of the Region and Subregions Which Might Affect ACD," Dennis J. Doolin and Yuan-li Wu;

Chapter 2, "The Extraregional Powers," Claude A. Buss, J. Chester Cheng, and Anthony E. Sokol, with the assistance of Joseph Chung and Jason L. Finkle;

Chapter 3, "Conflicts, Tensions, and ACD: A Country Survey," Dennis J. Doolin with the assistance of Leonard A. Humphreys;

In Part III, Chapter 1, "Attitudes of Regional Nations Toward ACD," Janet Colson and Leonard A. Humphreys;

Chapter 2, "Limitations and Possibilities of Arms Control and Disarmament in the Far East," Janet Colson and Yuan-li Wu in conjunction with Dennis J. Doolin and Leonard A. Humphreys;

Chapter 3, "Implications for the National Interests of the United States," Dennis J. Doolin and Yuan-li Wu in conjunction with Janet Colson and Leonard A. Humphreys.

Throughout the preparation of all these chapters, Claude A. Buss, Janet Colson, Dennis J. Doolin, Leonard A. Humphreys, Anthony E. Sokol, and Yuan-li Wu have been in continuous consultation; they have benefited from general discussion and review by Ernest M. Moore and Robert C. North, as well as James J. Dalton, F. Tomasson Jannuzi, and George J. Lerski (the last three of the Asia Foundation). They have been especially fortunate in being able to draw upon the experience and advice of Kia-ngau Chang, Chung-sieu Chen, Shen-Yu Dai, Franklin W. Houn, Lawrence J. Lau, Hsien C. Ling, Grace Hsiao Wu, and Roland Yu-min Wu in matters concerning Communist China. In the use of Soviet literature, the assistance of Andrea H. Chadwick has been most valuable.

Certain working papers dealing with each of the regional countries have had to be prepared preliminary to the final draft of this report. Though not included in the present volume, the following attributions may be made for these papers. Japan--Kia-ngau Chang, Leonard A. Humphreys, Nobutaka Ike, and Kurt Steiner; South Korea--Joseph Chung; Taiwan--Chung-sieu Chen, Hsien C. Ling, Grace Hsiao Wu, and Yuan-li Wu; the Philippines--Claude A. Buss; Indonesia--Anthony E. Sokol and Susan E. Young; Malaysia and Singapore--Anthony E. Sokol and Susan E. Young; South Vietnam, Cambodia, and Laos--Claude A. Buss, Dennis J. Doolin, and Somsak Rakwijit; Thailand--Claude A. Buss and Somsak Rakwijit; Burma--James J. Dalton and V. V. Ramana Murti; Ceylon--Dennis J. Doolin, George J. Lerski, and V. V. Ramana Murti; India--Amiya Barat, Andrea H. Chadwick, F. Thomasson Jannuzi, and V. V. Ramana Murti; Pakistan--Amiya Barat and George J. Lerski; Australia and New Zealand--Robert G. Boyd. Anthony E. Sokol has prepared a section on regional pacts and conferences.

In addition, Leonard A. Humphreys is responsible for all necessary studies on the armed forces of the regional countries. Janet Colson, with the assistance of Susan E. Young, has worked indefatigably to accomplish all the detailed checking and a myriad of other important tasks.

On would be amiss if one failed to mention the invaluable assistance the researchers have received from substantive discussions with representatives of the Arms Control and Disarmament Agency or to register the cooperative spirit in which such discussion has been held.

The project staff, Caroline L. Bliss, Joan R. Kleinman, Ramona Miranda, and Nessa L. Robosson, have given unstintingly of themselves in working long hours to meet deadlines. In addition to occasional secretarial and editorial assistance from a number of other persons, acknowledgement is due to Julia F. Austin, Sally J. Vanders, and the late Winifred A. Teague for their administrative assistance.

Finally, I should like to express my pleasure at having had the privilege of working with such a group of distinguished scholars and at having been given the opportunity to learn from them. While individual members of the research team may not fully endorse each point expressed in the report, they are in general agreement. All remaining errors and shortcomings are solely the responsibility of the undersigned and his immediate associates.

YUAN-LI WU
Arms Control Project
The Hoover Institution

TABLE OF CONTENTS

PREFACE v

PART I

CONCEPTUAL FRAMEWORK AND PRINCIPAL ACD MEASURES

CHAPTER 1: CONCEPTUAL FRAMEWORK

Introduction 1
Some Preliminary Questions 2
Questions Applicable to Each Country in the Region 4
Acceptability of Different ACD Measures on the Basis of Benefit and Cost Comparison Independent of Adjustment Problems 7
Acceptability of ACD Measures Based on Ease of Adjustment. 8

CHAPTER 2: PRINCIPAL ACD MEASURES SINCE WORLD WAR II AND THEIR RELEVANCE TO THE FAR EAST

Introduction 11
Procedure 11
Analysis of the Attitudes of Major Powers 12
Regional Responses to Nonregional Proposals 12
Regional and Communist Chinese Proposals for ACD 14
General Subject Matter 15
Major Regional Proposals 15
Summary 16

PART II

REGIONAL AND EXTRAREGIONAL FACTORS AFFECTING ACD

CHAPTER 1: GENERAL CHARACTERISTICS OF THE REGIONS AND SUB-REGIONS WHICH MIGHT AFFECT ACD

Introduction 18
Common Characteristics of the Region as a Whole 20
Alternative Subregional Groupings 24

CHAPTER 2: THE EXTRAREGIONAL POWERS

Introduction 28
The Communist Powers 30
The Non-Communist Powers 35
The Strategy and Tactics of the Communist Powers 38
Policies of the Non-Communist Powers Since 1946 42
Historical Attitudes Toward Arms Control and Disarmament . 45
Conclusion 50

CHAPTER 3: CONFLICTS, TENSIONS, AND ACD: A COUNTRY SURVEY

Introduction 53
East Asia 53
Southeast Asia 60
South Asia 70
Southwest Pacific. 74

PART III

ATTITUDES, LIMITATIONS, AND POSSIBILITIES OF ACD

CHAPTER 1: ATTITUDES OF REGIONAL NATIONS TOWARD ACD

Introduction 76
Method of Determining Attitudes 76
Test Groupings 77
Weapons 81
Armed Forces and Deployment. 90
Military Expenditures 91
Aspects of Implementation, Organization, and Verification 92
Conclusion 103

CHAPTER 2: LIMITATIONS AND POSSIBILITIES OF ARMS CONTROL AND DISARMAMENT IN THE FAR EAST

Introduction 104
Acceptability of Arms Control and Disarmament Measures. . . 105
Sources of Threat to Regional Security and Their Effects on the Feasibility of Arms Control and Disarmament 106
Possible Arms Control and Disarmament Arrangements for the Region. 110
Possible Regional and Extraregional Response to Arms Control and Disarmament in the Far East 117
Implementation -- Sequence and Priority 119
Conclusion 120

CHAPTER 3: IMPLICATIONS FOR THE NATIONAL INTERESTS OF THE UNITED STATES

Introduction 124
Proposal I: A Guarantee of Defense Aid to India By One or More of the Nuclear Powers, Excluding Communist China 125
Proposal II: A Series of Voluntary Renunciations on the Part of the Regional Countries 126
Proposal III: The Formation of a Regional or Subregional Joint Defense and Mutual Assistance Arrangement 127
Proposal IV: Regional Police Force for Limited Peace-Keeping Functions Such as Observation of Border Armistices and So Forth 128
Proposal V: A Series of Joint Technical, Economic, and Scientific Programs 128
Proposal VI: Sponsorship of Regional Informal Discussions and Educational Programs with Regard to ACD Problems 129

APPENDICES

APPENDIX I, PART A: MAJOR NONREGIONAL ACD PROPOSALS 135
PART B: REGIONAL ACD PROPOSALS 138
PART C: THE MATRIX. 140

APPENDIX II: REGIONAL ATTITUDINAL MATRIX 175

APPENDIX III: REGIONAL CONFLICT AND TENSION CHART 203

INDEX 205

LIST OF TABLES

Asia -- Area and Population 19

Intra-subregional and Inter-subregional Trade (1962): Imports 22

Intra-subregional and Inter-subregional Trade (1962): Exports 23

Regional Response Toward the Regulation of the Use of Outer Space and Other ACD Measures 121

Response of Individual Countries to the ACD Measures by Major Categories 122

Suggested ACD Proposals -- United States National Interests 131

PART I

CONCEPTUAL FRAMEWORK AND PRINCIPAL ACD MEASURES

CHAPTER 1: CONCEPTUAL FRAMEWORK

INTRODUCTION

Scope of the Study

The present study on regional arms control and disarmament measures in the Far East has been undertaken by the Hoover Institution under contract with the United States Arms Control and Disarmament Agency. According to the terms of the contract, the area of investigation consists of three major categories of problems. These are:

1) ". . . the content of arms control and disarmament measures (ACD) and the possibilities and limitations of arms control and disarmament arrangements in the regions of the Far East and in such subregional areas as may be considered to represent appropriate groupings for these purposes."

2) ". . . the interaction of regional matters with arms control and disarmament arrangements which might be concluded among the great powers," and

3) ". . . organizational and procedural matters."

In general, Parts I and II of the report deal with problems in the first category; Part III is concerned with inferences based on the first two parts and with policy and operational issues which constitute the second and third categories of problems stated in the terms of reference.

Definitions

To begin with, certain definitions are necessary. The following are adopted for our purpose. First, we understand by arms all instruments of violence which can be used to inflict physical harm or damage. Second, by arms control is meant any control or regulation of the possession of, use of, experimentation in, and/or traffic in arms by nation-states, as well as the creation of conditions under which arms control might be possible. Disarmament is therefore a special form of arms control. Third, for the purpose of this study, we shall consider as "intraregional":

1. Japan, including Okinawa, 2. South Korea, 3. Taiwan, 4. the Philippines, 5. Indonesia, 6. Malaysia, including Singapore, 7. South Vietnam, 8. Cambodia, 9. Laos, 10. Thailand, 11. Burma, 12. Ceylon, 13. India, 14. Pakistan, 15. Australia, and 16. New Zealand.

On the other hand, we shall consider as "extraregional":

1. the United States, 2. the Soviet Union, 3. Communist China, 4. North Korea, and 5. North Vietnam. Disregarding the Asian extraregional powers, it is clear that the 16 countries in the region can be further grouped into "subregions." For instance, 1 to 3 inclusive may be regarded as the geographical subregion of East Asia; 4 to 11 inclusive constitute Southeast Asia; 12, 13 and 14 are often described as South Asia; 15 and 16 represent the Southwest Pacific subregion.

Furthermore, it is understood in this study that the purpose of any arms control proposal or agreement is not to eliminate conflict *per se*, but rather to eliminate (or markedly reduce) the possibilities that nation-states may attempt to resolve conflicts by force or violence, or, at the very least, to reduce the damage caused by such acts as well as any other adverse effect of such acts if their occurrence cannot be prevented. This is, of course, not to preclude the possibility of eliminating or resolving some conflicts.

Research Attitude

Finally, it should be pointed out that while this report aims at the development of ideas which would be useful at the level of policy determination and ACD negotiations, its usefulness is predicated upon an objective analysis of the nature, feasibility, and limitation of ACD measures in the region. Accordingly, in considering these problems in Parts I and II, value judgments are not permitted to intrude. The applicability of a given ACD measure in the region or one of its subregions, for instance, is examined without any judgment as to its desirability on the basis of the national interest of any individual state, regional or extraregional. It is important that this approach be understood by the readers of the report. Such criteria as national security, the leadership of the United States in the free world, the proper attitude in dealing with the Soviet Union and other Communist nations, etc., in so far as they affect ACD in the region and are affected by it, will be reserved for discussion in Part III and in the concluding observations only.

SOME PRELIMINARY QUESTIONS

A preliminary and general survey of certain aspects of ACD and of the region appear essential prior to any detailed analysis of the applicability of ACD to the individual countries in the region. Such a survey should afford us (1) an understanding of the characteristics of past ACD proposals and their relevance to the region; (2) an appreciation, albeit in broad strokes, of certain characteristics of the region which may bear on ACD, with particular reference to the homogeneous and heterogeneous factors in the region as a whole and in its subregions; and (3) a review of the attitudes and policies of the principal extraregional powers which must be taken into account by the regional powers. A discussion of these points is contained in the several chapters which follow immediately below.

Previous ACD Proposals and Their Relevance

A large number of ACD proposals and measures have been advanced since World War II. An analysis of the principal ones would constitute an appropriate starting point. A number of basic questions may be asked in this connection. For instance, what are the basic elements, common characteristics, and patterns of divergence of the ACD proposals made to date? What are the principal reasons for agreement or disagreement with regard to the objects, methods, and organization of control and inspection? How relevant are some of the major aspects of previous ACD proposals if applied to the Far East? Of what utility are previously established ACD treaties and agreements, collective security systems, and other international arrangements in minimizing, limiting, and prohibiting the use of force and violence? Primary attention will be given to the comparison of United States and Soviet proposals.

The analysis of previous ACD measures and proposals can be made by categorizing the major contents of said proposals under certain convenient headings, such as types of weapons, total or phased disarmament, inspection systems proposed or used, number of countries involved, adherence of countries not directly participating in the agreement, etc.

An attempt should be made in this connection to answer the question whether ACD measures and proposals advanced to date have any relevance to the countries in the Far East, and whether these countries have hitherto expressed any views toward these measures. Account will be taken of the basic attitudes of the United States as shown in her proposals and of the regional powers as seen in their responses and the proposals originating from them.

Nuclear Arms and the Nuclear Arms Race

In anticipation of such a survey, one can probably indulge in some speculations. Most ACD proposals that are more than pious hopes or bromides voiced for foreign and/or domestic consumption have been concerned with the Soviet-Western arms race involving nuclear weapons. It is widely held that nuclear warfare on a total war basis is intolerable. It is also generally agreed that there is danger of a limited war escalating to nuclear, total war, thereby making limited warfare more dangerous than it might be otherwise. Another widely shared view is that, in the course of the nuclear arms race, atmospheric testing entails serious health hazards to countries not directly involved as well as to countries conducting the tests. The question whether or not these beliefs have been fully verified is immaterial for our purpose, for it is clear that they are widely held and have caused many governments to advocate controls that would curb the nuclear arms race, reduce the possibility of accidental war or escalation of limited war, and diminish health hazards that might be caused by nuclear tests.

Given this context, there are many reasons for a country to express itself openly in favor of nuclear arms control, the nuclear test ban, and other related measures and proposals, especially if the country does not possess nuclear weapons at present and does not envisage either an absolute need to possess them or the possibility of possessing them in the foreseeable future. Since such controls and disarmament proposals would not directly necessitate any action on a nation's part beyond some general statement of views, its vital interests are not touched by any need to adjust its policies and activities.

The prohibition of nuclear weapons now possessed by only five states would automatically increase the relative power of some of those nations which neither have them nor expect to have them in the near future. The importance of conventional weapons and raw manpower (such as is possessed by Communist China) would be proportionately enhanced.

Consequently, past pronouncements in favor of control of nuclear weapons cannot be regarded *per se* as reliable indicators of a nation's real attitude toward limitation and/or control of conventional weapons.

Arms and Their Use

In the circumstances, how do we determine the possibilities and limitations of ACD arrangements for the Far East if the pronouncements of the governments of many countries in the region are not truly indicative of their real attitudes? We might approach the problem by postulating the following:

First, arms are coercive instruments. Their control or reduction will be resisted if conditions obtain or are expected to obtain where coercion is either required, will be required, or is contemplated. Such conditions include:

1) fear of conflict with another state or a domestic situation that may require coercive resolution;

2) a judgment that recourse to arms is the better and more expedient method of conflict resolution; and

3) a capability on the part of the country to maintain the requisite military establishment.

Second, although no conditions exist (or are expected to exist) that call for either an increase in armaments or even maintenance of the *status quo* in armaments, ACD may be resisted if a country perceives the costs incurred by ACD to exceed anticipated benefits. For example, the armed forces may be highly regarded as: (1) a status symbol; (2) a means of creating a sense of national identity; (3) agents for skill formation; (4) instruments needed under existing international or regional agreements; and (5) a vehicle for social mobility.

Third, arms control may be resisted because of resentment of any interference with a country's sovereign right to do as its pleases, independent of any considerations of benefit and cost.

Fourth, a military clique or elite and/or a political party may fear that it would lose power through being a party to an ACD agreement.

Fifth, there may be a lack of faith in extranational guarantees.

QUESTIONS APPLICABLE TO EACH COUNTRY IN THE REGION

Pursuing the question of those conditions which work against either the formulation or implementation of a viable ACD proposal or agreement, an attempt must be made to answer the following questions for each of the countries in the Far East.

Sources of Conflict

1) Is X (the given country) at present in armed conflict with any other country, either regional or extraregional? If so, what is the level of severity (i. e., total war, limited war, guerrilla activities, insurgencies, etc.)?

2) Does X anticipate a conflict with any other country, either regional or extraregional -- (a) as a result of continuing current policies and/or (b) as a result of changes in domestic or foreign policies? For example, is the power balance likely to be changed so as to affect X through the development of nuclear or other modern weapons systems by another regional power, or by an extraregional power, such as Communist China? Would such a development necessitate adjustments in the foreign policy of X? Would it directly or indirectly increase the probability of conflict?

X may not at present be faced with a situation which one would normally describe as conflict, but there may be a state of tension which can be aggravated, thus developing into a conflict. For example, a dispute between nationality groups or religious groups, which may or may not involve external powers, may create tension, and increasing tension may ultimately lead to open conflict. Such areas of tension would also need to be identified.

3) What is the nature of the present or potential conflict, real or perceived?

a) Border dispute? Dispute in international or territorial waters (e. g., over fishery rights)?

b) Subversion or other antiregime activity sponsored by a foreign country?

c) Civil war which either results from purely internal struggles or has either identified or unidentified foreign sponsorship?

d) Alliance with or favorable disposition toward the enemy or enemies of neighboring state(s)? Economic privileges, favored treatment, or aid granted to such enemy country(ies) of neighboring state(s)?

e) Problem of minority nationalities? Restriction of population movements?

f) Irridentist movement?

g) Discrimination by X against imports from another country? Against nationals of another country? Is discrimination reciprocated?

h) Competition in dealings with third country (for markets, sources of supply, foreign capital, foreign aid, etc.)?

i) Politico-economic claims of a state in the region or territory of a third regional state?

j) Politico-economic claims of a state in the region or territory of an extraregional state?

k) Misunderstanding of mutual intent?

l) Expansionist policy or sentiments of X toward neighbor(s)?

m) Unsatisfactory domestic conditions which are not or, possibly, cannot remain localized or which demand arousing national emotions to cover up real difficulties?

n) Fear of upsetting the present balance of power in favor of an opponent?

o) Expansionist policy or sentiments of an extraregional state toward state(s) in the region?

Whatever may be the basic cause(s) of the conflict(s), it should be borne in mind that conflicts may be self-reenforcing. One conflict may lead to another; domestic unrest for instance, may invite foreign intervention.

The Extraregional Context

In order to answer the last question in the list -- item (o) -- perceptions of United States policy by the countries in question must be determined. An attempt must also be made to postulate the policies of the Soviet Union, Communist China, North Korea, and North Vietnam, as perceived by the policymakers of country X, together with possible alternative policies on the part of these Communist countries. We must also gauge what effect the current Sino-Soviet conflict has on ACD within the region as a whole, as well as the effect upon ACD in subregional groupings and individual countries within the region. This will be treated more fully in points (16) and (17) below.

Intensity of Conflict

4) We must also estimate the intensity and historical significance of a given conflict or state of tension. Is it a conflict of long standing? Is it being aggravated by propaganda? Does the conflict have a rational basis or has the basis become primarily an emotional one?

The Power Potential: Arms or Other Means for Resolution of the Conflict(s)

5) What is the power potential of the country in question? In determining the power potential, we must consider such factors as geographical location, communications net, area, population, natural resources for its own use, natural resources needed by other states, industrial capacity (including transportation facilities) and prospects for expansion of this capacity, ideological/national characteristics and traditions, leadership, motivation, morale of the populace (or the politically relevant sector of the populace), etc. What countries in the region are potentially capable of developing nuclear weapons and modern arms systems in the near future? What are the incentives for the development of such weapons in these countries? What factors would tend to discourage such development?

6) Can conflict be resolved by means other than war? If so, what are these means? What is the role of communications in conflict resolution?

In other words, what <u>principal alternatives are there to armaments</u>? Here we must deal with the possibilities for collective security through the United Nations, SEATO, or some other organization, either for the entire region or for smaller segments of it. Attention should be given (as mentioned earlier) to past successes, or lack of same, in collective security arrangements as well as the feasibility of such arrangements for the Far East or subregions therein.

It would also seem that there are certain prerequisites for any ACD system worthy of the name. Collective action of any type is impossible without agreement among the participants on certain fundamentals. First and foremost, the parties concerned must either see the advantages of such action <u>or</u> some form of pressure must be available which will move a given state, against its will, to participate in a collective agreement. It should be recognized that, to secure a meaningful agreement, coercion of some kind (political censure or economic sanctions, for instance) may have to be used in lieu of another form of coercion (military force) as a means of resolving conflicts.

Minimum Level of Armaments

7) At the outset, we stated that ACD proposals should seek to eliminate or reduce military resolution of conflicts, rather than to eliminate conflict

itself. Just as conflict is an inescapable concomitant of a dynamic world, it is virtually impossible to envisage a world (or an area of the world) without arms. Every nation requires a certain level of coercive hardware (determined by both the nature of the society and the perceptions of the elite) for routine police functions. In other words, certain domestic conditions require coercive measures, and the absence of such measures might allow what would otherwise be a localized evil to spread outside a given country. Thus, we must give some attention to the level of armaments and armed forces necessary for domestic tranquility (or, at least, for the isolation of a malaise). As the level of armaments and armed forces will obviously vary from state to state, the reasons for this disparity will have to be understood by, and must be agreeable to, the parties to any ACD arrangement. Furthermore, steps will have to be taken to ensure that this disparity does not become a threat to other countries.

Supply of Arms and Capability of Armed Forces

8) What is the present level of armaments by major categories? How are such armaments obtained? What is the present capacity of domestic arms production? Is it possible that country X might produce nuclear weapons or other weapons that would appreciably affect the balance of power? Does country X have the material and/or technical resources to produce such weapons? If certain categories of arms are imported, where do they come from? Is the import overt or clandestine? If clandestine, how are the arms brought into the country? How are the imports financed? How much of the imports are financed through foreign aid. If imports predominate, can the imported arms be given proper maintenance locally?

What is the present level of the armed forces? Of trained reserves and untrained manpower? What is the method of recruitment? What is the organization for mobilization? Are the armed forces being expressly prepared for some specific (or specific category of) conflict?

Comparison of Levels of Armed Strength and Significance Thereof

It is important that we know (a) the present level of the armed strength of country X , (b) the level that X can maintain on its own, (c) the level that might be attained with outside help, and (d) the level X deems necessary for domestic or external purposes. These levels must be appraised on the basis of the effective strength that can be mobilized and brought to bear in a conflict within a given time with or without outside assistance. The relative levels of (a), (b), (c), and (d) will have an important effect on the acceptability of any ACD proposal and the meaningfulness of acceptance. It is not inconceivable that the present level may be too low to allow performance of essential tasks.

Economic Cost and Benefit of Arms

9) The economic cost of maintaining or adding to a given military establishment, including arms and manpower, must be measured in terms of the useful alternatives in which the resources devoted to it might otherwise have been engaged.

One should therefore ask: Would these resources have been unemployed if they had not been absorbed by the military establishment and its supporting industries? Are the resources and manpower such that, if freed from military use, they would be readily absorbed by the civilian economy? Or, would it be necessary to make special arrangements (retraining, relocation, employment exchanges, etc.) before they could be absorbed by the civilian sector? To what extent has the economy suffered because of the military sector, in terms of economic growth, for instance? Does country X have an economic development program which has been held back because of military expenditure?

Would some arrangement for regional economic cooperation (the Colombo Plan, for instance) be enhanced if some ACD measure is implemented? Could it be used as a starting point for ACD? Would the economic development of

X be otherwise advanced through greater international investment and greater trade?

How large is defense spending in relation to the GNP and the budget? Would arms reduction relieve fiscal and inflationary pressures and problems by increasing production in the civilian economy or would they cause unemployment? What is the effect on the exports of X if other countries (regional or extraregional) reduce their arms expenditures? What is the effect on imports if X reduces arms spending? What if a specific ACD proposal actually requires an increase in spending (because of the enforcement measures, for instance)? Is this likely in the case of the Far Eastern nations.

What advantages does the civilian economy derive from the maintenance of the military establishment apart from the role of military spending as a source of effective demand? Does military research contribute to the civilian economy? What is the state of military research and development? What is the training and educational role of the military?

Political Costs of Arms

10) Aside from the economic costs entailed in armaments or an arms race, we must consider the political costs of maintaining armed forces at their present levels; that is, the political costs measured in both domestic, intraregional, and international tensions. How can alternative solutions be provided to the problem of establishing a viable, effective ACD arrangement, maintaining a reasonable level of security, and proffering an attractive possibility of reducing the military posture?

ACCEPTABILITY OF DIFFERENT ACD MEASURES ON THE BASIS OF BENEFIT AND COST COMPARISON INDEPENDENT OF ADJUSTMENT PROBLEMS

11) The relative acceptability of different types of ACD measures, either unilateral or multilateral, should be determined in the light of the intensity of a given conflict (present or potential), together with the costs of armaments. Without going into the details that will be discussed in the "ACD matrix," some of the alternatives to be considered are, for instance:

a) Declarations against the use, testing, and/or dissemination of nuclear weapons;

b) Declarations against the use of various types of weapons (chemicals, heavy offensive weapons, biological weapons, and so forth);

c) Limitations on production or importation of certain weapons;

d) Limitations on levels of armaments and armed forces -- either an absolute ceiling, percentage reduction, or maintenance of specific ratios, allowance being made for specific, national needs (on this point, refer to (7) above);

e) Restrictions in regard to the deployment of forces or armaments;

f) Creation of neutralized or demilitarized zones between countries, with appropriate inspection;

g) A limitation of military budgets, presupposing the formulation of a standardized budget and accounts system;

h) International and/or regional agreements not to train, grant refuge, or otherwise support troops or voluntary paramilitary organizations of another country;

i) Prohibition of antiforeign propaganda.

ACCEPTABILITY OF ACD MEASURES BASED ON EASE OF ADJUSTMENT

12) It is conceivable that a country sees no current or prospective conflict, either domestic or foreign, that requires the maintenance of armed forces and freedom in their use and deployment at the present level. However, the nation might nevertheless be unable to effect the adjustments required by ACD. Similarly, while arms reduction as a general goal may be acceptable, certain methods of implementation may be unacceptable. The following sections include questions designed to provide data on these points.

Economic Adjustment

Acceptance of an ACD arrangment may hinge upon the successful conversion of the economy to a new basis with a different level of military expenditure (refer to (9) above). A crucial question is: Can the officers and men and capacity of arms production be employed elsewhere? What adjustments, tensions, dissatisfactions, etc. would be attendant on such a reemployment? What are these alternative sources of demand? Are the industrial and institutional structures sufficiently flexible? Does the economic interest most affected by the adoption of ACD also control the center of political decision making? Is the scale of economic adjustment manageable?

Political Adjustment

Politically, the problem of adjustment to ACD may be no less traumatic. First of all, is the military establishment of the country used in backing, maintaining, or strengthening the current ruling class or clique? What is the status of the military in the country? Will the source of the ACD proposal prejudice it in the eyes of country X? Will the form in which it is presented preclude its acceptance? What psychological preparations of the population and the political leadership are needed? What is their present attitude toward the concept of the "just war?" What is their present attitude toward ACD in general and toward the use or prohibition of specific weapons systems? How readily can the leaders become accustomed to working with limited freedom in the use of coercive means because of ACD? Will other parts of the power spectrum be substituted for the use of armed forces?

Possible Discrepancies Between Perception and Objective Conditions

13) Another problem (perhaps an insoluble one) concerns the possible divergence between national interests as perceived by the relevant decision makers and "real" or "true" national interests. It may be in the true national interest of a country to agree to participate in an ACD agreement, yet the decision makers may consider any such arrangement to be detrimental or humiliating. Conversely, it is possible that a nation may agree to some ACD proposal, yet when the proposal is implemented, it is found to be either resented or actually contrary to the nation's national interest.

However, a distinction should be made between the effects of actions <u>taken</u> on the basis of a mistaken perception and those of actions <u>not taken</u> because of a mistaken perception. If the costs of an ACD measure are underestimated or the benefits overestimated, the measure would prove unstable even though it may have been accepted. On the other hand, if the costs are overestimated or the benefits underestimated, rejection of the ACD measure would, by virtue of the rejection, preclude any opportunity to demonstrate by implementation the error of the original perception.

Conditions for Implementation of ACD Measures

14) Once the ACD arrangements considered feasible in this study have been determined, we must ascertain what measures are necessary to implement them. We must find out how and by whom such arrangements can be verified, controlled, and supervised; the possibilities of evasion; the reliability of various controls; and whether control methods will reduce or intensify

regional and/or international tensions. With reference to the Far East, what special kinds of inspection and verification would be most appropriate to the countries of the region? Which would be the most acceptable (or the least objectionable)? Who would set it up? The United Nations? Some other international agency? A regional agency? Would the same kind be effective for the region as a whole, or would it have to be differentiated according to individual countries or subregions? Would inspectors of certain races or of certain other states be welcomed or even allowed in these countries? What other ways exist, aside from control teams, to ensure that the ACD agreement is kept? Could civilian populations be utilized for that purpose? -- In brief, what political, economic, psychological, and/or organizational difficulties exist or are likely to exist that would make implementation of an ACD agreement difficult, infeasible, or unacceptable? What can extraregional powers do to reduce tensions and prepare the ground for effective ACD and attendant implementation? Under present conditions, it would be unrealistic to discuss an inspection-enforcement force that would be capable of operating contrary to the desires of the "great powers" or their interests, however construed. Thus, the question arises as to whether or not the "great powers" should be a party to the inspection-enforcement force. However, this may raise the spectre of "great-power chauvinism." Possibly the answer lies in a purely regional inspection force with firm commitments of the "great powers" not to interject themselves. It is probable, however, that such a commitment may itself require an inspection-enforcement force. (It would seem that escalation is inherent even in ACD proposals!) Furthermore, on account of local conditions, verification and inspection would have to be conducted on the spot rather than by technically sophisticated, long distance schemes such as have been advanced in regard to nuclear ACD proposals.

Finally, inasmuch as inspection would curtail the independence of a nation's decision making to some extent, we must seek to determine, through a consideration of various possible arrangements, the degree to which each would necessarily impinge upon national sovereignty and how each proposal would be received. This is particularly relevant in the event of violation (real or suspected) of the ACD agreement.

Nature of Sequential and Concentrated Action Required

15) Another variable that may make an ACD arrangement unacceptable or otherwise restrict its applicability or efficacy is the plethora of international agreements already in force, such as mutual defense pacts, alliances, and the various less formal relationships with intra- and/or extraregional powers. Hence the following questions:

What concurrent or sequential actions are required on the part of other powers if any particular arms control measure is to be applied to a particular country? Would concurrent action and a multination approach enhance the chances for acceptance of the measure and a successful implementation of the measure? In this regard, it will be necessary to attempt to determine specific actions needed to be taken by some other country for each country in the region.* Possibly (hopefully), specific common features can be identified for certain groups of countries.

Interaction with Extraregional Powers

The problems of interaction mentioned above lead to the second category of major problems in the "Statement of Work."

16) Why are some of the major extraregional powers deeply concerned with events in the Far East? How have these concerns been expressed? How important strategically, militarily, politically, and economically is the region under study to each major power? What are the possible effects on United

---

* Such as, would a basic reorganization of the United Nations be required?

States, Soviet, and Chinese Communist policies if certain arms control measures are introduced in the Far East? Each proposed arms control measure should be examined with a view to the following contingencies:

a) acceptable, and removes some cause(s) of conflict;

b) acceptable, but does not remove any cause of conflict;

c) unacceptable and unenforced due to failure to remove some form of conflict;

d) unacceptable and unenforced due to adjustment problems;

e) unacceptable for (c) and/or (d) but enforced from outside against the will of X.

And, finally, what are the possible effects of these agreements on the aforementioned "great powers' " policies toward one another and toward the countries in the Far East? This question must be pursued, for it is possible that, while reducing tensions for a time, an ACD arrangement for the Far East may indeed increase international tensions in the long run.

Effect of Extraregional ACD Measures on the Far East

17) As the reverse of (16), we should consider the possible effects of ACD arrangements reached among the "great powers" on countries in the Far East. Would such arrangements help to remove some of the causes of conflict, thereby making countries in the region more amenable to ACD arrangements?

United States Policy Implications

18) Finally, what specific adjustments in United States policy, if any, would the conclusions in (16) and (17) indicate?

Negotiation and Procedural Matters

19) Questions of procedure, organization, and negotiation (the third category of problems to be investigated in this report) would follow from the conclusions drawn on points (11) and (18).

CHAPTER 2: PRINCIPAL ACD MEASURES SINCE WORLD WAR II AND THEIR RELEVANCE TO THE FAR EAST

INTRODUCTION

In this chapter, we propose to examine the contents of past ACD proposals with five objectives in mind:

1) to determine the attitudes of the major powers, as evinced in the proposals, including -- (a) areas of substantial agreement between the United States and the Soviet Union; (b) areas of substantial disagreement between the two countries; (c) areas where earlier disagreements have been reduced, due to a shift by either the United States or the Soviet Union; and (d) areas where there was early agreement but now disagreement because of a policy shift by either country;

2) to determine the attitudes of regional (i.e., Far Eastern) powers to the proposals of the major powers on the basis of identifiable responses in public statements;

3) to determine the attitudes of regional powers as seen in their own proposals;

4) to determine the relationship(s), if any, of past proposals to the region under study; and

5) to determine those elements essential to certain ACD arrangements that have not been included in previous ACD proposals.

PROCEDURE

To this end, a matrix has been constructed that contains a total of 215 alternative ACD positions and/or propositions.[1] Against these 215 alternatives, a representative sample of major nonregional proposals (in the sense that the origin of each proposal, at least in part, was extraregional -- e.g., Western) was cast to determine consistencies, inconsistencies, similitudes, contrasts, and/or lacunae.

Numerous ACD proposals and counterproposals, as well as a plethora of official statements and opinions relating to ACD but distinct from formal positions taken in negotiations, have been advanced since the end of the Second World War. It was felt that an analysis of these proposals, counterproposals, statements, and opinions could serve as a starting point in studying the possibilities and prospects for ACD arrangements in the Far East.

The great majority of all post-1945 ACD proposals have been concerned primarily with the regulation of nuclear weapons and/or the prevention of great-power conflict(s). As a result, most proposals have dealt with United States-Soviet relations, with emphasis on their European aspects, and only a few of the proposals or provisions have touched, even tangentially, upon the problem of ACD in the Far East.

After completing a general survey of all ACD proposals and official statements from 1945 to July 25, 1963 (the date of the Nuclear Test Ban Treaty), 75 major proposals of nonregional origin were selected for closer examination.[2] The method of selection was based on one or more of the following criteria: (1) the special importance of the proposal in serving as a basis for negotiation; (2) the introduction of modifications or new aspects that, in retrospect, have proved to have an important bearing on later negotiations; and (3) apparent and/or direct relevance of the proposal to ACD in the Far East. For reasons of convenience, Communist China's proposals were not considered among the nonregional ones but were reserved for later examination with the regional proposals.

This general survey indicated that, even though the content of ACD proposals often varied considerably from one another, it was possible to develop a basic structure -- described in the matrix -- by means of which any and all ACD proposals could be compared, contrasted, and analyzed.

ANALYSIS OF THE ATTITUDES OF MAJOR POWERS

For our purposes, the evidence provided by both the matrix and the variant representation is relatively negative. While 23 points of "substantial agreement" are indicated, a closer look shows that the common ground is in reality less extensive than the figures might indicate. For example, 15 points of agreement deal with what should be controlled, but only 6 deal with how control should be effected.

Further, several points of crucial disagreement render the areas of agreement academic. General agreement on what should be controlled means little if one side is adamant in demanding that ACD should proceed before the establishment of control machinery (the Soviet position) while the other side is equally firm in demanding that the control machinery should be established before proceeding with ACD (the United States position). Other examples could be cited.

Third, it should be noted that of the 62 proposals advanced by the two major nations (27 United States and 35 Soviet), 47 (or 75% of the total) dealt with nuclear weapons. Of the six United States proposals that did not deal with nuclear weapons, only 2 dealt with other types of weapons systems: proposal U-24 (see matrix), which dealt with conventional force levels; and U-36, which dealt with the uses of outer space. Of the Soviet proposals that did not deal with nuclear weapons (of which there were nine), only four dealt with other types of weapons systems: R-4 (see matrix), which dealt in general terms with reduction of armed forces; R-25, which dealt with conventional arms and armed forces and was a counterproposal to U-24; and R-40 and R-42, which dealt with long-range and intermediate-range delivery systems for nuclear warheads.

Therefore, assuming that the United States and the Soviet Union will be parties to any ACD arrangement for the Far East, either formally or through tacit acceptance, a study of past nonregional ACD proposals provides little positive evidence as to the stand of the two major powers. However, Soviet insistence that the United States withdraw from her overseas bases and disband her security alliances is considered to be a disquieting indicator. And the 68 "N" items (comprising nearly one-third of the universe), many of them with direct -- even crucial -- relevance to ACD in the Far East, indicate that any proposed regional arrangement will deal with a virgin area where past experience has little relevance, either to the regional or the nonregional powers.

REGIONAL RESPONSES TO NONREGIONAL PROPOSALS

During the early post-World War II period, regional responses to Western proposals were few. At that time, Asia was far from being a region composed of independent states. Japan was under occupation, and most of the other nations were bound by colonial ties to the policies of either France, England, or the Netherlands.

Where nations were independent (e. g., Thailand), domestic matters left little time for commenting upon Western attempts to deal with the problem of controlling atomic weapons. The two exceptions were the Republic of China and Australia. The Communist victory on the Chinese mainland in 1949, however, markedly lessened the weight and importance of the Republic of China's support of the United States' position. In regard to Australia, it appears that her attitude was, and continues to be, influenced more by her Western ties and orientation than by either her regional associations or her geographic location. Further, the same state's ACD proposals, of the early period, did not differ significantly from one another -- another reason for the lack of any extensive or significant regional commentary. Finally, as mentioned earlier, the sum and substance of these proposals seemed to deal with areas and problems that were far removed from the more visceral needs and demands of the Far East.

Regional commentary on nonregional ACD proposals increased somewhat during the 1950's for four reasons: (1) independence and a sloughing-off of colonial ties; (2) the Korean War, which brought a violent cold war confrontation to Asia; (3) the rise of Communist China; and (4) an aching desire on the part of some Asian states to be recognized, accorded their due, and respected by others.

At the same time, United States and Soviet proposals were often polar opposites on a given point. Agreement with one or the other formulation amounted to a "choosing-up" of sides. Thus, it often appeared that regional powers were considering ACD proposals as little more than an exercise in power politics: i.e., a pro-Western state would support a United States proposal; a pro-Soviet state would support a Communist proposal; and a "neutral" state would either applaud both, condemn both, or abstain.

This approach can be seen from the following example. On January 12, 1952, the sixth major disarmament proposal (R-6) in our representative sample was advanced by the Soviet Union, calling for a Korean armistice and atomic control. In this plan, the Soviet Union seemed to be making a major concession, as the proposal agreed to continuing inspection, although asserting that there was to be no interference in the domestic affairs of any nation.

Feeling on this proposal ran high. Sides were carefully delineated and positions clearly defined. The Korean conflict was reaching a climax and the Soviet Union, well on the way to achieving a respectable nuclear force, was thus more concerned than heretofore with the possible loss of vital information to any international control agency.

Western reaction to the Soviet proposal was immediate, strong, and negative. The Western nations felt that if the prohibition convention were signed there, and later agreement on control methods proved impossible, they would be saddled with an inequitable and restrictive General Assembly resolution. This attitude was due to the fact that the proposal showed the Soviet Union still strongly opposed to the international operation of "nuclear plants." Thus, many Western observers viewed the Soviet proposal as a major propaganda move to convince the peoples of Western Europe and Asia that the Soviet Union wanted control over atomic energy and nuclear weapons badly enough to make major concessions, whereas the West (and the United States in particular) did not.[3]

Both Australia and the Republic of China approved the Western resolution to refer the plan to the newly-constituted Disarmament Commission, as did the Republic of the Philippines and New Zealand. Indonesia reacted by abstaining on any part of the Soviet proposal that was unacceptable to the Western powers. India expressed her regrets over the continuing great power dispute and stated that she would abstain on both votes, as a vote either for or against the Soviet proposal or the Western (Big Three) proposal would only widen the area of disagreement. Other examples of political considerations dictating (or, at least, greatly influencing) regional responses to Western ACD proposals could be given, but one must suffice for the sake of brevity.

In general, the majority of the Western proposals in our representative sample elicited no regional responses. This is understandable for at least three reasons. First, many of the proposals had, or appeared to have, little or no relevance to the Far East at the time they were made: since regional interests were not involved, there were no regional responses.

Second, since many proposals were really counterproposals, amplifications, or clarifications (rather than dramatic panaceas), regional powers apparently were loath to interject particular comments and possibly disturb the process of great-power negotiations. This is further illustrated by the very general tenor of response on those occasions when comment was made. In sum, most of these responses favored a continuation of United States-Soviet talks on outstanding issues, advocated coexistence, and pledged the respondent's good will and moral support to the cause of world peace.

Third, it should be noted that regional comment was not specifically solicited during the decade immediately following World War II. This approach changed in December 1957, however, when Marshal Bulganin sent a letter to President Eisenhower suggesting an East-West conference. Copies of the letter were delivered simultaneously to other countries, including India, and a note was appended to the Indian copy which stated that the Soviet Union would be willing to end nuclear testing within a month. While the above indicated that Asian opinions would be welcomed and recognized, it did not actually trigger any appreciable increase in responses -- the majority of Western ACD proposals were still perceived to be regionally irrelevant.

It appears that some Far Eastern countries attempt to play dual and often contradictory roles: (1) as a conscience or moral force; and (2) as a nation-state. India, for example, has projected an international image of peacemaker and arbiter (role 1). At the same time, she has refused to compromise perceived national interests -- Kashmir, etc. -- even to advance regional stability (role 2). This point is not made critically, but it does indicate that regional responses to ACD proposals not specifically concerned with Asia and not touching upon the national interests of Asian states provide no clear evidence as to possible or probable positions on the matter of ACD in the Far East.

REGIONAL AND COMMUNIST CHINESE PROPOSALS FOR ACD

On the basis of a fairly exhaustive sample of 36 regional and Communist Chinese ACD proposals,[4] several facts become apparent:

1) For several years after World War II, regional powers (with the exception of China) played but a negligible role in the international arena.[5] When ACD proposals were first advanced by the major powers in 1946, there was little or no regional response. Even in the first years of the United Nations, the regional powers had but a small international role to play -- indeed, they were neither expected to play such a role, nor were they in position to do so. However, as the capability and the desire (and, to a lesser degree, the skill) to play a greater role developed among the regional powers, there was little corresponding desire on the part of the great powers to share the responsibility.

2) Only 12 of the 36 proposals included in the sample were made before the United Nations Disarmament Commission or the Eighteen Nation Disarmament Conference (ENDC). The remaining 24 were either: (a) proposals sent by one or more regional powers to the United States and/or the Soviet Union; (b) speeches before national legislatures; (c) conference resolutions; or (d) policy statements by a *bona fide* national spokesman or decision maker. Thus, it could be argued that, in many ways, the majority of these proposals were in reality not formal proposals at all. They were not advanced through established channels and, therefore, did not evoke comment for several reasons: (a) the manner of submission was often outside of the usual channels; (b) there was little that was new in the proposals; and (c) as stated above, there was little likelihood they would be acted upon.

3) As an expansion of the last point, we may consider the general subject matter of these ACD proposals. In actuality, early proposals differed little from those advanced by the nonregional powers, as discussed before in this chapter.

GENERAL SUBJECT MATTER

(Note: the details add to more than 36 because some proposals dealt with more than one item.)

Nuclear weapons (use, test, or deployment)	26
General and complete disarmament with inspection and controls	8
Collective regional peace-pact (both by Communist China)	2
Conventional weapons	2
Regional countries to be consulted on matters of regional concern	1
Effect of disarmament on national economies	1
Disarmament impossible due to imperialism (Communist China)	1
Oppressed nations must not disarm (Communist China)	1
	42

Thus, whereas 75 percent of the nonregional proposals dealt with some facet of the nuclear weapons problem, some 70 percent of the 36 regional and Communist Chinese proposals dealt with the same issue. Only two (2) of the 36 proposals treated the question of conventional weaponry, and neither was advanced with specific reference to the Far East. Thus, these proposals may actually constitute a tropism; in any case, they follow the same general pattern of nonregional proposals.

4) It is also interesting to note that over half (19/36) of the proposals included in the sample were advanced by India. Communist China (9 "proposals") was a poor second. The breakdown is as follows:

MAJOR REGIONAL PROPOSALS

Originators	Number of Proposals Sponsored
India	19
Communist China	9
Ceylon	5
Pakistan	4
Burma	3
Indonesia	3
Japan	3
Australia	2
Cambodia	2
Malaya	2
Nepal[6]	2
New Zealand	2
Afghanistan[6]	1
Philippines	1
Thailand	1
	59[7]

Further, the vast majority of the Asian proposals were more akin to moral appeals than hard propositions dealing with either United States - Soviet Union points of disagreement or the as yet insoluble problem of ACD implementation.

5) Finally, it should be mentioned that only one regional reaction to an early regional proposal was noted.[8] This buttresses the observations in points (2) and (3) above: namely, that these proposals were advanced through extraordinary channels, and that they were markedly similar to nonregional proposals. Therefore, lack of response was understandable. The latest Indian proposal concerning guarantees for nonnuclear powers threatened with

nuclear attack is an exception. The cause for the proposal is, of course, India's concern over Communist China as a nuclear power. India, one of the nations most concerned over Communist Chinese military power, has been an initiator of this proposal, but other regional and nonregional nations share her uneasiness. Nations capable of developing nuclear weapons such as India, Japan, and Canada, and not wishing to take the path of France and Communist China in proliferating them, must feel the need for reassurance that their acceptance of a nonnuclear military status will not jeopardize their security. This gives India's proposal worldwide notice that other regional proposals have generally not had.

Post-Nuclear Test Ban Treaty Developments

The signing of the Nuclear Test Ban Treaty on July 25, 1963, was originally selected as a cutoff for the study of the nonregional ACD proposals because it formed a convenient and significant benchmark in the historical development of post-1945 ACD. Since that date, however, new proposals have been made by nonregional powers which should be given some consideration. Consequently, seven major nonregional post-Nuclear Test Ban Treaty proposals have been selected from among the slate of the primarily United States and Soviet proposals and counterproposals. These have been added as a separate section of Appendix I, Part A.

In general, it can be said that these later proposals change the observations and results of the foregoing pages very little, but some general comment is in order. First, each of these proposals is concerned primarily with nuclear weapons and each directs itself to the problem of proliferation which has become a matter of most urgent concern to both the nuclear and nonnuclear powers since two new powers, France and Communist China, have entered the "nuclear club." Second, no new subjects were broached except the United States proposition that the production of the raw materials used for manufacturing nuclear weapons be controlled. One interesting feature of these later proposals is that President Johnson's message to the ENDC on January 26, 1966, which expanded upon a statement in his speech of October 18, 1964, after the first Chinese nuclear explosion, embodies an answer to India's May 1965 appeal for the protection of nonnuclear states from the threat of nuclear attack. It seems clear that the President's statement was intended to be construed in this context, and his statement can thus be further construed as the first nuclear power response to the proposal (or appeal) of a nonnuclear (and, incidentally, regional) state.

SUMMARY

Extensive commentary would merely belabor the obvious: previous nonregional proposals, regional responses, and regional proposals give little insight into the content, application, or efficacy of possible ACD arrangements for the Far East. In the early years after 1945, special circumstances often precluded a response. Furthermore, some regional powers tend to treat ACD proposals as an extension of politics.

The positions and/or propositions included in the matrix were given little consideration by the regional states because (for various reasons) there was relatively little attention given to details in the nonregional proposals. Finally, on the basis of the objects of ACD in proposals to date, there seems to be little relevance to real possibilities for ACD among the regional nations. Therefore, it would appear that ACD in the Far East will have to start from scratch for three reasons: 1) nonregional powers have not considered the problem seriously; 2) regional powers have not considered the problem seriously; and 3) previous ACD proposals are largely irrelevant.

FOOTNOTES

[1]The matrix is contained in Appendix I, Part C.

[2]The 75 proposals are listed and numbered in Appendix I, Part A.

[3]Actually there was no major concession involved, as the question of international control remained unresolved.

[4]Though extraregional, Communist China has been included in this one instance to facilitate comparison. See list, Appendix I, Part B.

[5]The first recorded regional proposal was advanced at the Baguio Conference of May 1950, demanding that major powers take no action affecting the Far East without first consulting nations in that region.

[6]Nepal and Afghanistan will not be treated elsewhere in this study as regional powers.

[7]Some proposals were sponsored by more than one regional power. Corresponding to the total of 59 above, there were only 36 individual proposals.

[8]This was India's agreement with and amplification of Japan's proposal of September 23, 1957, that any disarmament agreement should provide for measures dealing with nuclear weapons, conventional forces, and aerial and ground inspection.

PART II

REGIONAL AND EXTRAREGIONAL FACTORS AFFECTING ACD

CHAPTER 1: GENERAL CHARACTERISTICS OF THE REGIONS AND SUBREGIONS WHICH MIGHT AFFECT ACD

INTRODUCTION

Twenty-nine per cent of the world's population (1962 estimate), or 913 million persons, live in the sixteen countries of the Far Eastern region, which constitutes just under 12 per cent of the world's land area. If Australia and New Zealand are excluded, the region would account for 28.7 per cent of the population and 6 per cent of the area, resulting in a density figure of approximately 111 persons per square kilometer.

In view of the relatively underdeveloped economies of the region, with the exception of Australia, New Zealand, Japan, and a few other areas, this relatively high population density corresponds with a low standard of living. Excluding Australia and New Zealand, available data show a per capita gross national income range in 1961 from US $52 (for Burma) to US $298 (for Malaysia). These compare with about US $1200 for Australia and New Zealand, over $2300 for the United States, and approximately US $700 for the Soviet Union.

During 1963, the United States derived 18 per cent of her total imports from the region and sent 19.5 per cent of her exports to it. However, if Japan (the largest trade partner of the United States in the region) were excluded, the region would account for only 9.6 per cent of United States imports and 12.2 per cent of her exports. If Australia and New Zealand were also excluded, the percentages would be 6.5 and 10.0 respectively.

In comparison, the Soviet Union derived 7.6 per cent of her total imports from the region in 1962 and sent 4.6 per cent of her exports to it in the same year. However, over 78 per cent of all Soviet imports from the region and 91 per cent of all Soviet exports to it resulted from trade with three states--Malaysia, Japan, and India.

In the case of Communist China, imports from the region to Communist China during the year 1963 amounted to 34 per cent of the latter's estimated total imports from the world, whereas China's exports to the region were 19.7 per cent of Communist China's total exports. These relatively large percentages are to be explained by the following facts: (1) On the side of Communist China's imports, by the large grain import from Australia and (2) on the side of Communist China's exports, by the relatively large exports to Malaysia and Japan. The grain import should be regarded as a temporary phenomena, not representative of the normal trade pattern. The large exports to Malaysia and Japan are partly to be accounted for by the contraction of China's total exports during the period of economic retrenchment and especially by the contraction of Communist China's exports to the Soviet Union. At any rate, none of these China trade figures is proportionately important to China's trade partners. Australia's exports to Communist China in 1963 were only 7.3 per cent of Australia's total exports, whereas imports from China in 1963 were only 1.1 per cent of Japan's total imports and 3.8 per cent of Malaysia's total imports.

These statistics show that, <u>in the very short run</u>, the trade impact of a shift of these countries, either to the Soviet Union from the United States or <u>vice versa</u>, would mean very little in the context of the world today. Coupling this fact with that of the underdevelopment of most of the countries (excepting

ASIA--AREA AND POPULATION (1962)

Region	KM^2	1962 Area: Percentage of Sub-Region	1962 Area: Percentage of Entire Region	Mid-1962 Population: Thousand	Mid-1962 Population: Percentage of Sub-Region	Mid-1962 Population: Percentage of Entire Region
Japan	369,661	73.3	2.3	94,930	71.5	10.4
South Korea	98,431	19.5	.6	26,520	20.0	2.9
Rep. of China[x]	35,961	7.2	.2	11,327	8.5	1.2
East Asia	504,053	100.0	3.1	132,777	100.0	14.5
Philippines	22,014	0.6	.1	29,257	13.9	3.2
Indonesia	1,491,564	41.1	9.2	97,765	46.3	10.7
Malaysia[+]	333,215	9.2	2.1	10,364	4.9	1.1
South Vietnam	170,806	4.7	1.1	14,929	7.1	1.6
Burma	678,033	18.7	4.2	23,183	11.0	2.6
Cambodia	181,035	5.0	1.1	5,740	2.7	0.6
Laos	236,800	6.5	1.5	1,882	0.9	0.2
Thailand	514,000	14.2	3.2	27,995	13.2	3.1
Southeast Asia	3,627,467	100.0	22.5	211,115	100.0	23.1
Ceylon	65,610	1.6	.4	10,442	1.9	1.1
India	3,046,232	75.1	18.9	449,381	80.8	49.2
Pakistan	946,719	23.3	5.8	96,558	17.3	10.6
South Asia	4,058,561	100.0	25.1	556,381	100.0	60.9
Australia	7,694,951	96.6	47.6	10,705	81.2	1.2
New Zealand	268,676	3.4	1.7	2,485	18.8	.3
Southwest Pacific	7,963,627	100.0	49.3	13,190	100.0	1.5
Entire Region	16,153,708	11.9	100.0	913,463	29.1	100.0
World Total	135,773,000	100.0		3,135,000	100.0	

[x]Excluding Quemoy and Matsu

[+]Including Malaya, Sabah (North Borneo), Sarawak, and Singapore.

Source: Demographic Yearbook, 1963, United Nations (New York: 1964), pp. 131-134, 138, 142.

Australia, New Zealand, and Japan) any long-range economic impact of a radical political realignment would not be felt before a sufficient time had elapsed in which considerable investment and development would have to take place.

This means that the importance of the area to the extraregional powers does not lie solely, if at all, in any possible shift in the economic sector. Its importance is determined by other considerations of either a political or strategic nature, or both.

Without anticipating the results of the more detailed country studies, it would be useful to enumerate some of the more important characteristics of the region. It would also be useful to see whether *a priori* it might not be possible to advance testable propositions with respect to the attitudes and policies of the regional powers toward ACD on the basis of these common characteristics.

COMMON CHARACTERISTICS OF THE REGION AS A WHOLE

1) Most of the countries in the region, whether situated on the continent of Asia or on islands surrounding it, may be regarded geographically as part of the Asian rimland. Therefore, they are exposed to varying degrees of pressure emanating from the powers located in the Asian heartland -- Communist China and the Soviet Union.

2) With notable exceptions, the regional powers (especially the newly independent nations) have strong feelings that may, in general, be described as "anti-imperialist," "anti-colonial," and "anti-Western," although these epithets are by no means identical. Having emerged from colonial status only in recent years, they may continue to see the reestablishment of colonialism as a threat, and the proposition that their attitudes and policies toward ACD may be affected by their past experiences would, *a priori,* appear plausible. As a corollary, one might advance the proposition that these newly independent nations, as well as some of the other regional powers, may perceive themselves as a singular moral force advocating peace and nonaggression.

3) With the exception of Australia, New Zealand, and possibly the Republic of the Philippines, the regional powers have what might be called fundamentally non-Western traditions and reflect non-Western cultural and social mores. Insofar as these can be generalized and contrasted with the corresponding characteristics of Western society, the following schema may offer an idea of the basic differences. It would be reasonable to assume that Western values concerning personal freedom, individual dignity, and morality would neither be held with the same degree of commitment nor interpreted in the same manner as they are in the West. One could therefore anticipate certain differences in outlook toward ACD between (a) the regional powers of non-Western tradition and (b) the regional powers of Western tradition and the *Western* nonregional powers.

Cultural Contrasts
between

"EAST"	and	"WEST"
Collective orientation with self-interest subordinated to group interest.		Orientation toward self whereby, to certain degrees, one can properly choose self-interest rather than group interest.

Particularistic viewpoint, with actions seen in relation to the actor himself.	Universalistic viewpoint, with expectation that actions will be the same regarding all persons who fall within the same category.
Perception of status in terms of ascription.	Perception of status in terms of achievement.
Diffuse -- no lines drawn regarding how far one will give in to the demands of another with whom one interacts.	Specific -- limits (such as contractual) set regarding giving in.

4) To date, no country within the region has developed a nuclear missile capability. Even though Communist China -- an extraregional (Asian) power -- has successfully tested atomic devices, this does not necessarily mean that she actually possesses, or will soon possess, a credible nuclear force.

5) Some regional states are unequivocally opposed to nuclear weapons. Little or no attention has been given to the fact that a variety of nuclear weapons with different delivery systems and effects exists. Japan, a regional state, is the only nation that has suffered nuclear attack. The level of emotion in regional opposition to nuclear weapons is thus understandable and is possibly a factor in regional attitudes toward ACD.

6) Another of the few common characteristics found in the region is that, with the exception of South Korea, South Vietnam, and the Republic of China the countries within the region are not -- by the standards of the great powers -- heavily armed. Thus, the extent to which these countries can project their influence by force of arms is relatively limited.

7) A final characteristic pertinent to the region is the variation in degree of economic integration or economic interdependence.

Tables 2 and 3 show that no nation purchased more than one-fifth of its total imports <u>from</u> its own subregion, with the exceptions of South Korea (28 per cent), the Republic of China (33.3 per cent), Malaysia (23.4 percent), and New Zealand (20.3 per cent). Likewise, no nation sold more than one-fifth of its total exports <u>to</u> its own subregion, with the exceptions of South Korea (45.1 per cent), the Republic of China (26.7 per cent), Indonesia (31.7 per cent), Burma (21.2 per cent), and Thailand (33.1 per cent). Finally, South Korea and the Republic of China were the only two countries whose intra-subregional imports and exports accounted for more than one-fifth of the total volume of their foreign trade; and in both cases, Japan was the major trading partner.

As far as inter-subregional trade was concerned, only one state sent over 30 per cent of her total exports to the other subregions (Burma, 32.2 per cent). Likewise, only one state bought over 30 per cent of her total imports from the other subregions (Ceylon, 30.6 per cent). In no case did a regional state's volume and direction of inter-subregional imports and exports exceed 25 per cent of total foreign trade.

Finally, in no case did the regional trade of a regional state amount to half of that nation's total foreign trade.

One of the purposes of this chapter has been to determine whether the question of ACD in the region can be examined from the point of view of the region as a whole. A tentative judgment in advance of the more detailed

INTRA-SUBREGIONAL AND INTER-SUBREGIONAL TRADE (1962): IMPORTS

Region	FROM East Asia Million US Dollars	%	Southeast Asia Million US Dollars	%	South Asia Million US Dollars	%	Southwest Pacific Million US Dollars	%	Entire Region Million US Dollars	%	World Million US Dollars	%
Imports of												
Japan	89.9	1.6	655.1	11.6	128.9	2.3	469.6	8.3	1,343.5	23.8	5,636	100
South Korea	116.4	28.0	20.3	4.9	1.0	0.2	6.5	1.6	144.2	34.7	415	100
Rep. of China	104.6	33.3	16.5	5.3	0.5	0.1	5.6	1.8	127.2	40.5	314	100
East Asia	310.9	4.9	691.9	10.9	130.4	2.0	481.7	7.6	1,614.9	25.4	6,365	100
Philippines	108.1	18.5	29.5	5.1	1.7	0.3	11.2	1.9	150.5	25.8	584	100
Indonesia	142.3	17.9	81.1	10.2	13.8	1.7	14.2	1.9	251.4	31.7	794	100
Malaysia	213.2	9.2	544.6	23.4	41.1	1.8	88.9	3.8	887.8	38.2	2,326	100
South Vietnam	69.6	26.4	17.8	6.7	2.0	0.8	-----	---	89.4	33.9	264	100
Burma	43.3	19.8	4.5	2.0	25.6	11.7	7.4	3.4	80.8	36.9	219	100
Cambodia	15.6	15.3	10.8	10.6	2.6	2.5	-----	---	29.0	28.4	102	100
Laos	. . .		. . .		. . .		. . .		. . .		24	100
Thailand	173.7	32.1	44.1	8.2	8.6	1.6	8.2	1.5	234.6	43.4	541	100
Southeast Asia	765.8	15.8	732.4	15.0	95.4	2.0	129.9	2.7	1,723.5	35.5	4,854	100
Ceylon	38.1	10.9	47.4	13.6	38.7	11.1	20.5	5.9	144.7	41.5	349	100
India	131.8	5.8	62.7	2.8	52.2	2.3	51.8	2.3	298.5	13.2	2,262	100
Pakistan	58.4	7.9	10.9	1.5	27.1	3.7	6.4	0.8	102.8	13.9	738	100
South Asia	228.3	6.8	121.0	3.6	118.0	3.5	78.7	2.4	546.0	16.3	3,349	100
Australia	110.9	5.6	98.8	5.0	70.7	3.6	30.4	1.5	310.8	15.7	1,982	100
New Zealand	23.5	3.5	14.9	2.2	19.5	2.9	138.0	20.3	195.9	28.9	679	100
Southwest Pacific	134.4	5.0	113.7	4.3	90.2	3.4	168.4	6.3	506.7	19.0	2,661	100

Note: . . . no information; ----- nil. Source: Yearbook of International Trade Statistics, 1962 (New York: United Nations, 1964), pp. 57-737.

INTRA-SUBREGIONAL AND INTER-SUBREGIONAL TRADE (1962): EXPORTS

Region	East Asia Million US Dollars	East Asia %	Southeast Asia Million US Dollars	Southeast Asia %	South Asia Million US Dollars	South Asia %	Southwest Pacific Million US Dollars	Southwest Pacific %	Entire Region Million US Dollars	Entire Region %	World Million US Dollars	World %
Exports of												
Japan	256.8	5.2	661.1	13.4	209.1	4.3	165.3	3.4	1,292.3	26.3	4,916	100
South Korea	24.8	45.1	1.1	2.0	-----	---	-----	---	25.9	47.1	55	100
Rep. of China	58.2	26.7	46.3	21.2	0.6	0.3	0.8	0.4	105.9	48.6	218	100
East Asia	339.8	6.5	708.5	13.7	209.7	4.0	166.1	3.2	1,424.1	27.4	5,189	100
Philippines	150.9	26.9	1.9	0.3	0.3	0.1	1.3	0.2	154.4	27.5	562	100
Indonesia	55.9	7.1	248.2	31.7	3.3	0.4	47.5	6.1	354.9	45.3	784	100
Malaysia	238.5	10.9	190.7	8.7	47.0	2.2	84.1	3.9	560.3	25.7	2,184	100
South Vietnam	3.2	5.7	3.9	7.0	1.9	3.4	-----	---	9.0	16.1	56	100
Burma	12.3	4.6	56.0	21.2	73.0	27.6	0.1	neg	141.4	53.4	264	100
Cambodia	0.9	1.7	7.7	14.3	0.2	0.3	-----	---	8.8	16.3	54	100
Laos	. . .		. . .		. . .		. . .	. .	. . .	. . .	1	100
Thailand	67.9	15.2	148.2	33.1	6.7	1.5	0.9	0.1	223.7	49.9	448	100
Southeast Asia	529.6	12.2	656.6	15.1	132.4	3.0	133.9	3.1	1,452.5	33.4	4,353	100
Ceylon	7.4	2.0	2.2	0.5	18.1	4.9	26.9	7.3	54.6	14.7	371	100
India	71.4	5.0	57.4	4.0	48.0	3.3	53.4	3.7	230.2	16.0	1,441	100
Pakistan	25.0	6.3	10.1	2.5	43.7	11.0	10.5	2.7	89.3	22.5	397	100
South Asia	103.8	4.7	69.7	3.1	109.8	5.0	90.8	4.1	374.1	16.9	2,209	100
Australia	418.7	17.4	87.8	3.6	84.0	3.5	131.6	5.4	722.1	29.9	2,413	100
New Zealand	26.1	3.3	3.6	0.5	3.1	0.4	30.3	3.8	63.1	8.0	790	100
Southeast Pacific	444.8	13.9	91.4	2.9	87.1	2.7	161.9	5.0	785.2	24.5	3,203	100

Note: . . . no information; ----nil. Source: Yearbook of International Trade Statistics, 1962 (New York: United Nations, 1964), pp. 57-737.

country studies would indicate the possibility that it cannot, as the paucity of "common characteristics" enumerated above shows. Further, the fact that exceptions and qualifications invariably have to be made indicates that the outstanding characteristic of the region as a whole is its heterogeneity. However, the possibility of making tentative generalizations on a subregional basis should be examined.

ALTERNATIVE SUBREGIONAL GROUPINGS

Geographic

A natural subdivision of the region can be made on the basis of geography, and the resultant subregions can then be examined in the same general manner as the region as a whole.

East Asia: Japan, South Korea, and the Republic of China. The cultural heritage that the three countries of this subregion have in common does not seem sufficient to serve as a basis for common action. The determinants of any joint action on ACD, it would appear, must be sought elsewhere. Presumably, there are certain elements that may be conducive either to common purpose or common action, or to both, as well as certain factors that may lead to discord -- both being crucial in view of the insufficient common cultural heritage and the absence of a clear homogeneity.

Of the positive elements, the following seem especially important:

1) From a strategic point of view, the three countries of this subregion may be regarded as occupying the same position as a first line of defense for the United States in the Far East that the Hawaiian Islands used to occupy before and during World War II.

2) These three countries are all dependent upon the United States for their defense and are aware of this dependence.

3) In return, the United States has a primary commitment to defend the subregion, which she evinced by participating in the Korean War and by making bilateral mutual defense treaties with the three countries, as well as in congressional resolutions and reaffirmations by high United States Government officials to this effect.

4) All three countries are relatively poor in natural resources, for the size of their populations, and are therefore dependent upon external trade with the West or aid from it (or both) for their economic viability and well-being.

5) Within the subregion Japan and the Republic of China have shown a high rate of economic growth in recent years, and the prospects for their continued economic development appear promising. Although still faced with economic problems, the 1964 growth rate of the Korean economy was most encouraging at 6.9 per cent.

On the other hand, several principal discordant factors merit attention:

1) Both Korea and Taiwan, until the end of World War II, were integral parts of the Japanese Empire. South Korea and the Republic of China may therefore harbor certain suspicions regarding Japanese intentions. This may also be true in areas in other subregions which were under Japanese occupation, or control, during World War II.

2) A great disparity in size between Japan, on the one hand, and South Korea and the Republic of China, on the other, exists. This disparity is sharply delineated in terms of productivity and other attributes of economic strength. It is possible that this disparity further accentuates the suspicions mentioned in the preceding point.

3) The perception of the degree of threat from the Communist side varies between Japan, on the one hand, and South Korea and the Republic of China, on the other.

4) Discrepancies between different segments of public opinion, which in its many forms is quite articulate in all three countries, both within the individual countries and among them, may render joint action difficult.

Southeast Asia: The Philippines, Indonesia, Malaysia, South Vietnam, Burma, Cambodia, Laos, and Thailand. The cultural and historical heritage of this subregion is not a unifying force here any more than in East Asia -- on the contrary, it is often divisive. Yet certain general characteristics of the subregion are pertinent in this connection.

1) This subregion extends more than 3,000 miles from east to west and more than 2,000 miles from north to south. The general division of the area into peninsular formations in the northwest and island chains in the southeast characterizes this subregion. An outstanding feature, therefore, is its topographical fragmentation. Furthermore, the subregion lies athwart (a) the natural route of expansion from the Asian continent toward the continent of Australia and (b) the trade routes between Japan and her trading partners in South Asia and Europe.

Superimposed upon these generally strategic geographical considerations is the high ratio of coastline to land area in the subregion. This means that, with the exception of such areas as Laos, the subregion is highly accessible by sea. With few exceptions, therefore, maritime links are particularly important for most of its parts. To date, however, topographical and physical conditions have rendered transport over the land routes difficult for heavy traffic.

2) Until recently, most of the countries in the subregion were colonies. Except in Thailand (which never was a colony) and the Philippines (for other reasons), anticolonialism and resentment toward former masters remain relatively strong. Nationalism, pride in their past, concern for their newly won independence, resentment of foreign interference (however construed), and demand that other nations recognize their peer status are characteristics shared to a greater or lesser degree within the subregion. Territorial disputes, such as the imbroglio over a part of New Guinea (West Irian) and the status of "North Kalimantan," are cases in point.

3) Yet most countries in the subregion have important minority nationalities, which give rise to what might be described as "subnationalism." On occasion, this "subnationalism" has led to open defiance, and even revolt, against the ruling or majority nationality, a tendency that is heightened when ethnic groupings transcend national boundaries. An example of the minority nationality problem is the existence of large Chinese communities within most of the Southeast Asian countries.

4) Most countries in the subregion are essentially producers of primary products for export and therefore compete with one another. The nature of the primary exports is such that the economic well-being of the countries is highly vulnerable to price fluctuations on the world market. This potentially destabilizing factor which is beyond the control of the subregional powers tends to make propositions from extraregional powers dealing with long-term, bulk-purchase agreements more attractive on the surface.

5) Although Malaysia and a few other countries are exceptions, economic development in the subregion since World War II lags behind its potential. In general, there is an abundance of fertile soil and ample water in the subregion. Together with a long growing season, easy access by sea, cheap coastal transport, and cheap labor, economic development would have been more rapid but for the absence of other prerequisites, such as political stability and realistic planning.

6) Finally, the nations of the subregion vary sharply in their perception of the nature of communism. This has tended to divide the subregion into anti-Communist, neutralist, and anti-Western groups.

South Asia: India, Pakistan, Ceylon.

1) All three states in the South Asian subregion were formerly parts of the British Empire. After the British had relinquished control, these nations did not sever their ties with the United Kingdom, but rather became full-fledged members of the Commonwealth. This status has resulted in certain defense arrangements and security guarantees involving the United Kingdom. Although no central organization to coordinate the defense strategy and resources of the Commonwealth exists, there has been valuable cooperation on a practical level, such as the standardization of weapons and combined exercises, together with specific bilateral defense arrangements.

2) The Colombo Plan for economic cooperation originated in this subregion and has spread to other parts of the Far East. The forming of this organization might indicate that certain types of cooperation are feasible; however, no judgment will be made at this point as to their efficacy with regard to ACD, other than as an influence on the general environment and will to cooperate.

3) In general, the subregion is economically underdeveloped and overpopulated. Although efforts to promote economic growth continue, the results have not equaled expectations.

4) A major factor impinging upon the economic development of the Indian subcontinent has been continuing friction and failure to resolve outstanding disputes (such as Kashmir) between India and Pakistan. Racial and religious differences were instrumental in dividing the subcontinent into two states -- India and Pakistan -- with Pakistan being on either side of India, in two sections over one thousand miles apart.

5) The divisive influence of political geography is accentuated by racial, social, cultural, and religious diversity rivaling that of the Southeast Asian subregion.

6) The nations of the subregion can be classified as either neutralist or anti-Communist, although with India and Pakistan the differentiation has tended to become blurred in recent months as a result of (a) the Sino-Indian border conflict of 1962 and (b) the Indo-Pakistan hostilities of 1965 and (c) the apparent rapprochement between Pakistan and Communist China.

Southwest Pacific: Australia, New Zealand.

1) In contrast to the other subregions, the Southwest Pacific subregion is distinguished by its homogeneity -- cultural, social, and political.

2) This homogeneity has been preserved by the fact that this subregion has remained somewhat aloof from the region as a whole. While some tendency toward greater participation in the affairs of adjacent subregions has been evinced, this has not been allowed to compromise the distinctiveness of the subregion.

3) Australia accounts for nearly 50 per cent of the total area of the region as a whole, yet she has only slightly more than 1 per cent of the population. Allowing for the existence of large stretches of arid and uninhabitable areas, Australia's low population density contrasts sharply with the overpopulation of many parts of the other subregions.

4) This subregion has the highest gross national income per capita (over US $1200 in 1961), which also contrasts sharply with corresponding data for the other subregions. Comparable disparity exists in regard to foreign trade.

5) Although Commonwealth ties similar to those between South Asia and the United Kingdom exist, this subregion as a whole is a party to a mutual defense arrangement with the United States (ANZUS).

Conclusion based on geographic factors. Even on the basis of the preceding cursory examination, certain conclusions emerge.

First, with the exception of the Southwest Pacific subregion, intra-subregional heterogeneity is an outstanding characteristic of all the subregions.

Second, the Southwest Pacific subregion, which is homogeneous, is extra-regionally oriented and, to a degree, distinct from the other subregions.

Third, all the subregions, save the Southwest Pacific, contain divisive intra-subregional factors that would seem to make joint action difficult. For this reason, joint action may have to be predicated on extraregional initiative.

Fourth, the possibility of serious inter-subregional friction and conflict is not to be neglected.

Nongeographic

The points enumerated above suffice to suggest the inappropriateness of any ACD arrangement formulated solely on the basis of geographic subregional or regional considerations. Whereas the specific conditions of individual countries in the region will be examined later in this report, nongeographic groupings can be examined briefly at this point.

Some such nongeographic groupings might be established as follows:

1) On the basis of "ideological proclivities":

a) anti-Communist countries, such as South Korea, Japan, the Republic of China, Malaysia, South Vietnam, Thailand, Australia, and New Zealand, which have joined the United States through either bilateral or multilateral defense arrangements.

b) "neutralist" nations, such as Ceylon, Laos, Burma, and India.

c) anti-Western and/or pro-Communist states, such as Indonesia until recently.

Not all countries fit neatly into these categories. Pakistan and Cambodia are cases in point.

2) On the basis of historical antipathies. In a sense, this amounts to a variant of (1), but different groups emerge as a result of applying such criteria as anti-French, anti-Japanese, anti-British, anti-American, and anti-Chinese. Therefore, it appears possible that countries in the region might react favorably to a given proposal as long as it would not entail close cooperation with a country or countries perceived to be a potential or actual danger because of these ancient antipathies.

3) On the basis of states having a common border with Communist states, such as South Korea, South Vietnam, Thailand, Pakistan, India, and Burma, in contrast with nations separated from Communist Asia by either land or water. _A priori_, it would seem that such contiguity could work for _or_ against a regional ACD arrangement. States with a common border might _be_ more amenable to an ACD proposal involving a Communist state or states (providing, of course, for satisfactory guarantees). On the other hand, regional states with no geographical contiguity with Communist Asia might be more receptive to such arrangements due to a perception that the threat is less immediate.

4) On the basis of the size, power, and influence of particular minorities, such as the Chinese, in given states. The presence of a substantial Chinese minority could influence opposite national policies regarding Communist China.

5) Among other possibilities, one should not ignore _ad hoc_ combinations which cross subregional lines for specific, and probably _limited_, purposes.

Conclusions based on nongeographic factors. While these nongeographic groupings provide somewhat different patterns (the most important, probably, being that the groupings transcend a given subregion), it can be seen that they ignore many cultural, economic, historical, and attitudinal factors, any of which may impose special constraints on foreign policy and influence reactions to ACD proposals. This brief chapter indicates many difficulties to be encountered in ACD, not only in the Far East region as a whole, but in its subregions.

CHAPTER 2: THE EXTRAREGIONAL POWERS

INTRODUCTION: NATIONAL INTERESTS AND IDEOLOGY

In the assessment of proposals for arms control and disarmament in the Far East, the attitudes and policies of the extraregional powers are probably as important as the reactions of the nations within the region.[1] This chapter analyzes the policies of the Communist and non-Communist extraregional powers and their anticipated reactions to ACD proposals in the Far East. Special attention is given to their perception of national interests as well as to their ideological commitments. The historical record of their actions in and statements on the Far East are examined with emphasis on the strategy and tactics they have used to implement their policies. A separate section is devoted to their historical attitudes toward ACD. In conclusion, an analysis is made of the characteristics of policy conflicts among the extraregional powers as a background for the Annex to this report where the policies, ideological commitments, national interests, strategy, tactics, and historical record of the regional powers themselves will be discussed.

The national policies of <u>all</u> nation-states are assumed to be based on the achievement of such invariant goals as self-preservation, territorial integrity, economic viability, enhancement of national prestige, and preservation of a chosen way of life. No ACD measure will be accepted which threatens or seems to threaten any of these goals seriously.[2] It is further assumed that all powers have a secondary level of vital objectives that are determined by ideological commitments as well as by perceptions of national interests. Such objectives will be pursued in accordance with long-range strategy and short-range tactics which must necessarily be adjusted in accordance with changes in local conditions or shifts in the global balance of power.

Since the three most powerful extraregional powers -- the United States, the Soviet Union, and Communist China -- are closely identified with conflicting ideologies, stress must be placed on their positions on questions of war, peace, armaments, and arms control. Although ideological tenets can remain constant over long periods of time, the process of development or interpretation may produce differences of opinion, rifts, or conflicts between leaders or nations with the same ideological commitments. These ideological cleavages may be as important as conflicts of national interest in anticipating the attitudes of extraregional powers toward ACD in the Far East.

One of the basic factors in the international conduct of any state is its commitment to an ideology as well as the functioning of a political-social system that, actually or ostensibly, is based on that ideology. A particular ideology may be highly organized, systematic, and cohesive; another may be largely pragmatic, unorganized, and eclectic; and still another may be somewhere between the first two. Nonetheless, when we refer to an ideology, wherever it belongs within this wide range, we speak of it as a belief system, as a perception of the universe and man's role within it; and not necessarily of the correspondence or lack of correspondence between its profession and the actual behavior of the individuals or groups that profess it.

Against this background, we see a considerable range of ideologies professed by non-Communist, extraregional states, including such diverse views as those of Franco Spain, parliamentary Britain, Gaullist France, federalist United States (with her complex equilibrium of centrifugal and centripedal forces), and the seeming hodgepodge of tradition, impulse, experimentation, idealism, and superstition emerging from some of the new states of Africa.

An extraordinarily complex pattern of ideological confusion and conflict is evident in the confrontation among the Communist and non-Communist extraregional and regional states in the Far East. The United States and other major non-Communist extraregional powers directly concerned with the area perceive themselves as upholding such principles as the dignity of the individual and the more or less pluralistic concepts of freedom as developed in Northwestern Europe, the United States, and the British dominions. In line with this generally unsystematic, somewhat pragmatic ideology or world view, the United States and her allies believe they are championing the right of peoples to choose their own ideology and system of government while they are containing the powers that seek to spread their system and ideology by force. It is thus an important aspect of the Western democratic profession that the United States and her allies have no particular creed they want to force upon the rest of the world. The asserted aim is to "live and let live," recognizing the right of each state to choose its own way of life as long as this choice does not intrude on the legitimate needs and aspirations of another sovereign state.

The Communist powers, on the other hand, fashion their policies in conformity with a world view that encompasses a fairly specific body of doctrine to which they adhere. In general, this ideology is based on an assumption of basic, inevitable, world-wide conflict in which the capitalist powers are seeking to retain and defend their own economic, social, and political advantage against the rising aspirations of "exploited" nations and classes. It is thus central to their belief system that Communist leaderships have perceived themselves as champions of the working class, of the various nationalist revolutionary groups in the "colonies and semi-colonies," and of other "oppressed peoples."

Traditionally, Communist leaders have perceived political struggle -- both in its violent and nonviolent aspects -- as a central and unavoidable process in human affairs. Only when the last vestige of capitalism has been uprooted will a classless society emerge in which nonviolent controversy becomes a norm and the need for violence on all political levels disappears. Within this context, then, the surest and, in the long run indeed, the only way to achieve lasting peace is to strengthen the proletariat under Communist leadership, and thus hasten the overthrow of capitalism, the disappearance of classes, and the emergence of a new, nonviolent order. Anything short of this end may be useful, but it remains impermanent and tends to be a kind of temporizing.

This view does not mean, however, that the traditional, orthodox Communist is opposed to nonviolent methods of conflict. The skilled Communist leaders pursue basic objectives by peaceful methods when possible and by force when necessary. Marxist-Leninist theory tells them, however, that the bourgeoisie will defend the capitalist order to the death -- by whatever means lie at their disposal. Consequently Communist leaders expect conflicts that are initially nonviolent to be forced into violent channels as the capitalists find themselves and their system increasingly threatened. A logical outgrowth of this theory is the belief that the capitalist always incites a given conflict and pushes it into a violent channel, whereas the Communist is always the defending champion of the oppressed.

Communist ideology has been differentially applied by successive leaderships in the Soviet Union. Stalin, Malenkov, Khrushchev, and Kosygin are identified with individualistic interpretations of supposedly immutable, inflexible dogma. To date, the "official" interpretation in Communist China has been the "thought of Mao Tse-tung," or "Maoism" as it is often referred to in the West. Historical deviations have failed to attract significant support in China, but it is impossible to predict the direction or directions of ideological development in any post-Mao period.

Although geography and other factors often work to preclude freedom of interpretation, the centrifugal (polycentric) tendencies in the Communist world are not confined to Eastern and Western Europe. North Korean and North Vietnamese leaders as well as Communist leaders in non-Communist Asian states wish to make whatever interpretations or adaptations of ideology they believe to be necessary for their purposes, with or without the consent of Moscow or Peking. Therefore, the major extraregional Communist powers are treated in some detail for a better understanding of the influence of the Communist world view on their attitudes and policies toward ACD.

THE COMMUNIST POWERS

The Communist powers are a bloc only in the sense that they profess a common adherence to Communist ideology. The Communist system, however, is by no means monolithic, for each state has its own interpretation of communism, which is under constant revision and development. Nonetheless, these powers are united by an uncompromising opposition to capitalism and imperialism with world revolution as the ultimate goal.

The Soviet Union's National Interests in Asia

The Soviet Union, the former undisputed head of the international Communist movement, is now regarded as the first among equals of the Communist powers. Russia sees no conflict between her own national interests and the spread of communism. Her policies in Asia, as in Europe, are designed to further her security and welfare and to benefit the states and peoples who are friendly and sympathetic to her.

By far the largest part of the Soviet Union is in Asia. Czarist Russia expanded to the Pacific littoral by a process suggestive of the westward movement in the United States. Her boundaries in inner Asia, on the other hand, were established by treaties with China. The Soviet Union now claims any land over which her flag once flew. She is determined to keep the heartland strong, to surround herself with a safety belt of buffer states, and to weaken the rimland as much as possible.

With almost 5 million square miles that contain important industries and vast reserves of raw materials, Siberia alone accounts for 60 per cent of Soviet territory and a rapidly growing population of 24 million people. From Siberia, the Soviet Union has access to the Pacific and with it, to the other oceans of the world. Hence, it is only natural that the Kremlin is deeply interested in the affairs of Asia. This interest, however, is graduated, being strongest when it concerns countries adjacent to Russia, such as Japan, Korea, China, Mongolia, and Afghanistan. In the Russian view, for instance, Korea is a necessary satellite of the Soviet Union, a strategic protection for Eastern Siberia and the Maritime Provinces.

The Soviet Union has little direct national interest, scant economic relations, and limited knowledge of the southeastern part of the region. Most of South and Southeast Asia is not connected with the Soviet Union by land, or is connected only over almost impassable mountain ranges and deserts. In these subregions, the primary motivation of Soviet policy would appear to be ideological as frequently as nationalistic.

The Soviets have provided military and economic aid to friendly governments, such as those in North Vietnam, Burma, Laos, Cambodia, and Indonesia. In addition, Russia deeply desires to maintain a favorable image in India. In Asian countries that are openly anti-Communist, the Russians may be expected to support any scheme that seemed likely to weaken American influence or to make Western assistance more difficult -- provided that Communist Chinese influence does not fill the void to the exclusion of Soviet influence. Such action would indicate a more studied Soviet approach toward Asian countries not bordering on the Soviet Union, irrespective of political coloration. Soviet policy (such as it is) toward Thailand is a case in point.

Communist China

Like any other state, Communist China is motivated by the promotion and protection of her national interests, although in the case of the China that the Communists have inherited, the concept of "nation" had at times been extended to imply "world empire" in past history. Like any other Communist state, she is dedicated to world revolution. But, because of her geographic location, she is perhaps the most vitally concerned of the extraregional Communist powers in the events of the Pacific-Asian region.

Communist China's national interests in Asia. Communist China, because of historical experience, looks first to her territorial integrity and has precise though by no means absolutely inflexible ideas about the meaning of that phrase. According to the Chinese Communists, the areas surrounding China may be divided into (1) "lost territories" subject to recovery, (2) former tributary areas deemed to fall properly within her sphere of influence, and (3) "zones of just ambition,") as determined by past conquests or ethnological relationships. The "lost territories," according to a 1954 Chinese Communist map,[3] include *inter alia* Taiwan, Tibet, Nepal, Bhutan, Sikkim, the Chamdo area of the Northeast Frontier Agency of India, the Aksai Chin part of Ladakh, the Ryukyu Islands and Outer Mongolia. The former tributary states of Burma, Thailand, Korea, Vietnam, Laos, and Cambodia are designated as areas where Peking "refuses to sit idly by while helpless states are ravaged by foreign powers." The "zones of just ambition" refer especially to the Maritime Provinces and Russian Turkestan. The conspicuous absence of current references to Hong Kong and Macao indicate some degree of pragmatic flexibility.

The Chinese willingness to barter land for land, or even land for political gains, was evidenced in the Sino-Burmese negotiations of 1956 and the Sino-Pakistani border settlement of 1963. In the former case, calculations of practical advantage were very important. In the latter case, Peking gave up as much as 700 square miles of mountainous territory in exchange for Pakistan's friendship vis-à-vis India and for her possible estrangement from SEATO and CENTO.

Taiwan and Tibet, however, are of more than practical significance to the Chinese. Both areas are regularly designated as inalienable or inviolable Chinese territory, and the "liberation" of Taiwan is never mentioned as anything less than a "sacred duty of the entire Chinese people." Full Chinese sovereignty in both areas is a matter of principle on which no compromise, again in principle only, is possible.[4]

Communist China has concluded a series of boundary settlements and friendship pacts with non-Communist neighbors, including new boundary agreements with Burma, Nepal, Pakistan, and Afghanistan; treaties of friendship and mutual nonagression with Burma, Afghanistan, and Cambodia; a treaty of friendship with Indonesia; and a treaty of peace with Nepal. Although these agreements do not provide for compulsory arbitration of any differences arising out of interpretation or application, the treaties normally contain a clause calling for the settlement of disputes by "peaceful negotiation" or through "normal diplomatic channels."

Communist China has a much greater and more direct national interest in most Asian countries than has the Soviet Union. It can be assumed that China would like the restoration of her position of superiority over adjacent countries and would like the unhampered right to use their resources for her own benefit. She also seeks a *cordon sanitaire* of friendly states similar to the protective screen provided for the Soviet Union by the Communist states in Eastern and Central Europe. She may conceivably look upon Southeast Asia as an ultimate stepping stone for an ethno-cultural and political, if not military, invasion of underpopulated and basically Western Australia.

The national interest of the Soviet Union and Communist China could clash in a number of instances. The main areas of potential conflict are Southern Siberia and the Soviet Maritime Provinces -- areas the Chinese regard as "lost territories." Sinkiang and North Korea are also possible areas of dispute. Mongolia has already been seen as a hard-put buffer between the two giant neighbors, with China apparently mindful of her past sovereign status. In other countries such as India, Japan, and Taiwan, the Soviet Union and Communist China have radically different perceptions of their interests. Chinese-Soviet rivalries thus remain as inflammable in the contemporary Far East as they have been throughout history.

Scarcely less important than security and territorial integrity as a vital national interest is the Communist Chinese drive toward recognized great-power status. This drive manifests itself in the tendency of the Chinese to issue pronouncements on all world events, great or small, and to interpret certain situations as encroaching on their world status when to others much less appears to be at stake. Communist China's intervention in the Korean War could be interpreted as partly, but only partly, due to the conviction that nonintervention would have amounted to a negation of her status as a great power. Nonintervention in Vietnam might also be regarded as relinquishing great-power status, although pragmatic considerations may have greater importance. Even continued aid to Mongolia, irrespective of the latter's utterly pro-Soviet attitude, may be viewed as an attempt to hang on to China's traditional paternalistic self-image.

On the whole, the principles of Chinese policy show certain characteristics: (1) The ideological outlook appears absolute, but, because national interest at some point may dictate a less militant stance and approach, elements of flexibility and inconsistence are often injected into Chinese foreign policy declarations and diplomatic behavior. (2) The ideological goals and national interests appear to be concerns of the elite and not to be questioned among, but only to be supported by, the ranks of the "people," who are often charged with tasks of practical diplomacy. (3) The reaction to any event that appears to threaten the more fundamental and concrete of the goals of China as a nation-state -- recovery of Taiwan and attainment of recognized great-power status -- is always energetic, especially if the event is open to the public view. But this by no means precludes pragmatic flexibility.

Ideology of Communist China. Communist China shares the heritage of Marxism-Leninism and under the aegis of Mao Tse-tung has added interpretations and extensions which are peculiarly her own. The orthodox line on an international anti-imperialist united front was expounded in 1949 by Liu Shao-ch'i:

> The working class must unite with all other classes, political parties, and around organizations and individuals who are willing to oppose the oppression of imperialism and its lackeys, from a broad and nation-wide united front and wage a resolute fight against imperialism and its lackeys.[5]

Fourteen years later, the Chinese Communist theoretical journal Red Flag continued to assert:

> A fundamental task is thus set before the international Communist movement in the contemporary world, namely, to support the revolutionary struggles of oppressed nations and people of Asia, Africa, and Latin America, because these struggles are decisive for the causes of the international proletariat as a whole.[6]

According to the Chinese, these areas constitute "the focus of the contradictions in the capitalist world and are the weakest links in imperialist rule."[7]

The Chinese accepted the orthodox Marxist-Leninist views on war and peace. As early as 1936, Mao wrote the following in his essay Strategic Problems of China's Revolutionary War:

> War is the highest form of struggle, existing ever since the appearance of private property and social classes, for the purpose of settling contradictions between classes, between nations, between states and between political groups at certain stages of their development. War, this monster of mutual slaughter among mankind, will eventually be eliminated through the progress of human society, and in the not too distant future. But there is only one way of eliminating it, namely, to oppose war by means of war, to oppose counter-

> revolutionary war by means of revolutionary war, to oppose national counter-revolutionary war by means of national revolutionary war, and to oppose counter-revolutionary class war by means of revolutionary class war.[8]

On the eve of the founding of the People's Republic of China, on the other hand, Mao considered the question of peaceful relations with the imperialists in the following terms:

> Meanwhile, we proclaim to the entire world that what we oppose is exclusively the imperialist system and its plots against the Chinese people. Provided that it is willing to sever relations with the Chinese reactionaries, refrain from conspiring with them or assist them, and adopts an attitude of genuine and not hypocritical friendship toward People's China, we are willing to discuss with any foreign government the establishment of diplomatic relations on the basis of the principles of equality, mutual benefit and mutual respect for territorial integrity and sovereignty. The Chinese people wish to have friendly cooperation with the people of all countries and to resume and promote international trade in order to develop production and further economic prosperity.[9]

These precepts were incorporated into the Common Program in September 1949 and into the Constitution of the People's Republic of China, adopted in September 1954.

Chou En-lai and Nehru of India enunciated the Five Principles of Peaceful Coexistence (Panch Shila) in 1954. These principles included mutual respect for territorial integrity and sovereignty, nonagression, noninterference in each other's internal affairs, equality and mutual benefit, and peaceful coexistence. They recur in the communiqué issued in 1955 at the close of the Bandung Conference.

In 1956, Mao Tse-tung further explained the general principles of Peking's foreign policy:

> To achieve a lasting world peace, we must continue to develop our friendship and cooperation with the fraternal countries in the camp of socialism and strengthen our solidarity with all peace-loving countries. We must endeavor to establish normal diplomatic relations on the basis of mutual respect for territorial integrity and sovereignty and of equality and mutual benefit with all countries willing to live together with us in peace.[10]

In the following year (1957), Mao commented further on war and peace:

> To strengthen our unity with the Soviet Union and with all Socialist countries -- this is our fundamental policy and here lies our basic interest. Then there are the Asian and African countries and all the peace-loving countries and peoples -- we must strengthen and promote our unity with them. As regards the imperialist countries, we should also unite with their peoples and strive to coexist in peace with these countries, conduct business with them and prevent any possible war, but under no circumstances should we harbor any unrealistic notions about them.[11]

North Korea

For the smaller Communist powers in Asia, a major factor impinging upon their ability to maneuver with some degree of freedom is their precarious position vis-à-vis the present conflict between Communist China and the Soviet Union. Thus, North Korea has not reached a stage where it exerts a significant influence on the formulation of Communist ideology. North Korea has generally supported the Communist Chinese hard line which holds that the ultimate goal of world revolution can be reached only by toppling the United States and imperialism by force and war. North Korea, like Communist China, has denounced Titoism, and maintains friendly relations with Albania;[12] however, she has been extremely careful never to slight the Soviet Union directly.

In the absence of information on the North Korean attitude toward the use of the nuclear weapons and related matters, some insight may be gained by examining the arguments used by North Korea to denounce the 1963 test ban treaty. According to an officially-inspired editorial, the treaty

> . . . serves only the U.S. imperialists' policy of aggression and war, for all the noisy clamor of its authors.
>
> As we have already pointed out clearly, the treaty on partial nuclear test ban has no binding on the nuclear war preparations of the U.S. imperialists in the least but, on the contrary, has attached legality to their nuclear blackmail policy and is increasing the danger of a nuclear war. . .
>
> Today, the U.S. imperialists are, in fact, becoming more frenzied in attaining nuclear supremacy and intensifying the nuclear blackmail policy taking advantage of the Moscow treaty.
>
> Under the signboard of this treaty, they are staging underground nuclear tests in an unbroken chain. They are vehemently pushing ahead with the plan for the establishment of a "multilateral nuclear force" while openly brewing intrigues for passing over nuclear weapons or nuclear secrets to West Germany, Canada, France and other "allies" and are preparing for atmospheric nuclear tests.[13]

North Vietnam

North Vietnam (the Democratic Republic of Vietnam) is the only Communist state in Southeast Asia. Her prime objective is the creation of a united and independent Vietnam under Communist leadership, and she is determined to overthrow the opposing government of South Vietnam and reap the advantages of economic unification. In fact, the creation of a firmly grounded, stable, economically viable, unified state takes precedence over her zeal for world revolution. North Vietnam is, however, mindful of her military strength vis-à-vis the other Indochina successor states and seeks commensurate diplomatic influence in the affairs of her neighbors, Laos and Cambodia.

A basic interest of North Vietnam is to avoid all-out war with the United States. At the same time, however, she doubts the credibility of United States security guarantees and the degree of United States resolve (i.e., staying-power). Thus, North Vietnam and her National Liberation Front (Viet Cong) have refused to negotiate with the United States and the Republic of (South) Vietnam which would effect a peaceful resolution of the conflict. Their "terms" amount to no less than a United States-Saigon surrender. This refusal injects a discordant element into North Vietnamese policy inasmuch as the security of the North cannot be guaranteed as long as the fighting in the South continues at its present level of severity.

It is equally important for North Vietnam to preserve her complete independence vis-à-vis her Communist allies, the Soviet Union, and Communist China. Ho Chi Minh does not feel indebted to either China or Russia because he won national independence by the strength and prowess of his own forces. The danger from the Soviet Union is less immediate because there is no evidence that the great European member of the Communist bloc, unlike China, looks upon Southeast Asia as an area of primary interest or concern.

As long as Sino-Soviet conflicts -- ideological or otherwise -- are of minor consequence, North Vietnam can afford to straddle the issues. When the controversy becomes vital, however, she is obliged to take into account the proximity of her powerful Chinese neighbor. All Vietnamese, North and South, nurse a deep sense of distrust and hostility toward the power of China. After the basic fear of a possible American ground attack in North Vietnam, the next greatest dread is that of a preventive Chinese occupation of North Vietnam in the name of mutual defense.

In matters of ideology, North Vietnam (like North Korea) is a victim of the Sino-Soviet conflict. She is obliged to accommodate both Peking and Moscow. Her own party leaders may be torn in their inclinations toward one Communist center or the other, but no deep schisms in internal party politics have appeared on the surface. Available evidence indicates substantial agreement in interpretation of ideological matters. The party leadership has been flexible in its acts and pronouncements, and it has a deep interest in preventing Sino-Soviet arguments from degenerating into an irreconcilable breach. North Vietnam sees herself as a prototype for other states in Southeast Asia that might wish to join the "socialist" camp.

THE NON-COMMUNIST POWERS

The non-Communist nations considered as extraregional powers include the United States, the United Kingdom, France, and the Netherlands. These powers and their allies have a common concern and a common interest in preventing any additional area in Asia from passing into the hands of the Communists. In general, they believe that the defense of the region and the achievement of political and economic stability should be a collective responsibility.

Another paramount aim of the non-Communist powers is to provide an atmosphere and a world environment in which peoples of underdeveloped countries can pursue their objectives without wars or the application of force. Harmony and understanding between non-Communist extraregional powers and the regional powers of the Far East must be achieved if the Communists are to be denied further gains.

As pointed out above, the non-Communist powers have no militant ideology to foster and no further territorial ambitions to gratify. The age of imperialism has been replaced by an era of partnership and recognized equality. Economic exploitation and cultural imperialism are now outmoded.

Ideology plays a lesser role in non-Communist states than in Communist states in determining foreign policies. Essentially, the non-Communist powers accept the supremacy of moral law and extol the concept of justice. They condemn aggression and the use of force, and they oppose war except in the name of self-defense. Their interests are ostensibly identified with peace, stability, universal prosperity, and peaceful methods for the settlement of international disputes.

The United States

The United States, with her preponderance of power, is sometimes thought of as the leader of the free world. She is rather *primus inter pares,* carrying heavier responsibilities than her allies because of her greater wealth and strength. In determining her vital interests, she is influenced by the same factors which shape the policies of other nations. In addition, she has an unusual faith in what she calls her own principles, however vaguely they may be defined or measured. She has no desire or intention to force these principles on others, although Americans would like to see them respected and emulated in other countries as appropriate.

Basically, the foreign policy of the United States and like-minded nations is one of live and let live; it becomes a policy of containment only when national interests are thought to be threatened by expansionist forces. In this connection, the Asian rimland acts as an advanced outpost for the national security of the United States -- a role that was previously played by the Hawaiian Islands.

Perhaps the most far-reaching analysis of the long-range objectives of the United States in the Far East has been made by Oliver E. Clubb, Jr., in his study of the United States and the Sino-Soviet bloc in Southeast Asia. These objectives are as follows:[14]

1) The primary responsibility of the United States is to provide for her own physical security, the welfare of her citizens, and the preservation of her democratic institutions.

2) The important segments of the world must be prevented from falling under the control of powers fundamentally hostile to the United States, thereby upsetting the world balance of power.

3) The Soviet Union and Communist China seek to extend their respective orbits, and Southeast Asia falls within the scope of their ambitions.

4) The physical security of the non-Communist Southeast Asian countries, together with their economic and political independence must be protected from either Soviet or Chinese Communist domination.

5) Economic and social progress in Southeast Asia should be promoted to strengthen the area against Communist exploitation.

6) Within the framework of each Southeast Asian country's culture, political moderation, democratic institutions, and representative government, as opposed to totalitarian and unrepresentative government, should be promoted.

7) The interests of the United States are best served by greater economic and political cooperation with the Southeast Asian countries.

Although these long-range objectives refer to Southeast Asia, they are generally applicable to all countries, including the entire region under study in this report. However, Southeast Asia currently receives more attention in the United States because United States policy there is in a greater state of flux than it is in the other subregions. Unstable conditions call for constant reassessment of the American interest in Southeast Asia. The subregion may have negligible military value in the event of total war; still it has significance in nonnuclear conflicts.

The present economic value of Southeast Asia is relatively small to the United States (and even to her allies), but it is important to deny the assets of the subregion to any potential enemy. Keeping Southeast Asia in the ranks of the free world may have a greater psychological benefit than is generally recognized. It is in the national interest of the United States, therefore, to help, when asked, any non-Communist state in the subregion to develop the capability to meet any military or nonmilitary threat to its existence or independence. The same would apply _a fortiori_ to the other more developed or more populated subregions.

The United States generally assumes that other non-Communist states will exert maximum efforts to improve their own individual and collaborative defense capability and to foster economic development. As stated by Deputy Under-Secretary of State U. Alexis Johnson:15

> It has been recognized as never before that what we in the United States are seeking in the less-developed world is not the building of military forces for their own sake, or economic development for its own sake, or pro-American propaganda for its own sake, but rather the use of all the available resources for assisting these new nations in building the kind of society and government that can maintain itself, develop in step with the modern world and above all, remain free from domination or control by Communist forces hostile to us. United States interests do not require satellites, colonies or subservience to all our ideas. I am convinced that our interests are well served if foreign peoples and lands are truly independent, and if that remains the objective they seek for themselves. Thus we have a basis for truly mutual cooperation.

The security of the United States is deemed to be protected in the present balance of world forces by the existing military establishment, the disposition of forces and weapons in the Far East, and the existence of bases and a system of alliances. However, security is not merely a matter of geography, strategic dispositions, and military forces; it embraces diplomatic, political, economic, ideological, and cultural relationships as well. Threats to security, therefore, range from infiltration and subversion to outright aggression by armed attack.

The Communist attack on South Korea was instrumental in the reassessment of United States interests in the Far East. It became a cardinal principle of United States policy to strengthen herself and her allies to prevent any further spread of Communist power throughout the region. Bases were brought to the maximum degree of effectiveness; and troops, fleet, and air dispositions were shuffled for instant and complete action. An energetic program was inaugurated for technical, economic, and military assistance.

A sharper concept of the United States objectives gradually came into focus. The immediate objective was to deter any Communist offensive, whether inspired or supported by Communist China, the Soviet Union, or indigenous Communists, and whether conducted by means of subversion or open aggression. It was also perceived that a military-political deterrent would be fundamental, but insufficient *per se*, and that it would have to be augmented by measures designed to promote economic, social, and political progress. The problem was to increase the awareness on the part of some regional powers of the danger of the Communist threat, to inspire them to greater efforts for self-defense, and to get them to work together for their individual and collective security.

The United Kingdom, France, and the Netherlands

The United States is not alone in the definition and defense of the vital interests of extraregional non-Communist powers in the Far East. The United Kingdom, France, and the Netherlands formerly controlled mighty empires in Asia, and they have residual interests where they were once supreme.

Great Britain retains Hong Kong and a protective interest in Malaysia as well as the naval base at Singapore which is of vital interest to the entire free world. The worldwide British system of transportation and communication depends on the security of Southeast Asia, and British investments and trade with Asia are as important as ever for the prosperity of Great Britain herself. Furthermore, Australia and New Zealand retain political, economic, and psychological ties with England. Any threat to the security or welfare of British dominions from the Far East is of vital concern to the entire Commonwealth of Nations. Great Britain is generally dedicated to the use of pacts and treaties for the preservation and expansion of the system of collective security. In addition, she has contributed substantially to the Colombo Plan and to other projects of assistance for underdeveloped areas.

France surrendered her political position in Indochina in 1954, but she retained her cultural affinity for her former colony. In addition, the French still have heavy investments throughout Indochina. The French sense of prestige therefore demands an influential voice in Asia, whether in making decisions in SEATO, conducting negotiations with Communist China, or participating in international discussions on ACD.

The Netherlands must also be considered an influential non-Communist power with vital interests in Asia. The Netherlands is not reconciled to the loss of her empire in Indonesia and feels that she was never treated with sympathy and understanding, even by her allies in the Western world. The Dutch had huge investments in the East Indies, which they lost as a result of World War II and the subsequent attainment of Indonesian independence. They salvaged but little of the wealth which their empire once represented, but they have a deep knowledge of the land and the people for whom they were once responsible. The Dutch are uniquely interested in the welfare of Indonesia, and they are not without hope in seeking new economic opportunities throughout the Far East. They are strongly anti-Communist yet uniquely tolerant in their attitudes toward people with ideologies different from their own. They are not likely to take a strong stand against Communist proposals unless their own security and welfare are clearly involved.

THE STRATEGY AND TACTICS OF THE COMMUNIST POWERS

The Communist powers, sometimes individually and sometimes in harmony or unison, have followed a constant strategy and an ever-changing line of tactics in pursuing their goals.

The Soviet Union

Of the Communist powers, the Soviet Union has the longest record of activity in Asia. An analysis of Russian statements and actions on general Asian problems may help explain the attitudes that may be anticipated on the part of the Soviet Union toward ACD in the Far East.

In contrast to Marx, Lenin was aware of the role played by colonies in the capitalist system. Believing, as did the capitalist thinkers of the time, that colonies were indispensable to the existence of the capitalist economy, he extended the concept of the struggle between the social classes to include the conflict between exploiting and exploited nations, which by necessity would lead to wars of liberation. He propounded the thesis that imperialism was the final stage of capitalism and that the collapse of the colonial system would mean the downfall of capitalism itself. This, he concluded, was one of the reasons why war was inevitable, and why the capitalists created tensions in the international situation and developed the arms race.

It remained for Stalin to extend both the theory and the practice of utilizing the colonial problem for the advancement of communism. As early as 1918 he published a tract in which he affirmed that the Soviets should infiltrate the colonial areas and aid local revolutionary movements against the imperialists. He is said to be the originator of the statement, "The road to Paris leads through Peking and Calcutta."

As the prospects for Communist takeover in Europe faded, the Kremlin concentrated on extra-European areas. Agents of the Comintern (Communist International) assisted in the formation of Communist parties in Indonesia and Indochina and in the creation of Communist-controlled fronts in the Philippines, Singapore, and Malaya. During the period of the United Front in Soviet policy, which began about 1935, the Comintern became less important because Stalin played down his assistance to revolutionary tides and assured his followers that the expected imperialist war was sure to unleash revolution and jeopardize the very existence of capitalism. The imperialist camp was bound to deteriorate because of its internal contradictions.

The Comintern was officially dissolved in 1943. In February 1946, Stalin began the shift of Communist policy to a hard line. This shift was formalized by the organization of the Cominform (Information Bureau of the Communist and Workers Parties) in October 1947. In rapid succession, every country in Southeast Asia except Thailand,[16] experienced a Communist-instigated and Communist-led rebellion directed against both colonial regimes and newly independent nationalist governments. A series of conferences in Bombay and Calcutta seemed to ignite explosions in Burma, Malaya, and Indonesia and aggravate the existing unrest in Indochina and the Philippines. The hard line called for the "liberation struggle" with means commensurate to "objective conditions" which existed locally. Local Communists were expected to execute whatever tactics they found useful in applying the Moscow line. When the hard line failed, the Communists changed their strategy.

The changes became apparent even before the death of Stalin, and evidences of a new soft line appeared in Stalin's last writings, Economic Problems of Socialism (1952). The post-Stalin contest for power within the Soviet Union, which led to a loosening of restraints on the lives of Soviet citizens, eased the transition to a softer line. Further manifestations of Soviet "reasonableness" appeared in the Korean armistice of July 1953, the Geneva Conference of 1954, the proliferation of the principles of peaceful coexistence culminating in the declaration of the Bandung Conference of 1955, and the Bulganin-Khrushchev visit to Southeast Asia. Ideologically, the Russians and Chinese seemed to be marching in step during this period.

However, both Moscow and Peking adhered to the two-camp theory -- the capitalist-imperialist camp versus the socialist camp -- and both maintained their faith in ultimate victory. They retained their invariant goals and sought new tactics to achieve success. The period was in a sense a return to the United Front period before 1928 and the second United Front period from 1937 to 1945. The Communists seemed to be successful in China, Korea, Vietnam, and Laos and felt that proffering a new olive branch would bring further successes. They inaugurated a trade and aid program, and stressed their willingness to cooperate on a government-to-government basis with their friends and neutrals in an atmosphere of peaceful coexistence. Encouragement to revolutionary movements was again played down, and priority was given to winning friends and wooing the uncommitted away from the West.

This new policy of peaceful coexistence was formally pronounced at the Twentieth Congress of the CPSU (Communist Party of the Soviet Union), and it exerted an immediate influence on Communist strategy and tactics in the Far East. The Soviet leaders cultivated the friendship of non-Communist governments by stepping up their program of political, economic, and cultural exchanges. They showed themselves to be extremely cautious in assuming any risks that threaten to precipitate a nuclear war; in fact, they were initially hesitant to assist Communist China in developing a native nuclear capability. However, the Russians did not abandon their interests in Laos and Vietnam. They neither disavowed the Communist rebellions in Burma, Malaya, and the Philippines nor used their influence to bring the rebellions to an end. In these countries, insurrectionist activities continued, presumably with outside support, despite friendly relations at the governmental level with the Soviet Union. Communist tactics embraced the policy of a "united front from below", or a temporary coalition with non-Communist revolutionary forces in "imperialist," ex-colonial, "feudal," or "national democratic" states. In the quest for victory, the tactics called for cooperating with existing governments or supporting insurgents, whichever seem appropriate for a particular objective.

Communist China

In comparing the strategy and tactics of Communist China with those of the Soviet Union, it is essential to underscore their different outlooks and preoccupations regarding the Far East. To the Soviet Union, the Far East is peripheral -- the main emphasis in her foreign policy must be Europe. To China, Asia is essential and vital. It is China's home base -- the possible menance to her security and the main hope for the fulfillment of her "destiny."

Communist China sees herself encircled, as the Russians saw themselves in the past, and she interprets her main actions in foreign policy as defensive. China insists that only the evidence of clear and present danger determines whether she follows a hard or soft line in international politics.

The analysis of Communist Chinese strategy and tactics may be divided into three chronological periods: 1949-1954; 1954-1957; and 1957 to date.

At the time of the inauguration of the People's Government (1949), Communist China's allies were conceived as certain social strata within various Asian countries rather than as national entities. While maintaining a cool attitude toward established governments, the Communist Chinese sought allies in the ranks of Asian labor organizations, the intelligentsia, and revolutionary groups. The term "people's diplomacy" is an apt one. The Communist Chinese support of left-wing political and social protest in other countries gave them more influence in the internal policies of other countries than would have been possible through support of orthodox revolutionary groups alone. Yet, this technique was hardly the way to gain international friendship, for it often alienated incumbent governments. They therefore shifted their immediate tactics from revolutionary uprisings to an outright stance of opposition to Western powers. They avoided criticism of the neutralists and instead sought to win their friendship.

This transition from "people's diplomacy" to a more normal style of conducting international relations on the state-to-state level came after the Korean armistice and the 1954 Geneva Conference on Indochina. The latter was particularly important in that it seemed to ratify Communist China's great-power status and made state-to-state dealings possible without compromising her dignity. The final step for the Communist Chinese was the Bandung Conference in 1955. Here the Communist Chinese made a new assessment of their preferred tactics. They transferred their support from political opposition in other Asian countries to the support of incumbent regimes.

The year 1957 marked the return of Communist China to the hard line. Peaceful coexistence lost its emphasis in Communist China at the precise moment it gained acceptability in the Soviet Union. The prevailing attitudes in Communist China after 1957 toward international affairs were generally reflected in six theses:

> First, the United States is "the common enemy of the people, the international gendarme suppressing the just struggle of the people of various countries and the bulwark of modern colonialism." Secondly, "the struggles among the imperialist powers for markets and spheres of influence in Asia, Africa, and Latin America and in Western Europe are bringing about new divisions and alignments." Thirdly, "the Socialist camp is the most powerful bulwark of world peace and of the cause of justice." Fourthly, contradictions exist between the "Socialist and imperialist camps," between the "old and new colonial imperialists and their lackeys on the one hand and the oppressed nations and peoples of Asia, Africa, and Latin America on the other," and among the "imperialist countries." Fifthly, contradiction cannot actually disappear between the "Socialist and imperialist camps." Sixthly, the "monopoly-capitalist class" is striving to strengthen its ruling position at home and its competitive position abroad.[17]

Peking became more vocally militant than Moscow in its support of national revolutionary or "liberation" movements. Communist China expanded her economic and military assistance programs and did not hesitate, as shown by her attack on India in 1962, to deviate from peaceful coexistence in order to make sure that the "East Wind" would continue to prevail over the "West Wind."

Within this strategic framework, the Communist Chinese took advantage of Lenin's advice to make all the tactical zigzags that were required. A differentiation was made in the treatment of socialist and capitalist states. The "proletarian, internationalist principle of mutual assistance," together with the principles of independence and equality, was followed in dealing with Socialist states. Full support was given North Vietnam and North Korea in alliances which had to be kept by China because the two countries were located in Communist China's primary security zone.

Different postures were adopted toward non-Communist states in the so-called "Intermediate Zone," and specific tactics depended on whether the particular state was small, like Cambodia and Burma, or large, like India and Japan. In the small states, Peking usually followed the policy of peaceful coexistence, signed non-agression and friendship pacts, rendered financial help and technical assistance, and settled boundary disputes and other questions which "were left over by history." Nevertheless, Communist China often brought pressure to bear upon them to form a kind of "popular front" with the Communist bloc. It also resorted to various means of subversion by encouraging and supporting local Communist parties, front organizations, Chinese schools, and active propaganda campaigns.

On the other hand, Peking has drawn a distinction between ruling cliques ("hostile," "militarist," and "reactionary") in Japan and the Japanese people ("peace-loving," "struggling for independence," and "desirous of friendship" with Communist China). Although official contacts have been curtailed with the "ruling cliques," Communist China has nevertheless made repeated efforts to cultivate the good will of the Japanese people, including influential politicians, businessmen, and intellectuals.

It would appear that economic considerations sometimes dictate particular Chinese Communist reactions to Japan that appear to be at variance with the overall hard-soft strategy. Further, this may also be related to the attitudes of particular Japanese cabinets regarding the improvement of relations between the two states.

In her policy toward India, Communist China was influenced by the strategic importance of the Aksai Chin part of Ladakh to Chinese Communist rule in Tibet and by Sino-Indian rivalry for prestige and influence among the other Asian nations. Chinese Communist policy appeared to be more constrained prior to the outbreak of border clashes in 1962, despite occasional allusions to the "government which serves as lackeys for imperialism." After 1962, Indian leaders were again described as "hysterical," "dependent upon American imperialism," and "anti-Chinese." The alternation between a hard and a soft line is clearly discernible in the relations between Communist China and India, and it illustrates the flexibility with which China has made necessary adjustments in the strategy and tactics used in the pursuit of Peking's invariant goals.

North Korea

The lesser Communist powers with significant interests in Asia have enjoyed only a slight initiative in the formulation and execution of their foreign policies. These limitations are reflections of their dependence on their more powerful allies.

North Korea's unique strategic goal has been the unification of Korea under her own Communist leadership. The Korean War and the continued presence of United States forces in South Korea has demonstrated the impossibility of unification by forceful means. North Korea has persistently called for the South to join her in a peaceful unification proposal which would contain some form of ACD. In the words of Kim Il-song,

> The U.S. Army should be withdrawn, and the North and South conclude a peace agreement that both sides refrain from attacking each other, and the armed forces of North and South Korea be reduced to 100,000 or less respectively. We have proposed this on a number of occasions and have done everything in our power . . . .[18]

The official pronouncements of intentions and attitudes concerning ACD were in direct contradiction to North Korea's actual performance as seen by her continued military buildup since 1953, in clear violation of the armistice agreement. However, the military buildup was explained as necessary in view of the presence of United States Armed Forces in South Korea as well as the streamlining of the South Korean Army itself.

To protect herself from the real, potential, or imagined threat of "American imperialism" and the Republic of Korea, North Korea concluded treaties of friendship, cooperation, and mutual assistance with both the Soviet Union and Communist China in July 1961. These two treaties of mutual defense were signed within a week of each other and are basically similar. Their essence is found in Article II of the Peking agreement:[19]

> The Contracting Parties undertake jointly to adopt all measures to prevent aggression against either of the Contracting Parties by any state. In the event of one of the Contracting Parties being subjected to the armed attack by any state or several states jointly and thus being involved in a state of war, the

> other Contracting Party shall immediately render military and other assistance by all means at its disposal.

The treaties seemed to represent the maximum response North Korea could elicit from her sponsors in answer to the two-month-old South Korean military regime that was dedicated to anticommunism and its own style of Korean unification.

For North Korea, Asia remains an area with both friendly and hostile states. Understandably, her leaders consider as enemies all governments aligned with the United States. Her attitude toward Japan has been extremely hostile from the very beginning, denouncing the incumbent Japanese administration as "militarists," "imperialists," and "colonialists." North Korea is especially jealous and inimical to any development that brings South Korea and Japan closer diplomatically and economically, such as the Japan-Republic of Korea normalization treaty. Despite the small volume of trade between the two, Japan has been North Korea's most important trade partner from the free world.

Although the North Korean regime has thus far established only limited contacts elsewhere in the region, it has been trying vigorously to establish contacts with the nonaligned nations of Asia as well as with those of Latin America and Africa by means of diplomatic relations, trade, cultural exchange, and technical cooperation. She has thus far established consulates in New Delhi, Rangoon, and Djakarta, for example. One of the long-run political objectives of seeking contacts with the non-Communist world seems to be to break through the political isolation and near embargo imposed on North Korea by the United States and her allies during and after the Korean War. Particularly, North Korea wishes to swing the sympathy of these countries toward her side. Indeed, the ever-increasing frequency with which she has sent trade and cultural missions abroad may be the expression and confirmation of this objective.

North Vietnam

North Vietnam, like North Korea, is dedicated to unification of the entire country under Communist leadership. Until 1956, she hoped for unification by means of "free" elections; after that date she resorted to infiltration, subversion, insurgency, and guerrilla warfare, but has shied away from the risks of all-out war.

The Sino-Soviet split has not been without its benefits for North Vietnam. The rivalry of these leaders has given the lesser members of the Communist camp a certain freedom of choice and action. Ho Chi Minh has enjoyed an occasional role as a peacemaker. He has not been a puppet of either China or Russia, and he has been wooed by both. Furthermore, he has obtained substantial amounts of aid from both and has been treated more generously because of their competition in making grants and loans. Ho has managed to retain the good will of Soviet and Chinese leaders -- in itself a substantial strategic and tactical achievement.

POLICIES OF THE NON-COMMUNIST POWERS SINCE 1946

Because of the lack of an overpowering ideological urge, the non-Communist powers seemed to have lacked a precise strategy or a recognizable tactical system in applying their policies in the Far East since 1946. This has been eminently true of the United States, which has carried the main burdens for the Free World in the Far East since the end of World War II.

The United States

The crucial frustration of American influence in Asia was the fall of mainland China to the Communists in 1949. Until the outbreak of the war in Korea, the United States had failed to give adequate attention to the problems of Asia. In the face of the cold war in Europe and domestic problems, Washington had tended to ignore its obvious embarrassments on the far side of the Pacific.

In the early part of 1950, the United States had no desire to establish military bases on Taiwan. Both President Truman and Secretary of State Acheson said the United States government would not pursue a course that would lead to involvement in the civil conflict in China or provide military aid or advice to Chinese forces on Taiwan.

On June 27, 1950, in his initial response to Communist aggression in Korea, President Truman announced that military support to the Philippines would be increased; that a military mission would be sent to Indochina; and that military assistance to France and the associated states of Vietnam, Cambodia, and Laos would be accelerated. On the same day, he ordered the Seventh Fleet to protect Taiwan from any attack and to interdict any Nationalist move against the Chinese mainland.

This newly aroused concern with Asia was reinforced in the months to follow by agreements and pacts with Thailand, the Philippines, Burma, Indonesia, Australia, and New Zealand for varying degrees of economic and technical aid and military assistance. Emergency aid was also provided to the French in Indochina.

With the formal Korean armistice in 1953, international attention shifted almost immediately to Southeast Asia where the Viet Minh, under Communist leadership, drove the French out of Indochina. After the fall of Dien Bien Phu, the diplomatic and political position of Vietnam, Laos, and Cambodia was determined by the Geneva Conference of 1954. The United States stated that she would refrain from the threat or use of force to disturb the agreements; however, President Eisenhower declared that the United States would view with grave concern the violation of the armistice through renewal of aggression.

On September 8, 1954, eight nations, including the United States, signed the Southeast Asia Collective Defense Treaty (SEACDT). The United States was prepared to counter direct aggression -- to go, if necessary, to the brink of war, according to Secretary of State Dulles. SEACDT also established the Southeast Asia Treaty Organization which was designed to save all of Southeast Asia, including Vietnam, Cambodia, and Laos, or at least the essential parts of it. At this precise moment, the Soviet Union shifted her strategy of peaceful coexistence (linked with subversion), and Communist China enunciated her own five principles of coexistence at the Bandung Conference.

At the same time, the United States took a stance aimed at deterring the advance of communism in Asia, and proceeded to tailor her policies country by country to achieve her fundamental objectives of security, stability and orderly development. In 1955, and again in 1958, the United States stood firm against the Communist Chinese challenge over the offshore islands of Quemoy and Matsu. United States policy was not to be uncompromisingly inflexible, however, as was indicated by United States willingness to meet representatives of Communist China in Geneva and later in Warsaw.

The United States abandoned the attitude that neutralism was immoral, obsolete, and shortsighted, and accepted the hypothesis that neutralism was preferable to a more pronounced attitude of pro-communism. The United States shifted from a philosophy of massive retaliation to flexible response and placed more reliance on conventional forces as a means of coping with the small wars that loomed on the horizon of Southeast Asia. This shift in strategy emphasized increased mobility of fighting forces, greater fire-power, better fighter aircraft, and specialized training and readiness -- in short, a greater nonnuclear capability.

United States policies met their greatest challenge in Laos and Vietnam. Since Laos was looked upon as a "finger thrust down into the heart of Southeast Asia," it was highly desirable to keep her on the side of the free world. However, the political forces in Laos fought to an inconclusive status of neutrality that resulted in a coalition government of right, left, and center.

The new arrangement served only to remove Laos from the protection of SEATO; instead of bringing peace, it provided a framework within which the Communist forces could continue their struggle for power.

An acceptable modus vivendi has been more difficult to find for the cessation of hostilities and the reduction of tensions in Vietnam. Ngo Dinh Diem, with United States support, provided a degree of stability and progress in South Vietnam until 1959 when he announced that his country was "a nation at war." Subversive elements destroyed the framework of his government and plunged the countryside into chaos and rebellion. South Vietnam has received practically unlimited aid and assistance, including ca. 250,000 troops from the United States, in addition to South Korean, Australian, and New Zealand forces. North Vietnam, on the other hand, has shown no disposition to compromise or to use methods other than force to end hostilities.

The United Kingdom, France, and The Netherlands

After World War II, the United Kingdom, France, and the Netherlands pursued policies designed to salvage some of the broad interests which they had built up during the long years of the colonial regimes. The British retired as gracefully as possible from Burma and the Indian subcontinent. They gave up political hegemony, preserved their economic investments, and stood by with military missions and agreements to assist in the protection of the new nations which had been their wards. Great Britain remodelled the administration of Malaya and Singapore and gave new status to her possessions in Borneo in a vain effort to cope with the rising tide of nationalism. The Communist insurgency in Malaya, however, upset British intentions and complicated the problems of independent nationhood. Brunei chose to continue its status as a protected state.

Although the British retired as a major colonial power, they retained their interest in the welfare of underdeveloped nations, in international investments and trade, and in the maintenance of collective security. They held fast to Hong Kong and, by agreement, kept military forces in Southeast Asia for the defense of Malaysia. (Australia and New Zealand shared with Great Britain the tasks which were allotted to the Commonwealth. All three nations have contributed to defense activities in Vietnam and Thailand in fulfillment of the terms of the Southeast Asia Collective Defense Treaty.)

Great Britain was a co-chairman of the Geneva Conference of 1954. On the questions of Vietnam and Laos, she acted as the leader and spokesman for the non-Communists in dealing with Russia, who represented the Communists. The British have also been active in the United Nations, presenting their own views but usually supporting the general position of the United States.

France returned to the Far East after World War II with diminished power and prestige. By a treaty with Nationalist China in 1946, she surrendered her historical privileges on the Chinese mainland. Her brief resumption of her imperial status in Indochina was marred by civil war and came to an inglorious end in 1954. After Cambodia, Laos, and Vietnam gained independence, France kept military missions in all the new states (except North Vietnam) and maintained cultural and economic connections throughout the peninsula. France joined SEATO in 1954, but she became increasingly reluctant to endorse any positive actions designed to contain Communist expansion. In 1964, de Gaulle extended diplomatic recognition to Communist China and opposed the United States by espousing a policy of neutralization for Vietnam. The independence de Gaulle showed in his attitudes in Europe was reflected in Asia.

The Netherlands was as reluctant as France to surrender her privileged position in Southeast Asia. World War II dealt the coup de grace to her empire in Indonesia, although she tried desperately to restore her colonial rule after 1945. The Dutch were finally obliged to surrender their sovereignty over all their former territories, except Western New Guinea, at the end of 1949.

The Dutch were bitter about their losses. They resented the lack of understanding, sympathy, and support which they believed they had a right to expect from their friends and allies. After the withdrawal of their military mission from Indonesia, the Dutch retained no special responsibilities for the maintenance of peace and security in a region where once they had been so powerful and influential and did not join SEATO. They suffered the final indignity when they were forced to turn over Western New Guinea to Sukarno in 1963. Because of their sense of injury, it is unrealistic to expect the Dutch to support ACD proposals, except where their own immediate and tangible interests are directly involved.

The United Nations

The United Nations has become a new and significant element in the solution of conflicts in the Far East.[20] The United Nations is neither Communist nor anti-Communist, but its influence has been on the side of stability rather than on the side of revolutionary change. Its presence is particularly felt in Southeast Asia where it is looked upon as an instrument of peace and an agency for assisting underdeveloped countries. Furthermore, it is accepted as a symbol of humanitarianism and justice, as a champion for the weak as against the strong. Any ACD proposals supported by the United Nations would tend to be more, rather than less, acceptable in the Asian region.

HISTORICAL ATTITUDES TOWARD ARMS CONTROL AND DISARMAMENT

Against this background of conflicting national interests and ideologies and of Communist strategy and tactics as opposed to the policies of the non-Communist powers, it is in order to review the attitudes and actions of extra-regional powers toward ACD.

Extraregional Communist Powers

Soviet Union. The demand for disarmament (without implementing it) is a Russian tradition. In 1816, for instance, after the Napoleonic Wars, Alexander I of Russia proposed one of the first concrete plans for ACD in modern times when he suggested that the European powers simultaneously reduce their armed forces. At that time, most European states had already disbanded the bulk of their armies, but Russia had kept her own on a war footing. The Tsar's government gave many reasons why, despite its proposal, it was compelled to maintain large forces. The result of this maneuver was an intensification of the suspicions with which the other nations regarded Russia. Even the British suggestion for at least the exchange of information on the extent of armaments failed to find acceptance because, as Metternich expressed it, ". . . [of] the difficulty always of obtaining any true data from the Russians . . . ." He also pointed out that any proportional reductions, as proposed by the Tsar, would still leave Russia the most powerful nation. Even at that time, Russian suspicion of outside inspection and verification was plainly noticeable.

At an early date, the Soviet Union also posed as the champion of peace and disarmament, although she engaged in war and proclaimed the doctrine of the inevitability of struggle and war. Suspicions of Soviet sincerity could not be avoided, however, in view of the expressed attitudes of their leaders. Lenin said:

> The main argument is that the demand for disarmament is the clearest, most decisive, most consistent expression of the struggle against all militarism and against all war.
>
> But this main argument is precisely the principal error of the advocates of disarmament. Socialists cannot, without ceasing to be Socialists, be opposed to all war.

and

> . . . Socialism cannot achieve victory simultaneously in <u>all</u> countries. It will achieve victory first in one or several countries while the others will remain bourgeois or pre-bourgeois for some time. This must not only create friction but a direct striving on the part of the bourgeoisie of other countries to crush the victorious proletariat of the socialist state. In such cases a war on our part would be a legitimate and just war. . . .[21]

Until the Soviet Union developed a nuclear capability of her own, she was inclined to minimize the power of atomic weapons and to rely on conventional weapons and methods of warfare. With the acquisition of a respectable capability of her own however, her attitudes changed, and she continued to build up her conventional and nuclear strength. However, she revised these policies when she realized that her enemies also possessed great destructive power and that she would suffer disastrously in a nuclear exchange.

Despite protestations of peacefulness and readiness to disarm, Soviet leaders mentioned the possibility of nuclear or other attacks in the same breath with peaceful coexistence. Their main theme was that the Soviet Union could bury capitalism by peaceful competition, without the necessity of nuclear destruction. At the same time, however, they maintained that even a policy of peaceful competition or peaceful coexistence required the continuance of sufficient armament in view of the fact that coexistence might be abandoned at any moment in favor of more expedient tactics. Consequently Soviet leaders made a number of ACD proposals directed toward weakening their opponents while gaining the approval of world opinion. At international disarmament conferences, they positively opposed American proposals for verification and inspection, which they considered Western attempts at legalized spying. They did, however, sign the partial nuclear test-ban treaty of 1963. The impasse between the Russians and the Americans, however, came about because of differences on a global scale, over and above specific influences emanating from particular conditions in the Far East.

<u>Communist China.</u> Before the Chinese nuclear explosion in October 1964, Communist China's attitudes on war and disarmament showed a strong attachment to manpower and politics, as opposed to modern weaponry. Fu Chung, Deputy Director of the General Political Department of the Chinese People's Liberation Army, commented in 1960:

> Dialectical materialists consider that not only the role of materiel but also that of man must be stressed during war . . . . The decisive factor is man, not materiel. The relative strength of powers is not only the relative strength of military power and economic power, but also that of man power and man's will. Military power and economic power have to be controlled by man. Those who "stress only weaponry" attempt to rely on the advances made in modern weapons to refute the Marxist truth that "man is the decisive factor in war" by means of the destructibility of atomic weapons. This effort will be futile. The atom bomb is a weapon of mass slaughter. The development of this weapon has caused and will continue to cause profound changes in military affairs. To understand it correctly and to deal with it effectively are of vital importance. But however advanced weaponry may be, this maxim shall not be altered.[22]

In another passage, Fu underscored his view on the limitations of the atom bomb.

> In actuality, although the atomic bomb possesses massive power to destroy and to kill, it still cannot occupy territories, and cannot decide a war. Occupation of territories

> and the ultimate outcome of war still rest with man. The victory or defeat of future wars does not depend upon guided missiles or the atomic bomb; it still rests with man. The atom bomb can never destroy mankind and cannot destroy the world.

The Chinese press gave no indication of a downgrading of reliance on manpower and politics. This attitude may very well be making a virtue of necessity because the Soviet government had declined in 1959 "to provide China with a prototype of an atomic bomb and technical data concerning its manufacture."[23] In 1959 and 1960, top military leaders including Marshall P'eng Teh-huai, General Huang K'o-ch'eng, General Hung Hsüeh-chih, and General T'an Cheng were deprived of their respective posts as Minister of National Defense, Chief of the General Staff Department, Director of the General Rear Services Department, and Director of the General Political Department partly because they had persistently esteemed Soviet military superiority and technological advances. The three successful nuclear detonations in October 1964, May 1965, and May 1966 may herald a change in attitude similar to the one that apparently occurred in the Soviet Union a decade earlier. To date, however, there is no outward indication of any shift in policy.

According to Maoist ideology, universal and overall disarmament can be realized only after imperialism, capitalism, and all systems of exploitation have been eliminated. However, the complete and thorough prohibition of nuclear weapons can be achieved while imperialism still exists. In its statement of July 31, 1963, the Communist Chinese government made clear its position:

1) All countries, both nuclear and nonnuclear, must declare that they shall prohibit and destroy all nuclear weapons;

2) All countries shall dismantle all military bases, including nuclear bases, on foreign soil, and withdraw from abroad all nuclear weapons and their means of delivery; they shall establish, *inter alia*, a nuclear-weapon free zone of the Asian and Pacific region, including the United States, the Soviet Union, China, and Japan; they shall refrain from exporting and importing in any form nuclear weapons and technical data for their manufacture; they shall cease all nuclear tests, including underground nuclear tests;

3) An international conference shall be convened to discuss the question of the complete prohibition and thorough destruction of nuclear weapons.[24]

In its disputes with Communist China over the partial nuclear test-ban treaty, the Soviet government complained that Communist China not only joined hands with the most aggressive-minded circles of the imperialist powers, but even assumed the role of those in the extreme right wing of the ranks of the "American madmen, the West German revenge-seekers, and the French extremists." The Communist Chinese had stated earlier that:

> Only by ceaselessly reinforcing the strength of the Socialist camp, strengthening the national-liberation movements and the people's revolutionary movements in all countries, uniting with all peace-loving countries the world over, resolutely opposing the aggressive acts and war preparations of the imperialist bloc headed by the United States, and isolating the forces of war -- only then, will they be compelled to sit down to serious negotiations. We believe that only in this way will the struggle for universal disarmament achieve positive results beneficial to the peoples of all the world.[25]

Peking considered that nuclear weapons in socialist countries should always be defensive weapons against the nuclear threats of the imperialists and accused the Soviet leaders of error in shipping missiles to Cuba ("adventurism") and later withdrawing them ("capitulationism"). The Communist Chinese, claiming dissatisfaction with the "timidity" of the Nuclear Test Ban Treaty and suspicious of its alleged advantages to the "imperialists," refused to become a signatory. As is now known, the Communist Chinese were at that time planning to conduct their own tests.

After her first nuclear test on October 16, 1964, Communist China withdrew her long standing support for the establishment of a nuclear-free zone. She was no longer willing to consider any proposal which might increase resistance to additional nuclear testing and thereby adversely affect her nuclear advancement. Instead, emphasis was placed on the no-first-use principle:

> Many countries are at present keenly interested in the establishment of nuclear-free zones. However, to really free the nuclear-free zones from the threat of nuclear war it is necessary in the first place for the nuclear powers to undertake not to use nuclear weapons. Otherwise, the establishment of nuclear-free zones would be impossible. . . . [26]

Behind this shift in position lay an apparent Chinese Communist concern over nuclear proliferation.

Following the third explosion, Chou En-lai revealed that earlier he had proposed at Warsaw that the United States and Communist China enter into a no-first-use agreement. The United States, however, rejected the proposal, saying that it did not represent "a constructive step toward the paramount problem of controlled disarmament." [27]

On the subject of peace, Maoism has been in the forefront of its ostensible "proponents." Mao Tun, leader of the Communist Chinese Delegation to the World Congress for General Disarmament and Peace held in Moscow during July 9-14, 1962, stated:

> Our country's peaceful foreign policy is determined by our social system. Under our socialist system we have no need of any war. We will never occupy an inch of another country's territory. Nor, naturally, will we tolerate other countries occupying an inch of ours. [28]

A similar theme was expounded in Red Flag:

> It must be pointed out that by the nature of their society the socialist countries need not, cannot, should not and must not engage in expansion abroad. They have their own internal markets, and China and the Soviet Union, in particular, have most extensive internal markets. At the same time, the socialist countries engage in international trade in accordance with the principles of equality and mutual benefit, but there is no need for them to scramble for markets and spheres of influence with the imperialist countries, and they have absolutely no need for conflicts and especially armed conflicts, with the imperialist countries on this ground. [29]

In the view of Peking, world peace can be securely safeguarded only by:

> . . . resolute struggle against imperialism headed by the United States through constantly strengthening the socialist camp, and through successively supporting the national and democratic movements in Asia, Africa, and Latin America, the people's revolutionary struggles in various countries, and the movement to defend world peace. [30]

The faith of Maoism is still the Marxist-Leninist faith that peace will come only after, not before, mankind has eradicated the system of capitalist imperialism. [31] Before that utopia, peace can exist only between countries with different socialist systems, not between oppressed and oppressor nations or between oppressed and oppressing classes. [32]

North Korea. The North Korean attitude toward the use of nuclear weapons and related matters is apparent in the arguments used by North Korea to denounce the 1963 partial nuclear test-ban treaty. According to an official source, the treaty:

> . . . serves only the U. S. imperialists' policy of aggression and war, for all the noisy clamor of its authors.
>
> As we have already pointed out clearly, the treaty on partial nuclear test ban is not in the least binding on the nuclear war preparations of the U. S. imperialists but, on the contrary, has attached legality to their nuclear blackmail policy and is increasing the danger of a nuclear war . . .
>
> Today, the U. S. imperialists are, in fact, becoming more frenzied in attaining nuclear supremacy and intensifying the nuclear blackmail policy by taking advantage of the Moscow treaty.
>
> Under the signboard of this treaty, they are staging underground nuclear tests in an unbroken chain. They are vehemently pushing ahead with the plan for the establishment of a "multilateral nuclear force" while openly brewing intrigues for passing over nuclear weapons or nuclear secrets to West Germany, Canada, France, and other "allies" as well as preparing for atmospheric nuclear tests.[33]

The North Koreans, in essence, support the Communist Chinese position on ACD matters.

North Vietnam. North Vietnam has shown two attitudes toward ACD proposals. On January 26, 1963, a joint North Vietnam-Czechoslovak statement issued at Prague indicated a preference for a "soft line." The statement recognized the primacy of the Soviet Union in the international Communist movement and paid lip service to the principles of peaceful coexistence and general arms control. The two nations stressed the urgency of general and complete disarmament. They attached particular importance to the end of nuclear weapons tests, and expressed themselves in favor of rapid liquidation of military bases abroad and withdrawal of troops from foreign territories. They indicated their willingness to assist in the realization of such measures as the formation of atom-free zones in Central Europe, the Far East, and other parts of the world; the conclusion of a nonaggression pact between the member states of NATO and the Warsaw Treaty Organization; and the prohibition of war propaganda. It was significant that North Vietnam dared to deviate to such an extent from the known tenets of Chinese policy.

On May 16, 1963, Ho Chi Minh and Liu Shao-ch'i issued a joint statement which followed the Chinese line more closely. North Vietnam and Communist China pledged themselves to wage an indefatigable struggle against the imperialist camp headed by the United States and its "lackeys." They announced their stand for general disarmament and for the total prohibition of the use, stockpiling, manufacture, and testing of nuclear weapons in the Pacific region and in the United States. The joint statement used the goal of ACD to explain Communist intransigence and China's nuclear weapons development. It was declared to be "possible to force imperialism to accept certain agreements on disarmament and an agreement to ban nuclear weapons." Because of imperialism's rejection of disarmament and preparations for a nuclear war, it was considered "highly necessary to strengthen the national defense might of the countries in the socialist camp, including the development of nuclear superiority of the socialist countries." It is to be noted that North Vietnam, following the lead of Communist China, refused to sign the partial nuclear test-ban treaty.

Extraregional Non-Communist Powers

According to her basic philosophy, the United States is sincerely interested in real disarmament; however, in the absence of peace-enforcement measures, the achievement of total and universal disarmament is impossible. The United States stands ready to explore and agree on any limited measure for the gradual reduction or control of arms that will not jeopardize her national security.

No disarmament agreement would be acceptable without adequate provisions for verification, inspection and enforcement. Satisfactory control of weapons of mass destruction is particularly important so as to prevent any possibility of a sudden, "first strike" attack. The advent of nuclear-armed intercontinental ballistic missiles (ICBM) has robbed the United States of much of her protective mantle and has exposed her tc the dangers of surprise nuclear attack. Until recently she could deliberate before involving herself in a major war. In the present era, however, new weapons systems and new obligations arising out of alliance agreements make this impossible. The increased sense of danger has intensified the traditional American abhorrence of war.

The United States, like most other Western nations, when she does become involved in war, is impatient to end it quickly so that people can return to their normal, peaceful pursuits. Out of this impatience arises the seemingly paradoxical situation that the United States combines her anti-war attitude with a predilection for an all-out conduct of war, using the most powerful weapons available, once she has decided that there is no other course. The aim is to finish the fighting quickly by a few mighty strokes. Although such a war is destructive, it is deemed to be more humane in the long run. The use of weapons conserves manpower and presumably abolishes the need for invasions and long drawn-out campaigns. The Vietnam conflict is a partial exception, mainly because the war remains more or less localized. However, some Americans have called for the United States to institute measures that will end the war as rapidly as possible, and not via pacific means such as withdrawal.

Thus, the United States has tended to rely on a nuclear stockpile rather than large conventional forces. However, these views have been modified by the experience with insurgency and limited wars in Asia. Nuclear weapons are regarded as a protective shield against a potential aggressor rather than as a sword with which to strike the enemy. Abolition of nuclear weapons (or other means of mass destruction) can be accepted only if there is an absolute guarantee that such weapons are abolished by potential enemies, and if such mutual abolition does not automatically give the Communists an immediate superiority in conventional weapons and forces.

CONCLUSION

One of the principal determinants of the policies of an extraregional country is its perception of the power of the other major extraregional countries and of the threat they might pose. The historical record shows that such perceptions have changed over time for the United States, the Soviet Union, and Communist China.

Inasmuch as most of the states of the region are relatively weak, they take special account of the policies of the extraregional powers in formulating their own. In particular, they look for outside sources of strength and assistance, and, at times, disregard the location, convictions, and idiosyncracies of potential benefactors. However, the search for assistance and security is often confronted with a set of inherent difficulties. In the first place, the perceptions on the part of the extraregional powers of the relative strengths of one another do not remain constant. As the power balance and gravity of threat change, there is often no immediate perceptual reaction and resultant change in policy.

Changes in the perceptions of any extraregional power will overlap with, and also occasion changes in the perceptions of others. This "perceptual dynamic" often enhances the actual or perceived state of insecurity and weakens the credibility of any arrangement for outside assistance. Further, it is one of the reasons that the regional states often feel obliged to play both ends against the middle, exploiting for their own benefit the conflicts and antagonisms between Communists and anti-Communists. The historical record would seem to confirm this conclusion, and its disturbing effect on ACD is obvious.

FOOTNOTES

[1] The extraregional powers may be divided into two groups: Communist (including the Soviet Union, Communist China, North Korea, and North Vietnam) and non-Communist (the United States and her major Western European allies).

[2] However, a hierarchy of priorities is possible since "permanent goals" may be mutually exclusive in a given situation.

[3] Liu P'ei-hua, ed., Chung-kuo chin-tai chien-shih. (A Short History of Modern China), (Peking: I-ch'ang shu chü, 1954), following p. 253. The map is reproduced with English translation of the information given in boxes on the map, in Dennis J. Doolin, Territorial Claims in the Sino-Soviet Conflict (Stanford: The Hoover Institution, 1965), pp. 16-17.

[4] For a recent statement of the Chinese Communist position on the Taiwan question, see Chou En-lai's four-point statement in an interview given to a Pakistani correspondent on April 10, 1966 (Peking NCNA International Service in English, May 9, 1966): "[The Taiwan question is one] . . . of principle, which admits of no concession whatsoever."

[5] New China News Agency, November 23, 1949.

[6] "More on the Differences Between Comrade Toglaiatti and Us," Red Flag, Nos. 3-4, 1963, p. 19.

[7] "Carrying Forward the Revolutionary Spirit of the Moscow Declaration and the Moscow Statement," Editorial, People's Daily, November 5, 1962; also Peking Review, Nos. 47-48, 1962, p. 26.

[8] Selected Works of Mao Tse-tung, Vol. 1, first edition (Peking: Foreign Languages Press, 1951), p. 168; pp. 171-172.

[9] Selected Works of Mao Tse-tung, Vol. IV, first edition (Peking: Foreign Languages Press, 1960), p. 1470.

[10] Mao Tse-tung, Opening Address to the Eighth National Congress of the Chinese Communist Party (Peking: Foreign Languages Press, 1956), p. 5.

[11] Mao Tse-tung, On the Correct Handling of Contradictions Among the People (Peking: Foreign Languages Press, 1957), p. 38.

[12] The People's Korea, August 28, 1963, pp. 2-3.

[13] Rodong Shinmun (Labor Daily), October 11, 1963.

[14] The United States and the Sino-Soviet Bloc in Southeast Asia (Washington, D. C.: The Brookings Institution, 1962), pp. 95-96.

[15] Foreign Service Journal, July 1962.

[16] The so-called "Manhattan Affair" of June 1951 was declared by the Thai Government to be a Communist-engineered plot.

[17] "More on the Differences," . . . , op. cit., pp. 20-21.

[18] Kim Il-song, Immediate Tasks of the Government of the Democratic People's Republic of Korea (Pyongyang Korean Central News Agency, 1962), p. 31.

[19] For the full text of the Sino-North Korean treaty of July 11, 1961, see Communist China Yearbook 1962 (Hong Kong: China Research Associates, 1963), pp. 490-492.

[20] See inter alia the discussion of India, Pakistan, South Korea, and Indonesia in Part II, Chapter 3 for more details with regard to the United Nations and conflict resolution in the Far East.

[21] "War Program of the Proletarian Revolution, 1917" in Lenin: Selected Works (Moscow: Foreign Languages Publishing House, 1952), pp. 569, 571.

[22] People's Daily, October 6, 1960, p. 7.

[23] Peking Review, No. 33, 1963, p. 14.

[24] Peking Review, No. 31, 1963, p. 8.

[25] People's Daily, February 19, 1962; also Peking Review, No. 8, 1962, p. 14.

[26] "New Starting Point for Strivings for Complete Ban on Nuclear Weapons," editorial in Jen-min Jih-pao, November 22, 1964.

[27] The New York Times, May 12, 1966

[28] Peking Review, No. 29, 1962, p. 6. Of course, this includes Taiwan.

[29] "More on the Differences . . . ," op. cit., p. 11.

[30] People's Daily, December 31, 1962.

[31] Red Flag, No. 304, 1963, p. 36.

[32] People's Daily, December 31, 1962.

[33] Rodong Shinmun (Labor Daily), October 11, 1963.

CHAPTER 3: CONFLICTS, TENSIONS, AND ACD: A COUNTRY SURVEY

INTRODUCTION

Full examination of the many issues described in Part I, Chapter 1, as they apply to the individual regional states, would make the present report extremely bulky. This chapter, therefore, is a country-by-country survey of conflicts and tensions in the Far East, together with a country-by-country survey of attitudes (explicit, implicit, and inferred) toward conflict resolution.

The countries are surveyed in four subregional groups: East Asia, Southeast Asia, South Asia, and the Southwest Pacific. Primary attention is given to internal conflicts and tensions, external conflicts and tensions, extra-regional conflicts and tensions, and the given country's attitude toward ACD.

EAST ASIA

Japan

Internal. The sources of internal conflict relevant to ACD stem from two interrelated causes -- the attitude of the Japanese people toward war and the Marxist-Leninist orientation of two important opposition parties, the Japanese Socialist Party (JSP) and the Japanese Communist Party (JCP). Of these two parties, the former is the more important from the standpoint of its numerical strength and parliamentary influence and from the greater impact its arguments have because JSP policies are not controlled from abroad.

Both parties argue that the United States is an imperialist power and that she will become involved in imperialist wars in the Far East. This leads them to the conclusion that the Japan-United States Mutual Security Treaty, signed in 1951 and revised and renewed in 1960, will, in addition to impairing Japan's sovereignty, drag the latter into war as an American ally. Thus, the JSP demands complete disarmament and the abrogation of the Security Treaty. In addition, the JSP advocates a position of unarmed neutrality for Japan, guaranteed by a quadripartite nonaggression agreement between Communist China, the Soviet Union, the United States, and Japan. All external danger is perceived to have its origin in the ruling Liberal Democratic Party's policy of "subservience" to the United States.

At present, most Japanese feel the JSP's position with regard to the Security Treaty is unrealistic and risky. However, the temperament of the Japanese public since World War II has made certain aspects of the opposition arguments very appealing. The internal tension between the Government and the Opposition over defense and security questions is constant, and it has sometimes bordered on civil violence.

External. Tensions of varying degrees of intensity exist between Japan and neighboring countries, but they are not of the type that are likely to lead to war. In other times and under other circumstances, they might have given rise to armed confrontations, but unless Japan were the victim of external aggression, there is little likelihood that she could be involved in a war today with any nation. The attitude of the Japanese people and the Constitution itself guarantee that country's pacifist and nonagressive posture.

Regional. The recently ratified Japan-Republic of (South) Korea[1] Normalization Treaty recognizes the Seoul government as the legitimate government for the entire peninsula. Whether or not a permanent improvement in relations will be attained depends largely on the spirit in which the two countries carry out the provisions of the Treaty. The Treaty cannot overcome the basic suspicion and latent hostility of the Korean people toward the Japanese which resulted from 35 years of colonial occupation. Nor does it erase the condescension that most Japanese feel for the Koreans. In addition, there have been long-standing tensions arising from (1) past disputes over fishing rights, (2) title to the barren and uninhabited island of Dokto, and (3) the split allegiance of the Korean minority in Japan between North and South Korea. There seems little possibility, however, that problems arising from these sources will proceed beyond diplomatic concern.

With regard to the Republic of China (Taiwan), relations seem to form the antithesis to Japan's relations with Communist China at a given time. Tensions arising from the "two Chinas" question, Japanese trade with Communist China, and possible recognition of the Peking regime are ever-present factors in Tokyo-Taipei relations. However, as is the case with Tokyo-Seoul problems, there is little likelihood that they will become more than diplomatic concerns.

Extraregional. Russia and Japan have been in conflict over various problems since the last century, especially those concerning territory and fisheries. But, unlike the Communist Chinese situation, where popular opinion seems to favor increased contacts and improved relations, the majority of the Japanese distrust and fear the Soviet Union. Furthermore, Soviet propaganda over the past decade and longer has played upon this fear by emphasizing Japan's vulnerability to nuclear attack.

Present territorial disputes between Japan and the Soviet Union involve the southern Kuriles and the islands of Habomai and Hikotan. The Soviet Union has incorporated the southern Kuriles into her territory and demands that the Japanese recognize her ownership as a precondition to negotiations for a peace treaty formally concluding World War II. Japan has refused to meet this precondition. The Soviet Union has promised to return Habomai and Shikotan, but has also stated that the promise cannot be fulfilled while foreign bases remain in Japan. The latter condition has precluded any resolution of the territorial problem.

The issue of the fisheries continues to be a source of tension in Russo-Japanese relations. The agreement of 1956 ending the state of war between the two countries contained a clause that virtually banned Japan from fishing in the Sea of Okhotsk. In the past, the Russians have further exacerbated relations by seizing Japanese fishing vessels, confiscating the catch, and imprisoning their crews for violating Soviet-imposed fishing limits.

None of the present elements of conflict are serious enough, however, to embroil Japan and the Soviet Union in open hostilities; nor, it may be added, have the Sato Government's statements supporting the fundamental position of the United States on the Vietnam conflict seemed to result in any marked deterioration in Russo-Japanese relations.

Japan's relations with North Korea have worsened since the conclusion of the Tokyo-Seoul Normalization Treaty on June 22, 1965. However, there is little that Pyongyang can do save protest to Tokyo and attempt to sway the Sato government through propagandizing among Korean residents in Japan. In any event, the tension is (within the Asian context) a very low-key one.

The major obstacle to bringing about normal relations between Communist China and Japan is the latter's close economic and military ties with the United States, together with Japan's continued recognition of the Nationalist Government on Taiwan as the *de jure* government of China. On this point, the Communist Chinese have stated on countless occasions that there is no possibility of a fundamental improvement in relations with them until Japan breaks diplomatic ties with the Nationalist Government and ceases to play the role of "lackey to U.S. imperialism." Inasmuch as the Peking government is engaged in the development of a nuclear weapons system which is impressive, within the region at least, the chances that Japan would completely sever diplomatic ties with Taiwan and (or) her defense alliance with the United States appear to be remote for the present. Communist China's three nuclear detonations had a definite negative impact on Japanese attitudes toward the Peking regime and certainly did little to reduce tensions between the two governments.

With regard to the United States, the most important element of conflict is in the field of military policy. The United States sees Japan as a vital link in the Pacific defense system and has pursued a policy that attempts to make use of Japan and Japanese bases for this role. In short, the United States would like to see Japan as part of the worldwide system of defense against Communist expansion.

Attainment of this goal has been hampered by a number of factors, the most important being the pacifist attitude of the Japanese people themselves since 1945. In general, they fear involvement in any war for any cause, abhor nuclear weapons, sincerely believe in complete nuclear disarmament, and are reluctant to rearm their country because of the dangers of war and the risks of a resurgence of militarism.

The instrument that binds Japan and the United States is the bilateral Mutual Security Treaty first signed in 1951 and renewed in a form more palatable to the Japanese in 1960. The treaty provides for the three basic points of United States military policy toward Japan: a safeguard to Japan from external aggression, a provision for the use of Japanese bases by American forces, and an agreement that Japan will build up her own defenses.

The United States has concentrated more and more of her military strength in Okinawa, now the key military installation in the Pacific. She is reluctant to compromise her strategic military position on the islands by returning them to Japan or even by allowing Japanese administrative jurisdiction over them on a limited basis, even though she recognizes that Japan holds "residual sovereignty" over the islands. This conflict of interest, both in its military and in its political aspects, has been most embarrassing to the Japanese government and is a key issue in the JSP-JCP campaign against the Security Treaty.

Other problems exist (mostly in the economic sphere over fishing rights, trade, and airline routes), but they are not the type to lead to open conflict.

Attitude toward ACD. The Japanese approach to ACD has largely been an emotional one, calling for disarmament as the *summum bonum,* but not taking cognizance of factors in the real world that bar its realization. The term "arms control" is generally unknown in Japan.

Japanese popular attitudes toward ACD are sharply divided into two diverging streams, represented most clearly by the Government and the Liberal Democratic Party on the one hand, and by JSP opposition on the other. If these two camps were represented by the letter "Y", the stem of the Y would represent their substantial aggreement on such matters as worldwide nuclear disarmament, the test ban treaty, the necessity of preventing nuclear proliferation, GCD, the United Nations as an effective international peace-keeping body, the United Nations or other international control atomic energy and so forth. The over-whelming majority of the Japanese people support these positions.

The divergence arises as a result of the JSP's Marxist view of the world. The Socialist Party's ACD program (represented by the left arm of the Y), if formally presented, would certainly include a demand that a law be passed preventing United States forces from bringing nuclear weapons into Japan (including

Okinawa); a declaration that Japan would never store, use, or produce nuclear weapons; the establishment of a nuclear-free zone in Asia; and the abolition of the Self-Defense forces and renunciation of the Security Treaty. The Socialists would have Okinawa and the Bonin Islands returned to Japan and all United States bases removed from them. They would also come to terms with the Soviet Union, recognize Communist China, admit Peking to the United Nations, and make Peking a party to all international ACD negotiations.

The Government-LDP position (represented by the right arm of the Y) is almost diametrically opposed to that of the JSP on all these issues. Although it agrees that Japan should not become a nuclear power even though she could if deemed desirable, and that the United States should not introduce nuclear weapons into Japan, the LDP would not preclude a policy reversal should some emergency arise. Moreover, actual developments and government policy have made such a prompt reversal technically feasible. The Liberal Democrats advocate the continuation of the Security Treaty until Japan can rely on the United Nations and her own forces for protection. This naturally rules out the abolition of the Self-Defense Forces. They consider both the Soviet Union and Communist China potentially hostile and would not expose Japan to the possibility of aggression by abandoning either the ties with the United States or the indigenous defense effort. Although they want Okinawa and the Bonins returned to Japan, they do not feel it would be in Japan's defense interest to press for United States withdrawal under present circumstances.

Thus it can be seen that the Japanese do not agree among themselves on what ACD measures should be accepted, but there is enough basic agreement on long-term ACD objectives to make Japan one of the most responsive of the regional nations toward ACD in general. The Japanese people will almost instinctively respond in a positive manner to most ACD proposals, and as one of the key regional nations, Japan's attitudes and actions could well be influential in determining the position of others.

South Korea

Internal. At this writing, there are no apparent signs of internal tension and struggle that might grow into large-scale insurrections. Communist-inspired guerrilla activities which once threatened the internal security of South Korea have been effectively reduced since the Korean War. The downfall of Syngman Rhee in 1960 and the military coup of 1961, which brought General Park to power, were not accompanied by any protracted internal struggle.

The Park government has nevertheless been faced with two major crises: the treaty with Japan and the economic difficulties dramatized by inflation and chronic large-scale unemployment. In 1965, student demonstrations staged in Seoul and other cities opposing the Normalization Treaty were frequent and widespread, but seemed to lack the massive support of the general public. Most observers believe that Seoul will go through with the treaty provisions.

With regard to domestic conditions, if the standard of living of the general populace is not substantially improved soon and if unemployment is not alleviated, internal discontent may someday become serious enough to engulf the nation. However, any large-scale, externally directed, and openly Communist-inspired insurrection seems highly improbable, for there is very little support for communism among the South Korean people.

Regional. South Korea's only major regional conflict in recent years has been with Japan. The Normalization Treaty, as well as the Park government's more realistic approach to the question of fishing rights, has resulted in a marked reduction of tensions between the two countries. The major problem remaining concerns the aforementioned divided allegiance in the Korean community in Japan, but it is not of sufficient gravity to warrant extended comment here.

Extraregional. Although the Republic of Korea regards the Soviet Union as the architect of both the North Korean regime and the latter's invasion of South Korea, recent South Korean official publications and pronouncements have been less vitriolic toward the Soviet Union, particularly since the signing of the partial nuclear test-ban treaty in 1963. The treaty was signed by the South Korean government and was unanimously ratified by the National Assembly in May, 1964. The Government officially regards the treaty as the "dramatic turning point" in the cold war, possibly "heralding a new era of peaceful and competitive coexistence."[2]

Following the nuclear tests by Communist China, developments in Vietnam and Laos, as well as France's recognition of Peking, South Korea has become even more apprehensive about Communist China. South Koreans are convinced that the direct intervention of Communist China turned the tide in the Korean War against South Korean-United Nation forces. Communist China's close ties with the North Korean regime, as well as those with Hanoi, preclude any basic Seoul-Peking rapprochement at present. However, there is little likelihood of a direct clash between these two countries alone.

Concerning the United States, who remains South Korea's closest and most influential ally, the only major outstanding issue (aside from problems arising from the large number of American troops stationed in the country) centers around the signing of a status-of-forces agreement but this may be resolved without difficulty.

South Korea's major conflict has been and remains with North Korea. South Korea insists that measures to unify the country should be discussed in the United Nations and implemented through that body, while North Korea opposes any United Nations intervention in Korean affairs. Pyongyang demands the complete withdrawal of American troops from South Korea as a precondition for any settlement. The South Koreans fear that this insistence is actually part of a plot to create those conditions that favored invasion in 1950 once again. Furthermore, North Korea proposes military parity (10,000 troops or less for each side), but only after the withdrawal of foreign troops from the South. South Korea, mindful of the 1950 attack, however, insists upon the continued presence of United Nation troops and places her trust in superior military strength. She remains convinced that her security is menaced from the North and cannot be safeguarded except through the use of United Nations channels supported largely by United States troops. This conviction underlies her basic attitude in foreign relations, including all matters relating to ACD.

Attitude toward ACD. Given South Korea's fear that recent events, such as the third Chinese nuclear test, indicate a shift of the balance of power in favor of the Communist states in the Far East, any ACD measure that would reduce South Korea's military power at this time would not be acceptable to, or popular in, South Korea.

However, in areas of ACD not directly related to military strength in South Korea, such as the partial test ban, South Korea has more or less followed the lead of the United States. Furthermore, there is no reason why Seoul would not concur in banning underground nuclear testing if the United States were a party to such an agreement. Inasmuch as South Korea is gravely concerned with the nuclear-weapons program of Communist China, it follows that she would therefore concur in a nonproliferation agreement.

At present, South Korea would be opposed to an agreement stipulating the unconditional abolition of all foreign bases. This is especially true with respect to the United States bases in Korea. North Korea insists on the complete withdrawal of United States troops from South Korea as a prerequisite to ACD, unification, or other negotiations. The South Koreans feel that, even though the Communist Chinese troops have withdrawn from North Korea, they can easily, and on short notice, cross the Yalu River to North Korea, just as the Russians can easily cross the Tuman River.

Established under United Nation supervision, recognized as the sole legitimate government of Korea, and "protected" by it, South Korea has given the United Nations full support and cooperation in various matters, including peace-keeping arrangements and the discussion of the Korean question. South Korea wants the continued presence of United Nation troops until unification is achieved under United Nation supervision. Considering Seoul's confidence and trust in the United Nations, an ACD proposal would be more favorably considered and studied if it originated in the United Nations or other international forum, such as the ENDC. On the other hand, any ACD proposal initiated by the Communist side would be met with great suspicion.

South Korea's attitude toward peace-keeping organizations other than the United Nations can best be demonstrated by her desire to participate in an Asian collective security system as a protection against Communist aggression. It should be noted that Seoul's interest in collective security is not confined to East Asia alone, but seems to encompass the whole Western Pacific area.

As long as conditions persist which cause South Korea to wish for the creation of a collective security system, she will insist on the formation of such a security arrangement as a protection against any possible violation of an ACD agreement. In other words, the creation of a Northeast Asia Treaty Organization, for example, might create an environment that would in turn induce South Korea to participate in an ACD agreement. But, more important, South Korea would definitely press for the continuation of the existing Mutual Defense Treaty with the United States as the ultimate guarantor of South Korean security.

Republic of China (Taiwan)

Internal. The main internal source of tension is the latent hostility between the native-born Taiwanese and the mainland Chinese who fled to the island in the face of the imminent loss of the mainland to the Communists. The mainlanders' domination over the top civil service and Central Government officials has been a persistent source of discontent and friction. It is not surprising that some Taiwanese desire independence or even a renewed association with Japan. In addition, the burden of supporting the military establishment and the large superstructure of the Central Government is, of course, borne by the local population, of which perhaps more than three-quarters are native Taiwanese. It should be noted, however, that the economic benefits of prosperity in the agricultural, as well as in the growing modern industrial sector of the economy, have accrued in large measure to those who were originally residents of Taiwan. Whether this discrepancy between political and economic power may actually increase internal dissension and instability remains to be seen, although the succession question will not pose any serious problems. At present, the domestic scene does not seem marked by any unmanageable or truly explosive tensions such as those that gave rise to the 1947 uprising and repression.

Regional. No conflict that might call for armed intervention by either side exists, or is in prospect, between the Republic of China and other regional states. However, a number of outstanding differences between Nationalist China and other regional countries would either preclude her cooperation with them or make it exceedingly difficult. Such obstacles are relevant in considering ACD measures, especially if the latter were to require joint undertakings, reciprocal responsibilities, and the exchange or presence of one country's nationals in another country's territory, such as ACD implementation and inspection would require. For instance, it would be difficult to envisage joint ACD agreement between the Republic of China and any one of the countries that do not recognize her (Laos, Cambodia, Indonesia, Ceylon, Burma, India, and Pakistan). Employment of nationals of these countries (or of Western countries such as Sweden, France, and Great Britain) in peace-keeping operations or on inspection teams involving Nationalist-held territory would probably not be acceptable to the Nationalist Government.

Concerning Japan, differences exist with regard to (1) the status of Taiwan, (2) the related issue of alleged Japanese tolerance of the Taiwan independence movement in Japan, and (3) Japan's expressed policy of keeping political and economic issues apart in her external dealings -- a policy which allows her to trade with both Communist China and Nationalist China even though she has confined diplomatic recognition to the latter. The Nationalists suspect that Japan may favor either a "two-Chinas"policy or a "one China - one Taiwan" policy. On the other hand, these discordant notes are to some degree offset by a sizable and growing trade (especially from Taiwan's point of view) between Japan and Taiwan; rising Japanese investments in, and technical cooperation with, Taiwan enterprises; and genuine efforts on the part of both governments to maintain friendly relations.

Finally, mention should be made of a potentially disruptive issue that may militate against full cooperation between the Republic of China and such Asian countries as South Vietnam, the Philippines, Malaysia, and Thailand, which might otherwise find that some of their national security interests coincide with those of Nationalist China. This issue arises from the presence of large Chinese communities in these countries. The "host" countries show fear of, and resentment against, the influence and traditionally China-oriented loyalties of these groups and have consequently discriminated against them. The presence of Chinese troops in their territories as peace-keeping forces or of Chinese nationals on inspection teams might conceivably meet with some resistance.

Extraregional. The Kuomintang's militant, anti-Communist attitude makes no distinction between the variant froms of communism -- Soviet, Chinese, Yugoslav, and so forth. This is expressed in the oft-repeated slogan Fan-kung k'ang-o ("Opposition to Communism, and Resistance to Russia"). Practical implementation of this policy, however, must be directed against the Chinese Communists because they possess the Chinese mainland. Thus, Taiwan's conflicts with the Soviet Union, North Korea, and North Vietnam are tangential or secondary to the basic conflict with the Peking regime.

Two cardinal principles have evolved as the ultimate criteria of all policy, external as well as internal. These principles are (1) anticommunism and (2) "Return to the Mainland" -- that is, destroy the Communist Chinese regime. Because a peaceful return without surrender by either side is admittedly impossible, and neither side has shown any inclination to surrender to the other, the second goal becomes one of "reconquest of the mainland" through a "counter-offensive" or other means. Because the ultimate goal of the Nationalist Government is to recover the mainland, the distinction between the requirements of pure defense and those of an aggressive nature is not always, and perhaps cannot be, clearly maintained. In this regard, the offshore islands, especially Quemoy, are regarded by the Nationalists both as (1) essential stepping-stones for the "return," and as (2) essential to the in-depth-defense of Taiwan in the event of a Communist Chinese assault. As a step toward reducing tensions in the Taiwan Strait, the United States has sought to persuade the Nationalists to evacuate the Quemoy and Matsu groups, but to no avail. This matter, together with defense problems in general, have led to tensions between the United States and Taiwan, on occasion. However, all other extraregional tensions pale before the deepseated and, to date, irreconcilable conflict between Taipei and Peking.

Attitude toward ACD. The attitude of the Republic of China toward most ACD measures would seem to be quite predictable, in spite of her relative reticence on a majority of them and the seemingly little attention she has devoted to the subject thus far. A summary of her potential positions, admittedly speculative, may be presented as follows.

First, in all matters relating to nuclear weapons, which she does not possess and is unlikely to try to develop in present circumstances because of their cost and her lack of technical personnel, she would be likely to accept international agreements, such as the test ban treaty, in order to forestall their possible acceptance by Communist China. She would also hope that her own earlier adherence might discourage the latter from participation, because Communist China is also averse to the notion of two Chinas. She would continue to insist that measures be taken to remove Communist China's nuclear-weapons plants, but failing implementation of such a proposal, she might not wish to commit herself on the question of "nuclear proliferation." With this reservation, the Republic of China would be likely to follow the lead of the United States in ACD arrangements concerning nuclear weapons on the assumption that their availability and effective use as a deterrent would be safeguarded by the United States in the latter's own interest. However, the Nationalist Government would not favor a denuclearized zone in the Pacific for fear that it might reduce the effectiveness of deterrence against Communist China.

Second, in all matters relating to nonnuclear weapons, including their production, use, transportation, and disposition (of stock), the Republic of China, being in a state of continued emergency (the island is still under martial law), is suspicious of ACD proposals. She will probably insist on maintaining her freedom of action on the grounds that it is necessary for her internal security and that her conflict with the Chinese Communists is an internal insurgency problem not subject to restriction under international ACD arrangements. At the same time, the degree of freedom that she will enjoy will always be restricted and will depend upon United States policy and on the nature of the latter's military and political assistance.

Third, the Republic of China is likely to display the same attitude toward the recruitment and training of the armed forces, their size and deployment -- an attitude that has already been seen in her resistance to heavy pressures from the United States to reduce their size and redeploy their forces.

Fourth, the Republic of China would most strenuously object to any prohibition of military alliances inasmuch as the Mutual Defense Treaty with the United States is a cornerstone of her present defense arrangements, while alliances with such countries as South Korea, South Vietnam, Thailand, and the Philippines are being actively sought. In particular, the Republic of China would seek to distinguish between "aggressive acts" and "acts of a defensive nature" and would not wish to view all "hostile acts" in the same category.

Fifth, because of her deep distrust of all countries that are not anti-Communist, the Republic of China would insist on controls before proceeding with ACD. Preference would presumably be given to the introduction of ACD measures in gradual stages as well as to political settlement prior to adopting such measures. A political settlement with Communist China is, however, ruled out for the present.

Sixth, in any control organization, she would probably prefer unanimity to other forms of decision-making if she were represented. It is fairly clear, however, that she would not accept nationals from Communist countries and from certain "neutral" countries, especially if such nationals were on regional or field staffs assigned to the Taiwan area.

Seventh, as to methods of control, such as those concerning nuclear weapons, Taipei would probably follow Washington's lead. However, if Communist China were included, she would prefer methods of inspection that could be enforced without requiring official recognition of the countries involved. Therefore, she would prefer long-range (i. e. external) detection methods such as those being used at present. The same consideration would apply to the territory covered by ACD. Preference might be given to arrangements which would include the Republic of China as a signatory, plus other specified areas. The "specified areas" may include mainland China, but Taipei would not wish to be a party to any formal agreement to which Peking is also a party.

Lastly, on sanctions for the violation of an ACD agreement, the Republic of China would probably take the same position as the West on nuclear weapons. It is likely, however, that she would again insist upon a distinction between acts of aggressive intent and acts of self-defense.

SOUTHEAST ASIA

South Vietnam

Internal. The civil war (or, more acurately, the Hanoi-directed Viet Cong insurgency) is obviously the major source of conflict in South Vietnam.

This requires little elaboration, save to add that it is possible that the conflict could spread to other areas in this already unstable subregion.

In addition, there is the clear and present danger of a civil war within the general insurgency. Concepts of the South Vietnamese national interest vary greatly according to the political orientation of distinct and divergent groups within the country. The "Establishment," which consists of the central bureaucracy, urban and provincial councils, and the armed forces, is split into dozens of hostile segments whose concepts of the national interest are often tantamount to perceptions of personal welfare. Influential social groups, whose membership may cut across political lines, include Buddhists, Catholics, Hoa Hao, Cao Dai, and various social or national minorities such as the Montagnards, together with the effectively coordinated (within the South Vietnamese context) Chinese minority. Within all these groups save the latter, factionalism is generally rampant, and group action is often subject to the whims and ambitions of the dominant leaders. The Venerable Tri Quang's continuing (June 1966) attempt to bring down the Ky government is an example. Yet these groups all remain avowedly anti-Communist, adding a ludicrous fillip to a vicious war. Further, this internecine struggle is being waged at a time when the overall military effort against the Viet Cong and Viet Minh forces is proceeding much more satisfactorily and effectively than it was a year ago. The situation remains in doubt at this time, and further developments will probably depend largely on whether or not the Ky government can survive until the scheduled elections.

Regional. South Vietnam is hostile toward the Pathet Lao, perceived to be puppets of the Viet Minh, because of the north-south traffic in military supplies and personnel which passes over the strategic Ho Chi Minh Trail. South Vietnam considers the Communist-controlled areas of Laos as inimical as Cambodia because of their joint help to the Viet Cong.

Cambodia's recognition of Communist China (1958) and her favorable attitude toward the Communist powers have aggravated the perennial tensions between Phnom Penh and Saigon. Incidents along the ill-defined border have been numerous. Prince Norodom Sihanouk, the Cambodian Chief of State, has stated that the whole of Cochin China belongs to Cambodia, but he has not pressed this claim. Since 1956, he has also sought international recognition of Cambodian sovereignty over islands in the Gulf of Siam held by South Vietnam, particularly the large island of Phu Quoc. In late 1964, the South Vietnamese government asked the United Nations to appoint an international jurist to mediate the border dispute, but Cambodia rejected the proposal.

Extraregional. South Vietnam sees North Vietnam as its immediate and most deadly enemy. As an extension of this, under no circumstances will the military administration in the South consent to a coalition government in which control would be shared with representatives of the Viet Cong, who are also regarded as puppets of Hanoi. Therefore, Saigon has not been willing to enter into unconditional discussions with either the Viet Cong or the Viet Minh. Saigon states that victory is the only solution. Every administration has expressed the belief that civil war in the South would present no problem if the umbilical cord to the north could be severed.

South Vietnam perceives Communist China to be the power behind North Vietnam and the ultimate source of the present conflict. Many students, religious groups, and members of the South Vietnamese military would not only march on North Vietnam but also wish the United States to carry out a nuclear strike against the Chinese mainland. The fear of China is deep and real.

With regard to the Soviet Union, South Vietnam realizes that Moscow has given much military and political support to the Viet Cong and Hanoi, providing them with military supplies often of greater sophistication (for example, rockets) than those from Communist China. However, Russia is far away, and thus there is no feeling of immediate physical threat, although Saigon would not under present circumstances show any sympathy toward any Soviet ACD position if said position was not also supported by the United States.

South Vietnam's relations with the United States are the most important of her contacts with anti-Communist extraregional powers. (Saigon broke ambassadorial relations with Paris soon after Marshal Ky assumed power in mid-1965.) The American commitment in men and materiel is essential to South Vietnam's success. Economically, South Vietnam would not constitute a viable state at present were it not for United States assistance. At the same time, South Vietnam is wary lest she lose her sovereignty, however unwittingly, to her American ally. This amorphous feeling of American domination contributed in large measure to the destruction of United States property at the hands of the anti-Communist South Vietnamese in Saigon, Da Nang, and Hue during the crisis in the Spring of 1966. However, knowledge that a cessation of the United States commitment would be tantamount to total victory for the Viet Cong inherently constrains the activities of the anti-American dissidents and has kept them within manageable proportions to date. In addition, and equally important, is the fact that at the time of this writing (mid-June 1966) it would appear that the anti-American protest is confined to a relatively small, though well organized, minority.

Attitude toward ACD. South Vietnam's attitudes toward future ACD measures depend upon internal factors, the political interplay among the great extraregional powers, and the prospects of ACD in Southeast Asia as a whole.

South Vietnamese political and religious groups have not initiated any ACD proposal for Vietnam. South Vietnam's reaction to Prince Sihanouk's proposal for the neutralization of South Vietnam, Cambodia, and Laos, for example, was completely negative. De Gaulle's April 1964 proposal for the neutralization of the whole of Vietnam also received an overwhelmingly negative response from all major groups in South Vietnam.

Successive South Vietnamese governments have taken the position that any political settlement prior to the complete withdrawal of Communist forces to the North would simply be playing into the hands of the Communists. The exigencies of war, together with the totally antithetical positions held by the belligerents, have unfortunately precluded the realization of a ceasefire (other than the holiday period of Tet), let alone a truce, armistice, or ACD.

Laos

Internal. For several reasons, Laos is scarcely a nation in spite of the long history of the kingdom. First, for more than a decade the country has been torn by civil war. Nearly half of Laos is at present in the hands of the Communist Pathet Lao, in reality an agent of North Vietnam. Second, large numbers of DVR troops are present in the Communist-controlled areas of Laos, in addition to the traffic in North Vietnamese men and materiel through Laos along the Ho Chi Minh Trail to South Vietnam. Third, and quite important in the long run, there is little or no feeling of national identity among large sectors of the population. Laotians not ethnically tied to Laos (the Kha, Black Thai, Red Thai, White Thai, Meo, Yao, and others) may constitute over half the total population -- variously estimated to be between one-and-a-half and three million. The overwhelming majority of the people live in isolated towns and villages far from Vientiane and Luang Prabang, the administrative and royal capitals respectively. The mountains and highlands are inhabited by primitive tribal groups which remain unexposed to the modern world.

Regional. In Laos, as in South Vietnam, it is difficult to separate external conflicts from internal ones. The major external tension at present is with Cambodia. The Laotian government has charged that Cambodia provides a sanctuary for Pathet Lao forces as well as supplies via the so-called Sihanouk Trail. Cambodia's close identification with Peking has also had an adverse effect upon Vientiane - Phnom Penh relations. Within the Southeast Asian context, however, this crisis is *in esse* a minor one.

Extraregional. Aside from a general fear of Communist China, Laos' most dangerous extraregional conflict is with North Vietnam. As noted above, Vientiane regards the Pathet Lao as an agent of North Vietnam and sees Ho

Chi Minh's ultimate ambition to be the unification of the whole of Indochina under his (i. e., Communist) rule. Vientiane's conflict with Hanoi cannot, in short, be separated from the internal Pathet Lao insurgency.

Attitude toward ACD. Laotians have little notion of what ACD is about, and their country does not constitute an independent factor in ACD. They are anxious to be left alone (to them, "food, fun, and peace" is the *summum bonum*). They fear the Vietnamese, the Communist Chinese, and to a lesser extent, the Thai. Operations of the International Control Commission are part of the same issues that confront its counterpart in Vietnam. In short, the Laotian situation is so closely related to the Vietnam conflict that the two cannot be treated as separate ACD situations.

Cambodia

Internal. Although the potential for internal difficulties in Cambodia is very high, the situation at present is relatively quiescent, in comparison with certain other states in Southeast Asia. However, the possibility that some of these difficulties could be aggravated should not be ruled out. Among the more important internal sources of conflict are (1) Khmer Serei revolutionary activities against the Sihanouk regime, and (2) Communist revolutionary subversion which is tied in with (3) the minority problem.

Khmer Serei influence has been strongest in the border provinces near Thailand. According to Cambodian authorities, the Khmer Serei has engaged in subversive activities with increasing intensity, including broadcasting from clandestine stations hidden near the Thai and South Vietnamese borders.

Communist influence has been strongest in the border provinces near where there is a large and potentially disloyal Vietnamese minority. On a number of occasions during the Indochinese War, the Viet Minh invaded these border provinces. They organized a Khmer People's Liberation Army and a "resistance government" to wage a guerrilla war against the French and the Phnom Penh regime. In recent years, the Viet Cong have used these areas as bases, although Sihanouk denies this.

From an analysis of minority groups in Cambodia, the Vietnamese pose a serious and long-run security problem which has had important ramifications upon Cambodian domestic politics as well as upon her foreign policy. Cambodia's prohibition of aliens from pursuing some eighteen professions hits the relatively skilled Vietnamese minority the hardest and creates resentment in Vietnamese communities. The Chinese also have suffered from government measures to strengthen Cambodian control over the stagnant economy.

Regional. Cambodia's primary concern is the preservation of her national independence and territorial integrity. Prince Norodom Sihanouk, the Chief of State, and his party, the Sangkum Reastr Niyum (People's Socialist Community), usually referred to as the Sangkum, constitute a political leadership which, for the purposes of this analysis, may be considered as synonymous with the country itself.

The sources of conflict between Cambodia and her neighbors, Laos, South Vietnam, and Thailand, are conflicting territorial claims, border violations and incidents, support of insurgency, minority problems, and political polemics. These conflicts are not dangerous in themselves, but they could develop into serious confrontations. Sihanouk is uneasy lest Thailand and South Vietnam take advantage of local unrest and either annex certain Cambodian territories or aid the Khmer Serei in effecting a coup. He remains convinced that Thailand and (or) Vietnam only await a fortuitous moment to invade Cambodia.

Extraregional. Sihanouk perceives the primary danger to Cambodian security as arising from great power conflicts in Southeast Asia -- conflicts which may lead to "wars of national liberation" and (or) foreign intervention, like those in South Vietnam and Laos.

This conviction of threat explains in large part the seemingly paradoxical aspects of Sihanouk's perceptions of Communist China. The Cambodian leader is acutely aware of the geopolitical realities of Southeast Asia, as well as those of the world. He believes Communist China to be the supporter of all Communist subversion in Southeast Asia. At the same time, he appears to doubt both the credibility of United States security guarantees (though recognizing that the United States is the only extraregional power able, to any degree, to counter Communist inroads into the subregion) as well as the staying power (however defined) of this country. Furthermore, Sihanouk sees the United States in alliance with his ancient enemies, the Vietnamese and the Thai. Thus, even though convinced that Communist China will dominate the entire Southeast Asian subregion in the long run, he is nevertheless prepared to accept Peking as Cambodia's "protector" -- that is, to come to terms with a future danger in order to deal with what he regards to be a clear and present one. As the Prince stated in October 1965 (in a talk to a Cambodian military delegation prior to its departure for Peking):

> When we become pro-American, the Chinese and [North] Vietnamese immediately become our enemies and bring insecurity to us. It is for this reason that I think that we have greater advantages in continuing to quarrel with the Americans. . . . The most important advantage is that we can maintain our peace, unity, and tranquillity. . . .
>
> If we try to reconcile with the Americans, the Reds will create troubles, and we will die. The Reds in our country are always ready to serve the foreign Reds. Meanwhile, the latter only wait for a favorable moment to attack us. Now we are left alone because we are quarrelling with the Americans.
>
> Dear Companions, <u>I think we can quarrel with any country we want. But with China and [North] Vietnam which are near us, we must do our utmost to maintain their friendship in order to safeguard our security. Our policy must be realistic. If we do not follow this path, our situation will be serious. That is the truth.</u>[3] [Emphasis added]

In sum, then, Sihanouk has lost confidence in the ability of the United States to maintain her position in Southeast Asia. He sees no course open to him other than to applaud Communist Chinese pronouncements (whatever his private feelings may be) and to work to strengthen Cambodia's accommodation with Communist China.

<u>Attitude toward ACD.</u> As noted earlier, Cambodia in the past has been interested in the neutralization of Cambodia, Laos, and South Vietnam. Speaking in Paris in mid-1964, Sihanouk urged a disengagement between the United States and "foreign" Communist forces in Laos and South Vietnam and neutralization of the three countries under international guarantees with "appropriate control." The term "appropriate control" has not been defined. However, in the past, the Prince was willing to accept a system of control similar to that of the ICC in Laos. The Prince disagrees with de Gaulle's proposal of August 1963: the neutralization of the whole of Indochina. According to Sihanouk, the "neutralized zone" should not include North Vietnam, although any ACD scheme in Indochina must include Hanoi and Peking as interested parties. This point was made clear in July 1964 when Cambodia rejected South Vietnam's proposal for the development of a United Nation police force to prevent Cambodian - South Vietnamese border violations.

It is difficult to say whether Cambodia is at present still interested in her former neutralization stand. Cambodia's withdrawal of her own proposal for neutralization in April 1965, suggests that Sihanouk no longer believes that neutralization will safeguard Cambodia's national security.

Cambodia's attitude toward ACD seems to depend very heavily upon the attitude of Peking. For example, Cambodia refused to sign the partial nuclear test-ban treaty but supported Chou En-lai's proposal for complete prohibition and destruction of nuclear weapons. It is safe to say that Cambodia is most likely to reject any ACD proposal that is patently unacceptable to Communist China, given Sihanouk's apparent belief that the United States is indeed a "paper tiger."

Thailand

Internal. At present, the Thai Government is deeply concerned about the Communist-led Patriotic Front activities in northeastern Thailand, and to a lesser extent, with those Communist elements from Malaya that escaped to the Thai side of the Kra peninsula during the late 1950's. The Thailand Patriotic Front is considered to be an immediate threat to national security, and the Government (with United States assistance) is working energetically to pacify and materially improve conditions in the depressed northeastern area.

In addition to Communist infiltration and subversion, there is a potential danger of irredentism in the northeastern provinces of Thailand near the Laotian border. Ethnic heterogeneity, close cultural bonds not rooted in loyalty to the Thai monarchy and the existence of large numbers of Laotian and Vietnamese refugees from Indochina are responsible for the weak sense of nationality as well as for the conflicting loyalties in the northeast. The Thai government had long neglected these people and learned with alarm only in the past few years that the people in that region had more knowledge of developments in Laos and North Vietnam than of developments in Thailand. The situation, as noted above, has improved in the last few years. However, the fact that many of the Vietnamese refugees, overwhelmingly pro-Hanoi, have refused repatriation leaves a serious and unresolved problem within Thai frontiers.

A final source of internal tension has centered around Thai relations with the Chinese minority, especially with regard to the possibility that Peking, rather than Bangkok, may attract the loyalty of many Sino-Thai in the event of a major crisis. Furthermore, it should be added, the Thai want the Chinese minority to prove its commitment to Thailand but are not explicit as to what act or acts will constitute this proof. The Sino-Thai, in turn, generally feel that they have already made this commitment. This uncertainty, together with acts of discrimination by the Government against the Sino-Thai, prolongs the confused situation. However, within the context of this report, the Chinese minority problem is not one of major proportions.

Regional. Thailand's only regional conflict of note is with Cambodia and centers around unsatisfied territorial claims. The border problem aside, another source of conflict has been the frequent practice of Cambodian opponents of Sihanouk to find sympathetic asylum in Thailand. Thailand's membership in SEATO as well as divergent Thai-Cambodian policies with regard to Communist China, are additional sources of conflict. There is little likelihood, however, that the conflict will progress beyond the verbal brickbat stage, perhaps punctuated by a border skirmish now and then. The game, in short, would not be worth the candle.

Indeed, what is noteworthy is that this is Thailand's only regional conflict of any moment, and this conflict itself is low-key. The problems in the northeastern region of the country notwithstanding, Thailand feels secure (having a strongly nationalistic populace plus a firm United States commitment) and prosperous. She is, in addition, playing an increasingly important role in Southeast Asia. Thai assistance in (hopefully) ending the Malaysian-Indonesian confrontation is clear evidence of this.

Extraregional. North Vietnamese military intervention and revolutionary subversion in Laos and South Vietnam are viewed in Bangkok as part of the attempt to establish Communist rule over the whole of Indochina. North Vietnam, the Thai Government feels, does not have sufficient power to conquer Thailand without massive Communist Chinese military support, even with the pro-Hanoi Vietnamese minority in the northeast.

The Thai view Peking as having greater expansionist ambitions than North Vietnam. Communist China, the Thai feel, wishes to dominate the whole of Southeast Asia, and Thailand, as the great rice supplier of Southeast Asia, is a tempting prize.

Thailand does not view the Soviet Union as a major and immediate threat -- Moscow is far away and, in the Thai view, has lost much of its revolutionary zeal during recent years.

Attitude toward ACD. The Thai attitude toward ACD is basically sympathetic. Thailand appears to have no aggressive ambitions, Cambodian fears notwithstanding. Anything that would assure or enhance the maintenance of peace would receive Thai support. The Thai government however, is highly suspicious of any simple, idealistic scheme resting on the basis of mutual trust and respect.

Thailand signed the limited test-ban treaty and has asked the United Nations to develop truly effective peace-keeping machinery. Thailand has proposed that the United Nations establish a "service for peace committee" to serve as mediator in any international dispute.

Thailand considers that nuclear ACD and the elimination of heavy offensive weapons systems are useful largely for the major powers. Such arms reductions are laudable in that they reduce the danger of nuclear or large-scale conventional warfare, but they do not reduce the possibilities of conventional wars or Communist "wars of national liberation." The banning of the latter type of activity would receive strong Thai support if accompanied by a strong control organization with adequate peace-keeping machinery for detecting violations as well as force for punishing the violators.

Burma

Internal. By choice the most isolated country in Southeast Asia, one of Burma's chronic problems has been a lack of internal political stability. This is a problem for all the newly independent nations of Asia, but it seems even more pronounced for Burma, which suffered greatly under the Japanese Occupation during World War II, the subsequent liberation struggle, and the postwar series of rebellions. Probably no other regional country save Vietnam and Indonesia, has suffered through such a continuing series of wars, revolts, and alterations in political regimes. These phenomena are significant in the case of Burma, since they put a premium on conflict in domestic affairs as a major and continuing problem characterizing the affairs of that country since the attainment of independence.

Regional. External tensions exist with both India and the Republic of China, although the situation is not serious enough with either country to warrant extended discussion here.

Concerning India, overall friendly relations between the two nations have been steadily subjected to certain pressures arising out of the nationalization policies of successive Burmese governments as applied to the Indian minority. This problem is significant in the context of Burma's basic needs and interests, inasmuch as India remains Burma's best rice customer, and historically, Burma has valued India's friendship.

Burma's relations with the Republic of China are the worst of any of the relationships she has with foreign powers. The problem centers around the remnants of Chinese Nationalist troops who fled into Burma in the face of the advancing Communists in 1950. Some of them joined insurrectionist groups; others resorted to banditry; still others trafficked in opium. A United Nations General Assembly resolution (1953) called for the evacuation of these forces, and some 6,000 men were removed. However, it was said that some 6,000 remained. The problem still exists today, but successive campaigns by the Burma Army in 1960 and 1964 succeeded in reducing Nationalist strength. It may be noted that the success of these campaigns was the result of the effective coordination of military operations at the local level between the Communist

Chinese Army and the Burma Army in the border regions.

Extraregional. No serious extraregional conflicts exist, although Burma is apprehensive of the great power of Communist China. The Burmese policy of nonalignment has had a calming effect on points of potential conflict.

Attitude toward ACD. Burma's attitude toward ACD can be deduced from several basic factors, the most important of which are her commitment to a policy of nonalignment and her strong desire to assert and maintain her independence. This caused Burma to reject Commonwealth membership and, consequently, the military and economic aid which would have been available to her as a Commonwealth member. This policy in turn has aggravated internal stability and in fact may have prevented Burma from solving her internal problems, with the result that a military regime was established. Internal instability and military rule cannot help but affect Burmese attitudes toward ACD proposals. At the same time, however, it should be remembered that Burma's policy of nonalignment is more genuinely neutral than that of many other countries.

During the years of deliberation at Geneva since 1962, the Burmese delegation has consistently urged the following measures: the negotiation of a comprehensive test ban treaty; the linking of the proposed International Disarmament Organization more closely to the United Nations and making the control body a principal organ like the Security Council; the adoption of international control measures in some defined sequence so as to attain GCD; the cessation of any and all nuclear weapons tests; the setting up of an impartial international scientific body to insure inspection under a test ban treaty; the destruction in stages of conventional as well as modern strategic weapons and their delivery systems; all steps necessary to prevent the further proliferation of nuclear weapons; the conclusion of a nonaggression pact between NATO and Warsaw Treaty countries; the stopping of all armament production and development beginning with the more dangerous weapons and proceeding all the way down to the simplest conventional weapons; a parallel agreement among the major powers to reduce their military budgets by 10-15 per cent as proposed by the Soviet Union.

Malaysia

Internal. The main source of internal difficulties in Malaysia is the racial, cultural, and economic heterogeneity of the people, as well as their relative lack of national feeling or identity with the state. This can be seen in the ejection of Singapore from the Federation of Malaysia on August 9, 1965 (although, under the terms of the Articles of Separation, the two states retain very close ties), as well as Sabah state's blaming Kuala Lumpur for interfering in Sabah's internal affairs. The problem is further complicated by the relative industriousness of the Chinese minority vis-à-vis the Malay majority. However, Commonwealth membership and the presence of sizable British and Australian forces in the Federation seem to be stabilizing factors that could work to hold Malaysia together in the event of extreme crisis.

Regional. Malaysia has a low-key territorial dispute with the Philippines over the Borneo territory of Sabah; however, it is highly unlikely that this will lead to an open or serious conflict. The main conflict has been with regard to Sukarno's policy of "confrontation;" that is, the Indonesian leader's announced policy of destroying the Federation and bringing the Borneo states into the Republic of Indonesia, as a first step toward the eventual assimilation of Malaya into what Sukarno has called Indonesia Raya (Greater Indonesia).

Sukarno's policy was not successful; "confrontation" now appears to be over, on the basis of an agreement concluded in Bangkok in June 1966. If this is indeed the case, and if the proposed association including Thailand and the Philippines in addition to the two former protagonists actually comes into being, a major source of regional tension will have been eliminated.

Extraregional. The major extraregional tension arises from Malaysia's general fear of Communist China and from the possible subversion on the part of the latter through penetration of the Chinese population in Malaysia and Singapore. Inasmuch as the insurgents during the Emergency of the 1950's were predominantly oriented toward China and Peking, rather than toward Moscow, Kuala Lumpur is loath to carry on normal relations with Communist China and would certainly resist any attempt on the part of Singapore to do so.

Attitude toward ACD. In view of the embryonic stage of the Malaysian-Indonesian rapprochement at this time, no ACD proposals relevant to Malaysia can be discussed here, although the climate would seem to augur well for ACD in the Southeast Asian subregion. This will be expanded upon in Part III of this report.

Indonesia

Internal. Indonesia's major internal tensions are the general crisis situation arising from the abortive Communist Party (PKI) coup of Autumn 1965 and its bloody aftermath; long-standing tensions with the Chinese minority which were aggravated by the PKI's attempted coup; separatist tendencies in Sumatra and the Celebes; and serious problems attendant upon a nearly bankrupt economy.

With regard to the PKI, the Party has now been outlawed, and the Indonesian Army, in *de facto* control of the country, is attempting to eliminate those members who survived the coup attempt. The PKI, once the largest Communist Party in a non-Communist State, has been shattered, and President Sukarno appears to be little more than a figurehead.

The savage reaction to the attempted coup has also been directed against the Chinese minority. Inasmuch as Peking was perceived by the Indonesian Army leaders to be the *eminence grise* in the September 30 uprising (actually, the uprising occurred in the early morning hours of October 1, possibly to coincide with Peking's National Day celebrations), many Chinese were indiscriminantly killed, imprisoned, or stripped of their assets or means of livelihood. The Chinese schools in Indonesia have been ordered closed, and further acts of this nature can be expected. It should be noted, however, that such acts have a dual nature. Whereas they tend to add to the current, general post-September 30 crisis, they may, in the long run, tend to reduce the separatist tendencies of an important minority group and, thus, be stabilizing in effect (although Draconic in execution).

Insofar as the general economic malaise is concerned, the situation at present is far from clear. With Sukarno becoming more and more isolated from the decision-making process, it appears that cooler and wiser heads (such as Foreign Minister Malik and ex-Vice President Hatta) may prevail in the economic as well as in the political sphere. Both Japan and the United States have offered emergency aid to Indonesia, and there are already indications that rational economic planning will be reinstituted.

Regional. Indonesia's major regional tension has been the "confrontation" with Malaysia after the latter Federation was established in 1963. However, as noted earlier, it appears that a pacific settlement of this dispute has been, or is about to be, effected. During the discussions between the two principals held in Bangkok during June 1966, consideration was apparently given to what would in effect amount to a merger of the Association of Southeast Asia (ASA) and Maphilindo, with Thailand indicating that Burma and South Vietnam would also be welcome to affiliate with the proposed organization.[4] Although such a membership would appear at present to be highly unlikely, given the diverse (even discordant) political orientations of the nations involved, it does indicate that the Southeast Asian subregion is in a state of flux and that certain previously held fundamental positions no longer obtain. As indicated earlier, trends in Southeast Asia may augur well for ACD, both within that subregion and in a wider context.

Extraregional. In analyzing Indonesia's relations with the major extraregional powers, a distinction must be made between the pre-September 30, 1965 and the post-September 1965 period. Prior to the abortive coup of September 30, Indonesia's confrontation with Malaysia, her arms purchases from the

Soviet Union, and her close ties with Communist China had been sources of political conflict between Indonesia and Great Britain and had caused her growing estrangement from the United States. Since the September coup attempt, however, Indonesia has apparently decided to end her confrontation with Malaysia and has announced her intention of recognizing both Malaysia and Singapore. As a result of these developments, relations with Great Britain and the United States may be eased. By the same token, relations between Indonesia, on the one hand and Communist China and the Soviet Union on the other hand, are likely to deteriorate even further, with the possibility of a virtual rupture in relations with Communist China. However, in spite of Communist Chinese support for the PKI and Indonesian attacks on Communist Chinese representatives and official missions in Indonesia, the distance between the two countries would seem to preclude any direct armed conflict. On the whole, therefore, Indonesian relations with the extraregional powers would appear to have improved since the September 30 coup.

Attitude toward ACD. As is also the case with Malaysia, little can be said with certainty on the question of Indonesia's future attitude toward ACD. Although a party to the partial nuclear test-ban treaty, Sukarno nevertheless claimed that Indonesia was working to develop an indigenous nuclear weapons capability -- a claim discounted by serious students of Indonesian affairs. With "confrontation" possibly a thing of the past, the chances for ACD would seem to be enhanced. However, it should be noted that: (1) the Army is in de facto control of the country; (2) the purge of PKI members and sympathizers continues; (3) the domestic scene is far from stable; and (4) as a corollary to the preceding point, the fissiparous tendencies and the danger of separatism on Sumatra and in the Celebes are felt to require a large military establishment to preclude and/or deal with future results against central authority. The foregoing does not mean that ACD arrangements (e. g., pacific settlement of disputes) are impossible with Indonesia's neighbors, but it does indicate that the internal situation may be a complicating factor.

Philippines

Internal. The major internal problems center around the remaining Communist (Hukbalahap) forces in Central Luzon and endemic unrest in the rural areas due to difficult economic conditions. However, the back of the Huk insurgency was broken during the mid-1950's under the forceful leadership of the late President Magsaysay. This situation could change, but within the context of this report, neither problem would seem serious enough to warrant extended comment.

Regional. To an outside observer, it is noteworthy how little the Filipinos interest themselves in the affairs of their subregion. No major regional conflicts exist. Any territorial claims, however spurious, to the Borneo state of Sabah appear to have been dropped, inasmuch as formal diplomatic relations between Malaysia and the Philippines have now been established. Historical antipathies toward Japan remain, and there is a continuing, low-grade tension with Taiwan with regard to the Filipino Chinese minority; however, neither tension would seem to have an adverse effect upon ACD.

Extraregional. The Philippine Republic has a general fear of Communist China. This might have an adverse effect upon ACD; however, it could also be counteracted by the fact that the Republic is an island nation, as well as the fact that the United States is recognized as the ultimate guarantor of Filipino sovereignty in the event of a major conflict.

With regard to United States - Filipino relations, some increase in anti-American feeling has been noted of late; it has arisen in part over a fear that the Philippines will be drawn into playing a sizable role in the Vietnam conflict. In addition, there is a problem with Washington with regard to parity in the exploitation of natural resources. Again, however, neither problem would seem to be of significant moment in the regional context.

Attitude toward ACD. Any ACD arrangement would have to promise greater security to the Philippines than now exists in Manila's treaties with the United States, membership in SEATO, and membership in the United Nations. Such an arrangement would be difficult to imagine. However, it is quite possible that Manila would desire to be party to a subregional or regional ACD arrangement that would reduce area tensions to which the Philippines is not an immediate party; hence, Manila's participation would require little in the way of concrete adjustments, merely formal assent. It is reasonable to assume that in any negotiations for ACD with reference to Southeast Asia, the interests of the Philippines would be closely identified with those of the United States.

SOUTH ASIA

India

Internal. India's internal problems are many and varied: the language-state (separatism) problem; internal Communist pressures; age-old inequities, such as the caste system; and extreme population pressure together with a limping economy.

In a country as vast and diverse as India, regional loyalty has been a preponderant factor that often runs counter to national loyalty. This has led to serious north-south conflicts and tensions, which, in recent years, have been principally centered around the question of a national language. The Indian Constitution called for Hindi to be adopted as the official national language on January 26, 1965. This was heatedly opposed by the people of Madras whose mother tongue is Tamil, a language very different from Hindi. It was argued that inasmuch as qualifying examinations for Government would henceforth be given in Hindi, the Tamil-speaking candidate from the south would be at a great disadvantage vis-à-vis the northern applicants. In addition, even in the north the adoption of Hindi as the national language is strongly contested by the Bengalis, who claim that their language is the superior one. The situation remains unresolved, with English continuing to serve as the lingua franca.

The domestic standing of the Communist Party of India (CPI) was greatly reduced as a result of the Sino-Indian border war of 1962, as well as by the continuing tensions arising therefrom. In the last national election (February-April, 1962), the CPI polled nearly 11.5 million votes (9.9 per cent) and won twenty nine seats (5.9 per cent of the total seats); however, it should be remembered that this election was held about six months prior to the Communist attack.

At present, the CPI is plagued by splits within the movement, Government harassment, and its general lack of appeal among the Indian body politic. The CPI split into rightist (CPI/R) and leftist (CPI/L) parties in 1964, primarily over the issue of cooperating with the ruling Congress Party. At present, the estimated membership of the two parties is 55,000 and 70,000 respectively.[5] The CPI/R is generally Moscow-oriented and favors cooperation with the Congress Party, whereas the CPI/L, some of whose leaders are strongly pro-Chinese, advocate militant opposition to the Congress Party and the establishment of an underground apparatus. The leftist program has gained little public support, although it has secured the support of the majority of Indian Communists and is now the stronger of the two parties. In March 1965, the CPI/L, running against a split Congress Party, emerged as the largest single party in the Kerala state elections with 44 seats, while the CPI/R won only three. However, most of the CPI/L leaders were forced to enjoy this electoral success from inside jail -- nearly a thousand of them were confined in late 1964 on charges of plotting with Peking to overthrow the Indian government. In addition, the CPI/L was placed in a very difficult position by the Indo-Pakistani conflict of September 1965, when they were loath to support the Indian government even at the height of the conflict, and they have since been compromised by further Communist Chinese actions with regard to Pakistan. This did not work to the benefit of the CPI/R, however, for Shastri and the Congress Party were able to reap all the credit for India's performance during the conflict.

Party membership has apparently continued to decline,[6] and the Congress Party has greatly strengthened its position as a result of the Sino-Pakistani courtship, the Indo-Pakistani conflict (where India regained some small amount of respect), and the Tashkent settlement, coupled with Prime Minister Shastri's untimely death. It would appear that a disunited CPI, faced with Mrs. Gandhi and the charisma attendant upon that name as well as a revivified Congress Party (compared with 1964-65), has little chance even of holding its own in the national elections scheduled for early 1967.

On balance, India's most serious domestic problem would seem to be a dual one -- overpopulation and underdevelopment. Population growth continues unabated; vagaries of the weather plague the predominantly agricultural economy that has to struggle to reach subsistence levels; and the huge, entrenched, and fossilized civil service bureaucracy has proved unable to come to grips with these and other kindred problems effectively Indeed, the most sobering thought of all is that the problems may *in esse* be insoluble -- at least without massive international aid of hitherto-unheard-of proportions.

Regional. Tensions exist with *Burma* (over the latter's treatment of the Chettyars or Indian minority) and with *Ceylon* (over the latter's treatment of the Indian Tamil minority and her attendant demand that India accept repatriation of the majority of the Tamil community in Ceylon). However, neither problem is considered to be of sufficient gravity to require solution by force of arms.

India's major regional conflict is, of course, with *Pakistan.* The dispute over the distribution of the waters of the six rivers of the Indus Basin was amicably settled in 1960, but the basic issue of Kashmir remains; indeed, it has become of increasing concern to India in view of the Karachi-Peking honeymoon of the past twelve months.

The Hindu ruler of the Province of Jammu and Kashmir ceded his state to the Union of India on October 27, 1947, even though 77 per cent of the population was Moslem. Bloody fighting ensued, until a ceasefire policed by the United Nations was effected in 1948. A plebiscite was subsequently recommended by the United Nations, but India and Pakistan were not able to agree on the conditions for it. While accepting the need for a plebiscite in principle, the Indian government maintained that the necessary "conditions" did not exist in the area. India also argued that a plebiscite would result in communal riots and religious war. Thus, the Indian Parliament ratified a permanent constitution for the state of Jammu and Kashmir on November 17, 1956, and it -- that is, the Indian-occupied portion of the state -- was incorporated into the Indian Union on January 26, 1957, as the seventh state. Pakistan had already incorporated some 31,250 square miles of Kashmir territory, roughly 40 per cent of the state, into West Pakistan. The resolution of this conflict to the mutual satisfaction of the two principals seems impossible at present, although the Indo-Pakistani war over Kashmir in September 1965 may have proved one critical point -- mainly, neither belligerent can afford a repetition because the costs in men, materiel, and loss of aid are too great. In any event, this remains the major conflict in the South Asian subregion.

Extraregional. India's major extraregional conflict is with Communist China. Communist seizure of Tibet, the subsequent bloody suppression of revolts in that region, the Sino-Indian border war of 1962 together with the continuing probes and resultant incidents along the ill-defined perimeters of Ladakh and the Northeast Frontier Agency, and the fear of an already militant Peking soon to possess a credible nuclear capability -- all combined to produce the trauma that has in turn caused a heated debate within India as to the efficacy, and even the reasonableness, of tenets previously held sacrosanct.

"The Five Principles of Peaceful Coexistence" and the so-called Spirit of Bandung are examples. Nehru's grand design tumbled like a house of cards, and India emerged from the border war as little more than an impotent idealist. In turn, however, this shock, together with the increased perception of threat from both Communist China and Pakistan, has tended to inject a sobering note of realism into Indian policy of late. There are also signs that a more pragmatic and searching look is being given to the many serious domestic problems facing India, inasmuch as internal stability and development is usually sine qua non to national security and foreign influence. In any event, future trends in the conflict between these two Asian colossi are far from clear.

Attitude toward ACD. The present attempts on the part of India to effect a nonproliferation agreement are well-known, although strong arguments have been advanced within that country in favor of an Indian tactical nuclear deterrent. Indeed, the ultimate objective of GCD has been one of the chief aspirations of India since the beginning of the national independence movement. The major reason for this is the deep and continuing influence of the fundamental teachings of Gandhi, especially his philosophy of nonviolence, which in turn is based on pacific Hindu and Buddhist teachings.

If ACD measures can meet the basic prerequisites -- pursuit of nonalignment, nonproduction of nuclear weapons, and maintenance of national security -- they may well receive earnest and sympathetic consideration from India. The chances of their acceptance will be enhanced if India perceives that they also constitute an immediate contribution to Indian security, particularly with regard to Communist China and Pakistan.

This does not constitute a very comprehensive analysis of India's position with regard to ACD, but it is doubtful if a more exact evaluation can be made in view of the internal difficulties and potential external threats from Communist China and Pakistan. The need for GCD will be readily conceded in India, but the realization that, in an imperfect world, the "is" is not always (or even usually) the "ought" still sends shock waves throughout that country.

Pakistan

Internal. Pakistan's major internal problems concern tensions between East and West Pakistan (which are separated by nearly one thousand miles of unfriendly territory), as well as the general malaise resulting from a sluggish economy.

Although Pakistan has not suffered from civil war, the geographical makeup of the country poses serious problems. The leaders of Pakistan have relied upon the bonds of Islam and the fear of India to cement the diverse linguistic, racial, and cultural groups into one polity. However, no clear sense of Pakistani nationalism has emerged, and East Pakistan (i.e., East Bengal), culturally and geographically distant as it is, remains more concerned with its own grave problems than with problems concerning Pakistan as a whole. For instance, it does not share the Central Government's preoccupation with the Kashmir problem and, being about equal in population to the western part (though smaller in area), demands an equitable share in the Government the allocation of financial resources, and the economic development plans. The strong Central Government in the West is dominated by the Punjabis, and the President, Mohammed Ayub Khan, is also a westerner, although a Pathan rather than a Punjabi. The major economic problems center around Pakistan's large population and the fact that the price of jute, a major Pakistani product, has been depressed on the world market since the end of the Korean conflict.

In sum, fundamental differences between the two wings of Pakistan are likely to remain, and they constitute a serious source of tension for the country as a whole. The ultimate danger posed by these political, cultural, and economic problems is the possible secession of East Bengal.

Regional. Pakistan's major external conflict is with India and centers around the state of Jammu and Kashmir. Pakistan believes that the adjacent

Moslem territory should, by its very nature, belong to her. Strategically, Kashmir is also very important to Pakistan for defense, as well as for economic reasons. For example, all the rivers that flow through Pakistan rise in the Vale of Kashmir, and hence Pakistan fears possible Indian diversion of the courses of these rivers because India controls the headwaters.[7]

Extraregional. Pakistan has a latent fear of the Soviet Union. In addition, she resents United States aid to India. Neither problem, however, would seem to be serious enough to warrant comment within the context of this report.

Attitude toward ACD. The possibility of Pakistani participation in regional or subregional ACD arrangements has to be evaluated against Karachi's perception of her own defense requirements as well as against the possibility of Communist aggression. Until Pakistan becomes convinced that aggression against her is highly unlikely from India (over Kashmir), the Soviet Union (in the event Russia should seek Gwadar as a warm-water port,) or Afghanistan (over the creation of an independent Pakhtoonistan from the Pushtu minority in the two countries), the chances of her agreeing to reduce her armed strength is very slight. Any such agreement on the part of Pakistan would probably have to entail positive and tangible reduction in India's military strength.

As indicated above, the major obstacle to Pakistani participation in ACD arrangements is the conflict with India. However, if the causes of Indo-Pakistani tensions can be resolved to the satisfaction of both parties, Pakistan could at least redeploy her armed forces from Kashmir and the Indo-Pakistani border. In fact, Pakistan may eventually even accept a demilitarized and independent Kashmir under United Nations guarantees. This would of course augur well for South Asian as well as regional ACD.

Ceylon

Internal. Ceylon's major internal problems are a sluggish economy and the tensions generated by Sinhalese-Tamil rivalries. Negotiations in the Fall of 1964, however, have produced some positive results in this matter. India agreed to accept 525,000 Tamil immigrants as Indian citizens while Ceylon agreed to accept 300,000 as naturalized Ceylonese citizens. The problem of ascertaining the citizenship of the remaining 150,000 immigrants has yet to be formally resolved, although a spokesman for the Indian government stated that this group would be repatriated over a fifteen-year period. The two Governments are now taking steps to carry out the agreement.

Regional. The only regional tension of note has been the Sinhalese-Tamil problem mentioned above.

Extraregional. Ceylon has no serious problems with the extraregional powers.

Attitude toward ACD. Ceylon is unique in the Far East in that she would have everything to gain and nothing to lose through regional or subregional ACD arrangements. Any reduction in the military power of the greater and potentially antagonistic nations would be to Ceylon's advantage. But ACD measures would have little or no direct effect on the size and composition of her own small armed forces, nor would they be likely to cause problems of economic or psychological adjustment. The major benefit of an ACD arrangement to Ceylon would be the possibility that it would increase international security at no increase in cost to her. This is especially true with regard to a nuclear-free zone in the Indian Ocean, an arrangement desired greatly by Ceylon.

SOUTHWEST PACIFIC

Australia - New Zealand

Internal. No serious internal tensions or conflicts exist in either country.

External. Geographically isolated from the other countries of Southeast Asia by many miles of ocean, neither country has any serious regional conflict, save Australia's latent problem with Indonesia over the status and ownership of the New Guinea territories. However, with the Indonesian - Malaysian confrontation hopefully at an end, there would appear to be little possibility that this relatively minor problem would suddenly assume great importance.

Extraregional. Aside from a general fear on the part of both countries of Communist China, the only extraregional tension arises from the Vietnam conflict, inasmuch as both Australia and New Zealand have committed combat forces to the war. However, it is not foreseen that either country would take a position antithetical to that held by the United States concerning this conflict.

Attitude toward ACD. Australia and New Zealand see little hope for satisfactory ACD arrangements in the Far East. Their pessimism in this context can be summarized in two statements: the prospects for further Communist gains in Southeast Asia are considered so favorable that no serious interest in ACD can be assumed to exist on the Communist side; and, even if those prospects could be greatly reduced by a decisive Western strategy, any ACD arrangement acceptable to the Communist side would be observed only until its violation became expedient.

Australia and New Zealand cannot be expected to develop serious interest in any ACD arrangements for the Far East (especially Southeast Asia) unless the balance of power in those areas changes definitely in favor of the West and unless there is evidence that the revolutionary commitment in Communist China's foreign policy has been greatly reduced. However, it should be noted that this overt resistance (or lack of interest) may be reduced by means of repeated and concrete affirmations of the United States to stand by her defense commitments to Australia and New Zealand. This is not to indicate or imply that the latter two countries question the authenticity of the United States commitment, but merely that a promise, like a protestation of undying love, is worth repeating. In any event, should ACD agreements be effected among other nations in the region, there is little if anything that these two remote Southwest Pacific countries could do about it.

In order to summarize the multiple tensions among the regional nations, a chart is appended at the end of this report (Appendix III) and serves to bring together on one sheet a short resume of national internal conflicts and tensions, regional armed hostilities and tensions, and extraregional armed conflicts and tensions. For the sake of brevity, some examples of conflict and tension which appear on the chart are not covered in the text. Marked by asterisks, these conflicts are usually low key, only potential in nature, and primarily of historical importance.

FOOTNOTES

[1]The regional and extraregional states have been underlined to indicate interrelationships.

[2]*Hengjong baekso* (Administrative White Paper; Seoul: Dae Han Kong Ron Sa, 1964), pp. 102.

[3]Phnom Penh Domestic Service (in Cambodian), October 26, 1965.

[4]Thai Premier Thanom Kittikhachorn at a press conference, Bangkok Domestic Service (in Thai), June 6, 1966.

[5]Bureau of Intelligence and Research, *World Strength of the Communist Party Organizations, 18th Annual Report* (Washington: Department of State, January 1966), pp. 98-100 *passim.*

[6]*Ibid.*

[7]For a further discussion of Indo-Pakistani tensions, see the preceding section on India.

PART III

ATTITUDES, LIMITATIONS, AND POSSIBILITIES OF ACD

CHAPTER 1: ATTITUDES OF REGIONAL NATIONS TOWARD ACD

INTRODUCTION

This section deals with the attitudes of regional nations -- expressed or implied -- toward various ACD measures. These apparent attitudes have been collected and analyzed; and hopefully, certain valid conclusions can be drawn from the results.

The analysis continued in this section is based on a regional attitudinal matrix which closely parallels, but expands upon, the matrix contained in Appendix I, Part C dealing with the principal ACD measures proposed since World War II.* The attitudinal matrix, however, differs from the preceding one in that it poses specific questions concerning ACD to each country in the region. Answers to these questions were derived from an individual attitudinal matrix filled out for each country. An assessment of each country's attitude was based upon (1) government statements concerning the ACD measures in question, or lacking this, from (2) our own deductions of the probable attitude of the country, based on information contained in the country papers. All questions were designed to elicit answers that showed attitudes strongly favoring, conditionally favoring, strongly opposing, or conditionally opposing each ACD measure considered; however, certain noncommittal answers were allowed. It was assumed that all regional nations responded to the questions in the matrix simultaneously so that the answers of one country would not prejudice those of another. It was further assumed that each question was posed in the same manner, "Would your country consider entering into an ACD agreement that would provide the following . . . "

METHOD OF DETERMINING ATTITUDES

At first an attempt was made to determine the individual countries' responses to all the specific questions in the attitudinal matrix, each question dealing with one of the ACD measures or its variant.

The attitudinal matrix resulting from this attempt consisted of 439 questions answered hypothetically for each of the fifteen countries (Australia and New Zealand have been considered as one country in this study), giving a total of 6,585 responses. These results not only proved too unwieldy for meaningful analysis, but certain additional difficulties resulted. The first of these was that the questions, although designed to be simple and direct, could not help but be subject to some slight differences in interpretation when applied to different countries. And the second was that despite a careful analysis of each question, some countries, if actually put to the test, would probably not take the position we have attributed to them. It seemed more logical, therefore, to approach the problems by considering trends shown in answers to groups of related questions. Closer examination further revealed that certain questions could be grouped together without loss of meaning, whereas other questions could be omitted because they were too detailed to be of real value. The result was a more manageable matrix consisting of eighty-seven questions, with no significant loss of depth or clarity.

The next problem was to correlate the answers. This was done by making a series of independent "test groupings" according to geographic, cultural, political, economic, and military factors in order to determine patterns of response. As might be expected, some of the test groupings had no bearing

*For the regional attitudinal matrix see Appendix II.

whatsoever on regional attitudes toward ACD proposals, and they were eventually discarded. Other test groupings, however, showed many points of similarity with groupings made on the basis of answers given in the attitudinal matrix.

Test Groupings

The following is a list of the test groupings considered. Asterisks are affixed to those categories found to be relevant when tested against the attitudinal matrix.

TEST GROUPINGS

1. Geographic Location
   a. Nations touching Communist China, North Korea, or North Vietnam (First Tier)
      - Burma
      - India
      - Laos
      - South Korea
      - South Vietnam
      - Taiwan
      - Pakistan

   b. Nations close to, but not touching, Communist China (Second Tier)
      - Cambodia
      - Indonesia
      - Japan
      - Malaysia
      - Philippines
      - Thailand

   c. Nations relatively far from Communist China
      - Australia - New Zealand
      - Ceylon

   d. The island nations
      - Australia - New Zealand
      - Ceylon
      - Indonesia
      - Japan
      - Philippines
      - Taiwan (not an island nation in her own view)

2. Cultural Factors
   a. Racial groupings
      - Mongoloid (including Chinese)
         - Japan
         - South Korea
         - South Vietnam
         - Taiwan
      - Thai
         - Laos
         - Thailand
      - Mon-Khmer/Tibeto-Burman
         - Burma
         - Cambodia
      - South Asian peoples
         - Ceylon
         - India
         - Pakistan
      - Caucasian
         - Australia - New Zealand

   b. Religious orientation
      - Predominantly Buddhist - Theravada*
         - Burma
         - Cambodia
         - Ceylon
         - Laos
         - Thailand
      - Predominantly Buddhist - Mahayana *
         - Japan
      - Predominantly Hindu
         - India
      - Predominantly Moslem
         - Indonesia
         - Malaysia
         - Pakistan

Predominantly Christian

Australia - New Zealand | Philippines

Other

South Korea | South Vietnam | Taiwan

c. Large or significant Chinese minorities

Burma | Malaysia | South Vietnam
Cambodia | Indonesia | Thailand

3. Political Factors

a. Type of government and ideological orientation* (in a broad sense)

Pro-Western democracies

Australia - New Zealand | Malaysia

Pro-Western military regimes

South Korea | Taiwan
South Vietnam | Thailand

Neutralist military regimes

Burma

Neutralist democracies

Ceylon | India

Other neutralist countries

Cambodia | Indonesia | Laos

Countries difficult to classify

Pakistan

b. Influence of British, or British Commonwealth, ties

Commonwealth members

Australia - New Zealand | India
Ceylon | Malaysia

Other British ties

Burma

c. Policy of pursuing national interests by aggressive military action*

Indonesia (prior to early 1966)
Pakistan (Tashkent Agreement may end this aggressive role for Pakistan)
Taiwan

d. External threat perceived as:*

An intraregional threat

Australia - New Zealand (from Indonesia)
Cambodia (from South Vietnam and Thailand)
India (from Pakistan)
Malaysia (from Indonesia)
Pakistan (from India)

An immediate threat from Communist China, North Korea, and North Vietnam

India | South Vietnam | Thailand
Laos | Taiwan

A considerable threat from Communist China, North Korea, and North Vietnam

Burma | Cambodia | South Korea

A less immediate threat from Communist China

Australia - New Zealand | Malaysia
Indonesia | Pakistan
Japan | Philippines

A remote threat from Communist China
- Ceylon

As an extraregional threat from nations other than Communist China, North Korea, and North Vietnam
- Cambodia (from the United States)
- Indonesia (from the United States and the "imperialists")
- Japan (from the Soviet Union)
- South Korea (from the Soviet Union through North Korea)
- Pakistan (from the Soviet Union)

e. Internal dissidence and armed rebellion *

Active
- Burma
- Indonesia
- Laos
- Malaysia
- South Vietnam

Possibly active in future
- Cambodia
- India
- Pakistan
- Philippines
- Thailand (Fall 1965)

Little or no activity
- Australia - New Zealand
- Ceylon
- Japan
- South Korea
- Taiwan

f. Attitude toward ACD arrangements if Communist China did not participate in discussions and did not follow resulting ACD arrangements*(Taiwan not considered)

Might participate
- Cambodia**
- Ceylon
- Laos

Would probably not participate
- Australia - New Zealand
- Burma
- Japan
- Philippines

Would definitely not participate
- India
- Indonesia
- Malaysia
- Pakistan
- South Korea
- South Vietnam
- Thailand

4. Economic factors

a. Economy and standard of living

Advanced
- Australia - New Zealand
- Japan

Progressing
- Malaysia
- Taiwan
- Thailand

Making limited progress
- Burma
- Ceylon
- India
- Pakistan
- Philippines
- South Korea
- South Vietnam (before 1960)

** Although Cambodia might welcome any ACD agreement that would improve her position with her neighbors, it is quite possible that she would refuse to enter any agreement that did not have Peking's approval or support. Because this question is designed to test attitudes toward Chinese participation in discussions and observation of agreed-upon ACD measures, Cambodia still qualified as a nation favoring the principles of ACD in this context.

Stagnant or retrogressing

Cambodia
Indonesia
Laos
South Vietnam (since 1960)

b. Cost of military establishment

Hinders economic development

Burma
India
Indonesia
Pakistan
South Korea
South Vietnam
Taiwan
Thailand

Does not significantly hinder economic development

Australia - New Zealand
Cambodia
Ceylon
Japan
Laos
Malaysia
Philippines

c. Possible effects of ACD measures on employment

Unemployment problem might result

South Korea
Taiwan

Unemployment problem probably would not result

India
South Vietnam

Unemployment problem definitely would not result

Australia - New Zealand
Burma
Cambodia
Ceylon
Indonesia
Japan
Laos
Malaysia
Pakistan
Philippines
Thailand

5. Military Factors*

a. Country's own perception of ability to defend itself

Confident

Indonesia

Can defend with outside military aid (United States or other)

Australia - New Zealand
India
Pakistan (if threatened by India)
Philippines
South Korea
Taiwan

Might be able to defend with outside military aid

Japan
Malaysia
South Vietnam
Thailand

Has little or no confidence even with outside military aid

Burma
Cambodia
Ceylon
Laos
Pakistan (if threatened by Communist China or the Soviet Union)

b. Countries whose armed forces are insignificant as military instruments (from standpoint of size or efficiency)

Cambodia
Ceylon
Laos
Philippines

c. Countries whose armed forces are small in terms of size or population of the country

Australia - New Zealand
Japan
Philippines

d. Countries whose armed forces would be ineffective against an outside aggressor

Burma
Cambodia
Ceylon
Laos
Philippines

e. Countries the size of whose armed forces and/or equipment indicates that their purposes go beyond the purely defensive
   Indonesia
   Taiwan

f. Countries with numerically large armed forces
   India
   Indonesia (borderline case)
   South Korea
   South Vietnam (borderline case)
   Taiwan

The preceding outline shows some of the many test groupings that have been considered and which, on the surface at least, appear to be the most relevant.

Application of the test groupings to the attitudinal matrix could proceed in a number of ways. We have elected to attack the problem by first eliminating those areas of substantial agreement on ACD among the regional nations. The remaining ACD measures are then treated separately; inferences are drawn from each group of measures tested.

If the results of this approach are to be of any value, three points must be kept in mind: (1) National positions on ACD questions are not static and may change dramatically with the impact of a single major event. (2) The positions of politically unstable countries, shown in the test groupings, can change rapidly. (3) Many of the ACD attitudes attributed to the regional nations depend upon the definition of the terms we have chosen to use. Much flexibility in interpreting results is necessary in order to avoid stereotyping a nation's attitude or overemphasizing its response to any single question.

WEAPONS

Concerning the regulation of nuclear weapons; long-range unmanned delivery systems; and chemical, biological, and radiological weapons (Locus of Regulation, Part I, on the attitudinal matrix); almost all nations approved the control measures considered. The single exception was Indonesia, which consistently opposed controls. It would be unprofitable to apply the test groupings against these ACD questions to determine the countries choosing to accept, or in Indonesia's case to oppose, the controls. It should suffice to say that the regional nations have no reason to oppose controls on weapons of mass destruction which they do not possess, especially since they perceive them as a threat to themselves or to mankind. On the other hand, Indonesia's negative response was in keeping with her aggressive attitude toward her neighbors, and it is based upon the fact that Indonesia was allegedly striving to produce nuclear weapons of her own.

Another area of substantial agreement is in the control of the uses of outer space (Locus of Regulation, Part V, of the attitudinal matrix). All countries approve regulations controlling the use of outer space for military purposes, with the exception again of Indonesia. The reasons for this agreement, and for Indonesia's disagreement, remain the same as those for the control of nuclear weapons.

A third area of substantial agreement that can be eliminated from the test groupings concerns denuclearized zones and nonproliferation (Locus of Regulation, Part VI, of the attitudinal matrix). To all three questions in this set, twelve countries favored denuclearization and nonproliferation; three countries, Australia - New Zealand, Indonesia, and Taiwan opposed such measures. Inasmuch as each of the nations opposed had its own reasons for rejecting the denuclearized zone idea -- reasons apparently unrelated to those of other countries -- nothing further could be gained by applying the test groupings to them.

A final area considered unprofitable for inclusion in the test groupings is the section on sanctions (Control Aspect of ACD, Part V, C, of the attitudinal matrix). The answers to these questions are uniform, there being no worthwhile points of exception. All countries except Indonesia and Taiwan favored sanctions.

Having eliminated the ACD areas unproductive for analytical purpose, the relevant test groupings can now be applied to the remaining ACD questions. Before doing so, it should be pointed out that there are instances of spurious correlations. For example, countries whose economies show signs of development appear to oppose prohibition of the production of conventional weapons. It is doubtful whether any of the countries in question would oppose this prohibition for such a reason since it had already been determined that acceptance of ACD measures by most regional countries would affect their economies very little. The correct conclusion seems to be that these countries oppose prohibitions on the production of conventional weapons for other valid reasons and that the economic factor is coincidental. Several groupings of this kind have been rejected and will not be discussed further.

Heavy Offensive Weapons *

The analysis of attitudes toward the control of heavy offensive conventional weapons showed several interesting patterns. First, the cultural influence of Theravada Buddhism revealed a definite alignment:

Countries predominantly Theravada Buddhist in religion	Countries favoring general control of heavy offensive weapons
Burma	Burma
Cambodia	Cambodia
Ceylon	Ceylon
Laos	Japan
Thailand	Laos
	Philippines
	Thailand

Without intimating that Japan is greatly influenced by religious considerations in such matters, it is interesting to note that the one other Buddhist country does join this grouping very conveniently. India, the cultural wellspring from which the Theravada Buddhist countries derive their cultures, is not included among those favoring controls on heavy offensive weapons, but had the question been posed in 1960 instead of 1965, she most probably would have approved them. This change in attitude shows that practical considerations override philosophical values when the two conflict. These comparisons show a recurring pattern. That the Theravada Buddhist countries line up solidly in favor of controls on this question does not in itself constitute positive proof of a valid connection, but other patterns, which emerge in later questions, tend to support the validity of this grouping.

One might expect countries perceiving an immediate military threat from Communist China to approve controls on heavy offensive weapons. They do not, however. For example:

Countries perceiving an immediate threat from Communist China, North Korea and/or North Vietnam	General attitude toward controlling heavy offensive weapons
India	opposes
Laos	favors
South Vietnam	opposes
Taiwan	opposes
Thailand	slightly favors **

* See Appendix I, Part C, p. 138.

** In determining a "slightly favoring" or "slightly opposing" attitude, we have

Countries under considerable threat from Communist China, North Korea, and/or North Vietnam	General attitude toward controlling heavy offensive weapons
Burma	favors
Cambodia	favors
South Korea	opposes

At first glance, it would appear that no particular pattern arises from these two groupings. However, if we inject a second factor by asking "Which of those countries seriously threatened by Communist China, North Korea, and/or North Vietnam have decided to oppose this threat by force?" an interesting correlation results.

Countries that will oppose Communist China, North Korea, and/or North Vietnam by force	General attitude toward controlling heavy offensive weapons
India	opposes
South Korea	opposes
South Vietnam	opposes
Taiwan	opposes
Thailand	slightly favors

Conversely, if we ask "Which of these countries have decided to meet this threat by other means?" the following pattern emerges.

Countries that will oppose the Communist threat by other means	General attitude toward controlling heavy offensive weapons
Burma	favors
Cambodia	favors
Laos	favors

Here the important groupings, which later evidence tends to confirm as valid, emerge. Notice also that Burma, Cambodia, and Laos fit into the Theravada Buddhist cultural grouping. Thailand is the exception to the rule, both in deciding to oppose the Communist threat by force and in being the only country in that group to favor the control of heavy, offensive weapons even slightly -- hence the conflict between her current policy and her tradition is evident.

Three of the regional states having more or less aggressive attitudes toward their neighbors in the pursuit of national policies also take similar positions on this issue:

Countries pursuing aggressive national policy	General attitude toward controlling heavy offensive weapons
Indonesia	opposes
Pakistan	opposes
Taiwan	opposes

Pakistan's position in this group is based solely on her attitude toward India with regard to Kashmir. Taiwan's aggressiveness stems from her determination to reestablish the Nationalist Government on the mainland of China, which, from the Nationalist point of view, is an internal Chinese problem, although

** taken into consideration the element of strong and conditional responses, giving more weight to "strongly favoring" and "strongly opposing" positions than to their conditional counterparts. For this reason, a strictly numerical tabulation does not always indicate a country's attitude.

from the point of view of ACD, it should be considered as an aggressive attitude and a regional problem.

Another illuminating grouping can be made from the countries that perceive a serious threat from within the region:

Countries perceiving intraregional threat	General attitude toward controlling heavy offensive weapons
Australia (from Indonesia)	opposes
Cambodia (from Thailand and South Vietnam)	favors
India (from Pakistan)	opposes
Malaysia (from Indonesia)	slightly opposes
Pakistan (from India)	opposes

Malaysia's opposition is more qualified than that of some of the others, perhaps because she sees the possibility of imposing controls on Indonesia which in turn might lessen the Indonesian threat. Indonesia claims to see a threat from her neighbors, but these claims may be regarded as a political tactic and therefore not valid. Again, if we add the second criterion -- the manner in which a country proposes to meet this perceived threat -- we find all the countries that have decided to meet it by military resistance opposing controls on heavy offensive weapons; and Cambodia, the one nation that has decided to use other means to repel the threat, favoring these controls. Combining these results with the results of the question on the perception of a threat from Communist China, North Korea, and/or North Vietnam, a reinforcing pattern appears:

Countries seeing serious intraregional or North Korean, North Vietnamese, Chinese Communist threat and willing to oppose it by force	General attitude toward controlling heavy offensive weapons
Australia - New Zealand	opposes
India	opposes
Malaysia	slightly opposes
Pakistan	opposes
South Korea	opposes
South Vietnam	opposes
Taiwan	opposes
Thailand	slightly favors

If Indonesia, the only country aggressively pursuing her national objectives (until early 1966) and not listed, is added to this group, then all countries opposing control of heavy offensive weapons will have been included in the grouping. Again, Thailand is an exception.

When the countries confident of their ability to defend themselves, either alone (like Indonesia) or with outside aid (from the United States and/or other countries) are brought together another pattern results:

Countries confident of ability to defend themselves with outside aid	General attitude toward controlling heavy offensive weapons
Australia - New Zealand	opposes
India	opposes
Indonesia	opposes
Pakistan (against India)	opposes
Philippines	favors
South Korea	opposes
Taiwan	opposes

That the Philippines is the exception in this group may reflect two important outside factors: (1) Philippine confidence in United States willingness to defend her and (2) her insular position, which makes defense easy, particularly if heavy offensive weapons are not brought to bear.

The pattern is not quite so strong, however, among the countries having little confidence in defending themselves:

Countries with little or no confidence in ability to defend themselves	General attitude toward controlling heavy offensive weapons
Burma	favors
Cambodia	favors
Japan	favors
Laos	favors
Malaysia	slightly opposes
South Vietnam	opposes
Thailand	slightly favors

Ceylon is not considered because she perceives little or no threat. Pakistan is considered in her attitude toward India only because Pakistan thinks of defense primarily in terms of an Indian threat.

In evaluating the regional nations' attitudes toward ACD with regard to Communist Chinese (PRC) participation the results are according to expectations:*

Countries that might accept ACD without PRC participation	General attitude toward controlling heavy offensive weapons
Cambodia	favors
Ceylon	favors
Laos	favors

Countries that probably would not accept ACD without PRC participation	General attitude toward controlling heavy offensive weapons
Australia-New Zealand	opposes
Burma	favors
Japan	favors
Philippines	favors

Countries that would definitely not accept ACD without PRC participation	General attitude toward controlling heavy offensive weapons
India	opposes
Indonesia	opposes
Malaysia	slightly opposes
Pakistan	opposes
South Korea	opposes
South Vietnam	opposes
Thailand	slightly favors

Again, Thailand is the only country that lines up somewhat inappropriately.

The final significant groupings in this category have to do with the correlation between the size and effectiveness of a country's armed forces and its attitude toward heavy offensive weapons.

Countries having numerically large armies	General attitude toward controlling heavy offensive weapons
India	opposes
Indonesia	opposes
South Korea	opposes
South Vietnam	opposes
Taiwan	opposes

Countries whose armed forces would be ineffective against outside aggression	General attitude toward controlling heavy offensive weapons
Burma	favors

---

* Taiwan is not considered in this test grouping.

Cambodia	favors
Ceylon	favors
Laos	favors
Philippines	favors

It is obvious that countries with armed forces that would be ineffective against aggression would favor controls on heavy offensive weapons. The grouping of countries with numerically large armies in solid opposition to controls on heavy offensive weapons would not have been so impressive if India had not changed her attitude quite recently.

From the preceding analysis we can conclude tentatively that the regional nation favoring controls on heavy offensive weapons has the following general characteristics. It is a militarily weak nation lacking confidence in its ability to defend itself from threatened aggression; it may, therefore, have decided to defend itself by other than military means; and it is more likely than other countries to accept ACD measures without Communist Chinese participation. Most of the nations in this category are Buddhist in religion and cultural outlook.

On the other hand, a nation opposing controls on heavy offensive weapons tends to have a larger, more effective military establishment (there are noteworthy exceptions); it is more confident of its ability to defend itself if assisted from outside the region; and it has decided to defend its borders from aggression by military means. These countries are unlikely to accede to ACD controls without the assurance of Communist Chinese observance.

Inconsistencies in attitude abound. India, Pakistan, the Philippines, South Vietnam and Thailand all exhibit unusual attitudes at times. It may easily be explained that these exceptional attitudes of India, Pakistan, and South Vietnam arise from the practical consideration of existing circumstances, but those of Thailand and the Philippines seem to arise from more complex reasons. Culturally, Thailand favors the peaceful way, but she has sided with the West and has decided to fight in her own defense. Her ambivalence in attitude toward ACD controls on heavy offensive weapons may arise from a conflict between her culture and practical considerations. India has faced this same conflict, but perhaps because she has had to repel actual aggression, her attitude has suddenly reversed and has been firmly established outside the context of its normal cultural pattern.

The Philippines, as a relatively isolated island group, feels some security in her geographic position, and her independence is backed by strong guarantees that the United States will defend her. She can apparently afford the luxury of maintaining a military force limited in size and, of the countries confident of defending themselves, takes a different attitude in favoring ACD controls on heavy offensive weapons. Despite her strongly anti-Communist attitude, the Philippines perceives the Communist threat primarily as an internal matter, one in which heavy offensive weapons would not be expected to play an effective part.

Other Conventional Weapons

Only five of the fifteen regional nations generally favor control of other conventional weapons, whereas seven favor control of heavy offensive weapons, and fourteen favor controls on weapons of mass destruction. The reasons for this dwindling number of favorable response should become apparent as the examination of other conventional weapons proceeds. In comparing test groupings with the responses of the countries to the question of controlling other conventional weapons, several new trends come into focus.

Let us first examine the Theravada Buddhist grouping of nations to see the change that takes place among them:

Theravada Buddhist nations	General attitude toward controlling	
	Heavy offensive weapons	Other conventional weapons
Burma	favors	opposes
Cambodia	favors	favors
Ceylon	favors	favors
Laos	favors	slightly favors
Thailand	slightly favors	opposes

The almost unanimous approval shown toward control of heavy offensive weapons completely breaks down for other conventional weapons. Japan, the other Buddhist nation, continues to approve controls, and India, the country from whose culture traditional Buddhist attitudes stem (though not predominantly Buddhist herself), continues to oppose controls. In the matter of threat perception, attitudes on the control of other conventional weapons change significantly when compared with attitudes on heavy offensive weapons.

Countries perceiving North Korean, North Vietnamese and/or Communist Chinese threat and willing to oppose it by force	General attitude toward controlling	
	Heavy offensive weapons	Other conventional weapons
India	opposes	opposes
South Korea	opposes	opposes
South Vietnam	opposes	opposes
Taiwan	opposes	opposes
Thailand	slightly favors	opposes

These countries are now in complete agreement on the control of other conventional weapons.

The three countries that have decided to meet the Communist Chinese threat by nonmilitary means and which favor control of heavy offensive weapons no longer have a unified opinion on the control of other conventional weapons:

Countries perceiving North Korean, North Vietnamese and/or Communist Chinese threat and planning to meet it by nonmilitary means	General attitude toward controlling	
	Heavy offensive weapons	Other conventional weapons
Burma	favors	opposes
Cambodia	favors	favors
Laos	favors	slightly favors

Expanding the question,

Countries perceiving serious intraregional or North Korean, North Vietnamese, and/or Communist Chinese threat and willing to oppose it by force	General attitude toward controlling	
	Heavy offensive weapons	Other conventional weapons
Australia - New Zealand	opposes	opposes
India	opposes	opposes
Malaysia	slightly opposes	opposes
Pakistan	opposes	opposes

South Korea	opposes	opposes
South Vietnam	opposes	opposes
Taiwan	opposes	opposes
Thailand	slightly favors	opposes

To summarize, countries perceiving any type of outside threat seem reluctant to accept controls on other conventional weapons if they intend to meet the threat by force.

An examination of some political factors may help us to understand this change in pattern. From the point of view of governmental structure and ideology, no particular pattern emerges with respect to the control of heavy offensive weapons, except that military regimes usually tend to oppose controls. However, when the control of other conventional weapons is considered, an interesting change occurs.

Pro-Western democracies	General attitude toward controlling	
	Heavy offensive weapons	Other conventional weapons
Australia - New Zealand	opposes	opposes
Japan	favors	favors
Philippines	favors	slightly favors
Malaysia	slightly opposes	opposes

Pro-Western military regimes	General attitude toward controlling	
	Heavy offensive weapons	Other conventional weapons
South Korea	opposes	opposes
South Vietnam	opposes	opposes
Taiwan	opposes	opposes
Thailand	slightly favors	opposes

These two groups taken together show an increasingly negative attitude toward controls. Japan, however, shows an exceptional willingness to accept weapons controls under all conditions, a willingness that illustrates the strong neutralist strain running through Japanese attitudes.

Next, when the internal dissidence factors in the countries are examined, the following patterns become evident.

Active internal dissidence	General attitude toward controlling	
	Heavy offensive weapons	Other conventional weapons
Burma	favors	opposes
Indonesia	opposes	opposes
Laos	favors	slightly favors
Malaysia	slightly opposes	opposes
South Vietnam	opposes	opposes

Where no pattern appeared for heavy offensive weapons, a clear pattern of opposition emerges for other conventional weapons. Internal dissidence is probably a prime cause for opposition to the application of ACD measures to other conventional weapons within the region. Further examination shows:

Potential internal dissidence	General attitude toward controlling	
	Heavy offensive weapons	Other conventional weapons
Cambodia	favors	favors
India	opposes	opposes
Pakistan	opposes	opposes
Philippines	favors	slightly favors
Thailand	slightly favors	opposes

The trend in the "moderate" countries, although less pronounced, is unmistakable. Countries with dissidence problems appear to be reluctant to control other conventional weapons, their most important means for suppressing dissidence. In negative confirmation of this fact, there is no change among those nations undisturbed by dissidence problems.

Internal dissidence factor slight to none	General attitude toward controlling Heavy offensive weapons	Other conventional weapons
Australia-New Zealand	opposes	opposes
Ceylon	favors	favors
Japan	favors	favors
South Korea (repressed)	opposes	opposes
Taiwan (repressed)	opposes	opposes

No significant change occurs among those nations able to defend themselves and their comparative attitudes toward control of heavy offensive and other conventional weapons. Except the Philippines, they continue to oppose controls, but:

Countries with little or no confidence in ability to defend themselves	General attitude toward controlling Heavy offensive weapons	Other conventional weapons
Burma	favors	opposes
Cambodia	favors	favors
Japan	favors	favors
Laos	favors	slightly favors
Malaysia	slightly opposes	opposes
South Vietnam	opposes	opposes
Thailand	slightly favors	opposes

Here a rather weak pattern favoring the control of heavy offensive weapons disintegrates into one showing opposition to the control of other conventional weapons. This change can be explained in terms of internal dissidence as well. Even countries unable to defend themselves effectively against an outside aggressor are more confident of their ability to quell internal dissidence, and conventional arms are needed for the purpose.

Finally, among those countries that might accept ACD measures even if Communist China did not (Cambodia, Ceylon, and Laos), there is no significant change. These same countries which favor control of heavy offensive weapons still favor control of other conventional weapons, although Laos' attitude is now less favorable.

Countries that would probably not accept ACD unless observed by PRC	General attitude toward controlling Heavy offensive weapons	Other conventional weapons
Australia-New Zealand	opposes	opposes
Burma	favors	opposes
Japan	favors	favors
Philippines	favors	slightly favors

Among countries that would definitely oppose ACD measures not also applied to Communist China the trend is toward greater opposition to the control of heavy conventional weapons.

Countries that would definitely not accept ACD unless observed by PRC	General attitude toward controlling Heavy offensive weapons	Other conventional weapons
India	opposes	opposes
Indonesia	opposes	opposes
Malaysia	slightly opposes	opposes
Pakistan	opposes	opposes
South Korea	opposes	opposes
South Vietnam	opposes	opposes
Thailand	slightly favors	opposes

In summary, we can make the following observations on the attitude of the regional states toward control of other conventional weapons.

1) The Theravada Buddhist nations, which had maintained considerable solidarity in favoring the control of weapons of mass destruction and heavy offensive weapons, have lost their cohesion in this case.

2) Countries facing aggressive threats, although favoring controls on the weapons of mass destruction, are opposed to ACD controls on conventional weapons even more strongly than they are to controls on heavy offensive weapons.

3) While the pro-Western governments unanimously approve of controlling weapons of mass destruction and are divided on the question of controlling heavy offensive weapons, they are quite united in opposing the controls of other conventional weapons.

4) The presence or absence of internal dissidence in a country appears to play a primary role in determining whether it will favor control of other conventional weapons generally useful in cases of small counterinsurgency operations, but plays a lesser role in determining the control of heavy offensive weapons, and plays almost no role in determining attitudes toward control of weapons of mass destruction.

5) There seems to be very little chance that regional nations will accept ACD arrangements unless the same controls are applied to Communist China; this attitude is even more pronounced on the question of controlling other conventional weapons than it is on that of heavy offensive weapons.

Several conclusions can be reached from the foregoing: First, among the regional nations, conventional weapons will, in general, be more difficult to place under ACD arrangements than either weapons of mass destruction or heavy offensive weapons. The unstable countries in this area require conventional weapons to maintain government control over internal dissidence; they would not easily relinquish their most effective weapons. Second, favorable responses to ACD measures concerning weapons depend to a great degree upon whether a nation possesses (or aspires to possess) the weapons under discussion. Third, further evidence proves that countries will abandon general, traditional cultural attitudes when faced with real problems which defy traditional methods of solution.

ARMED FORCES AND DEPLOYMENT

Application of the test groupings to the Armed Forces and Deployment sections of the ACD attitudinal matrix (Sections II and III) reveals no significant new patterns but confirms many of the patterns established earlier. The nature of the ACD problems in the Armed Forces section makes it difficult to consider the section as a single entity; consequently, each group of questions has to be treated separately. To the questions relating to the regulation of the size of armed forces, responses vary widely. There is a substantial favorable response to placing numerical ceilings on manpower and to agreeing on national ratios to determine armed strength, but the idea of cutting military establishments down on a percentage basis is not well accepted, apparently because percentage cuts would generally be disadvantageous to the smaller and weaker nations.

On the questions concerning conscription, length of military service, and paramilitary formations, the attitudes are very uniform. Nations with internal dissidence problems or those perceiving strong outside threats tend to oppose these restrictions.

As might be expected, countries with military governments generally oppose restrictions on their armed forces; the same is true of the countries pursuing aggressive national policies.

On the problem of the deployment of armed forces, the neutral nations tend to be most favorably disposed toward restrictions in this field, and for the first time, Indonesia approves of an ACD measure, presumably because foreign bases and alliances hamper her own aggressive national policies. The largely favorable response to the question of putting limitations (jurisdiction over entry of weapons, personnel, etc.) on foreign bases seems to be a subjective reaction by several countries having American bases on their soil. They would not want to eliminate them, but would like to control them. Japan, the Philippines, South Korea, Taiwan, and perhaps, Thailand fall into this group.

One peculiar tendency in the responses to the two questions on prohibition of military alliances should be noted. Seven nations favor prohibiting military alliances with regional powers, but only five would prohibit such alliances with extraregional powers. On the opposite side of the same question, only three nations strongly oppose prohibiting regional alliances, but seven strongly oppose prohibiting extraregional alliances. Despite the strong nationalistic tendencies of the regional countries, they seem to agree that as long as a strong military threat to the region exists, they must depend on extraregional support to maintain security. Only five nations generally approve the various ACD measures on armed forces. In addition, it is often difficult to predict the attitude of two others (Laos and Pakistan). Indonesia apparently approves of the ACD measures on military alliances, not so much because they are ACD measures, but because these particular items might advance her own regional ambitions.

Countries generally approving ACD measures on:

Armed forces	Other conventional weapons
Burma	Cambodia
Cambodia	Ceylon
Ceylon	Japan
Japan	Laos
Philippines	Philippines

Four of the countries appear in both the preceding groupings. Laos could possibly be added to the list favoring control of the armed forces if it were possible to analyze her position. Burma's apparent ambivalence is logically explained by the important counterinsurgency role of her armed forces, even though she remains firmly neutralist. Like those countries approving measures to control other conventional weapons, the nations generally approving ACD measures controlling the armed forces are most often neutralist, either in outlook or in fact, they are militarily weak; they either perceive only an indirect external threat or perceiving a strong threat, they have elected to face it by means other than force.

A general tendency appears for the island nations (other than Indonesia and Taiwan, whose pursuit of national policy is aggressive) to show a more relaxed attitude toward ACD questions than mainland powers. This tendency is particularly marked in the instances of the Philippines and Japan. Ceylon responds in a very favorable fashion, but this is to be expected. The exception is Australia - New Zealand, whose sparse population and fears of hostile Asian peoples may counterbalance the feeling of security usually attributable to island countries. At any rate, those sections dealing with control of the armed forces and other conventional weapons show that the island nations do display a slightly greater sense of security.

MILITARY EXPENDITURES

This very short section adds nothing new to previous observations or conclusions, but again tends to reinforce established patterns. All three questions in the section elicit a generally favorable response. Those countries taking a negative attitude fit into three general categories: (1) nations aggressively pursuing national objectives, (2) nations perceiving a threat from Communist China and deciding to oppose this threat by force, and (3) nations having military governments. It is interesting to note that India, in this particular set of questions, has returned to a neutralist attitude by strongly favoring all three proposals. This may be explained by India's strong realization of defense costs in terms of economic development.

ASPECTS OF IMPLEMENTATION, ORGANIZATION, AND VERIFICATION

Regional attitudes toward the sequence in which an ACD arrangement is adopted, toward the nature of the control organization, and toward the measures of control to be exercised by a control authority are somewhat less specific than those attitudes toward the objects of control and/or regulation: weapons systems, armed forces, military alliances, and so forth. A possible reason for this vagueness is that few regional states have given serious consideration to those aspects of ACD. Their attention has instead been focused on what is to be regulated and on how such regulation might affect their individual security. Nevertheless, it is still possible to make some predictions about what kind of control organization might be accepted by the various regional powers. In this context, five general aspects of control have been considered: (1) the sequence of ACD arrangements, (2) the nature of the control organization itself and the composition of the field staff and inspectorate, (3) the method of inspection and verification, (4) the establishment and composition of an international police force, and (5) the determination and punishment of violations of ACD arrangements.

Sequence of ACD

On the basis of the attitudinal matrix, three general categories of sequence in which ACD might be adopted are considered: ACD measures prior to, simultaneous with, or following the establishment of control machinery; phased implementation of ACD measures with or without controls; and political settlement of issues prior to, simultaneous with, or following ACD arrangements.

With regard to ACD measures and their relationship to the establishment of control machinery, the positive responses can be arranged as follows:

Nations that might favor ACD measures *		
Before the establishment of control machinery	Simultaneous with the establishment of control machinery	After the establishment of control machinery
Burma	Burma	Australia-New Zealand
Cambodia	Cambodia	Burma
Ceylon	Ceylon	Cambodia
	India	Ceylon
	Japan	India
	Pakistan	Japan
	Philippines	Laos
		Malaysia
		Pakistan
		Philippines
		South Korea
		South Vietnam
		Taiwan
		Thailand

* When regional nations favoring ACD are listed under a category, it should be understood that those not listed oppose the measure, unless otherwise noted. This notation also applies to the forthcoming sections.

The pattern is now a familiar one. The three nations favoring ACD measures before any control machinery is established fit the neutralist, militarily weak, Theravada Buddhist grouping and continue to be the most representative of that group. If the grouping is expanded to include nations that would accept ACD measures simultaneously with the establishment of a control machinery the following may be added: one more neutralist state, India; a pro-Western nation strongly disposed toward neutralism and amenable to ACD measures in general, Japan; a nation feeling relatively secure from outside attack because of her island position and strong ties with the United States, the Philippines; and Pakistan. With the exception of Indonesia, which disapproves of any type of control machinery, all nations would consider ACD measures after appropriate control machinery has been established. At one end of the spectrum are those nations that most ardently advocate neutralism and those that will not respond militarily to a Chinese Communist threat -- Laos excepted, presumably because of her continuing adverse experience with one type of ACD control machinery. At the other end, the nations correspond exactly to the lineup on nuclear weapons control, with Indonesia taking the exceptional position.

On the two questions concerning the phased implementation of ACD a very similar pattern appears:

Nations favoring phased implementation of ACD	
Without controls	With controls
Burma	Australia - New Zealand
Cambodia	Burma
Ceylon	Cambodia
Indonesia	Ceylon
	India
	Japan
	Laos
	Malaysia
	Pakistan
	Philippines
	South Korea
	South Vietnam
	Taiwan
	Thailand

The lineup of the nations would be identical with the two extreme positions in the preceding question, except for the exceptional attitude of Indonesia on phased implementation of ACD without controls. The only logical explanation for this unexpected shift is that circumventing the controls may appear relatively easy to the Indonesian policy makers, and acceptance might even aid Indonesia in attaining her expansionist foreign policy goals. All in all, this question merely reinforces the pattern of the previous one.

Considering now the three questions concerning the sequence of political settlement of international issues and implementation of ACD, the following positive answers appear:

Nations favoring political settlement of issues		
Following ACD	Simultaneous with ACD	Prior to ACD
Burma	Burma	Australia - New Zealand
Cambodia	Cambodia	Burma
Ceylon	Ceylon	Cambodia
Japan	Indonesia	Ceylon
	Japan	India
	Malaysia	Indonesia
	South Korea	Japan
		Laos

Malaysia
Pakistan
Philippines
South Korea
South Vietnam
Taiwan
Thailand

The answers to these questions form a pattern that does not differ greatly from those of the two previous sets, but certain variations should be noted. Countries taking the most lenient view toward acceptance continue to be the three hard-core neutralist states, joined this time by Japan, whose positive views on ACD have by now been well established. Again, at the other end of the spectrum, no nation disapproves ACD after outstanding international political settlements have been made.

The group of countries that might accept ACD if political issues were settled simultaneously follows no particular pattern except that the neutralist countries and countries with neutralist tendencies predominate, but again, India and Laos are excepted for reasons that are now quite clear. Although Indonesia's motives continue to be suspect, it is significant to note that for the first time Indonesia and Malaysia both favor the same solution to an ACD problem. South Korea's somewhat surprising positive response to political settlement simultaneous with the adoption of ACD is not easily explained, but it might reflect the fact that more than ten years have passed since the end of the Korean War, and few signs of serious aggressive intent have been shown on either side.

Without actually presenting the test groupings in comparison with the answers from the attitudinal matrix in great detail, but from the patterns established earlier, we can now draw the following conclusions:

1) Pro-Western countries take these positions on adopting ACD measures:

They favor

a) ACD following the establishment of control machinery
b) Phased implementation of ACD with controls
c) Political settlement prior to ACD

They oppose

a) ACD before the establishment of control machinery
b) Phased implementation of ACD without controls
c) Political settlement after the establishment of ACD (except Japan)

On questions of a more intermediate nature, such as establishing controls simultaneously with the adoption of ACD measures and political settlement simultaneous with ACD, some pro-Western countries, such as Japan, Malaysia, the Philippines, and South Korea, break away from their "natural" groupings and favor one or both of these measures, whereas all other pro-Western countries oppose them.

2) The neutralist countries of Burma, Cambodia, and Ceylon favor all alternatives considered with regard to the sequence of ACD and given their choice of nonmilitary means to oppose external threat, they do not much care how ACD is implemented. But in a number of instances, India and Laos, the other neutralists, take an opposing position and follow the pro-Western countries, for considerations of practical experience and reality. In addition, India's perception of an immediate threat from both Communist China and Pakistan and her military involvement with both countries prevent her from taking a strictly neutralist position.

3) Countries perceiving a threat from Communist China, either direct or indirect, and willing to respond militarily (India, South Korea, South Vietman, Taiwan, and Thailand) and countries having some confidence

that they can defend themselves (Australia - New Zealand, India, Indonesia, Pakistan, the Philippines, South Korea, and Taiwan) take the following position on the adoption of ACD measures:

They favor

a) ACD following the establishment of control machinery (except Indonesia)
b) Phased implementation of ACD with controls (except Indonesia)
c) Political settlement prior to ACD (except Taiwan, whose position is not predictable)

They oppose

a) ACD before the establishment of control machinery
b) Phased implementation of ACD without controls (except Indonesia)
c) Political settlement after establishment of ACD

Concerning political settlement and the establishment of controls simultaneously with the adoption of ACD, the above groupings are not so clear-cut. India, Pakistan, the Philippines, Malaysia, and South Korea favor one or the other, but none favors both.

4) Countries perceiving a threat from Communist China and planning to deal with it by nonmilitary means (Burma, Cambodia, and Laos), and the one country that perceives relatively no threat (Ceylon) favor all the alternatives considered -- except Laos. Evidently these countries are willing to enter a looser form of ACD arrangement than those that are preparing a military response to perceived threats with a fair degree of confidence that they can defend themselves -- with outside aid.

5) Countries opposing ACD measures not also applied to Communist China (India, Indonesia, Malaysia, Pakistan, South Korea, South Vietnam, and Thailand) also oppose the adoption of ACD prior to controls and phased implementation of ACD without controls, but are not unanimous with regard to political settlement and controls simultaneous with ACD. Their positions closely follow those of the countries that feel they can defend themselves with outside aid.

6) Countries with relatively large armies (India, South Korea, South Vietnam, and Taiwan) take the following positions on adopting ACD measures:

They favor

a) ACD following the establishment of control machinery (except Indonesia)
b) Phased implementation of ACD with controls (except Indonesia)
c) Political settlement prior to ACD

They oppose

a) ACD before the establishment of control machinery
b) ACD simultaneous with the establishment of control machinery (except India)
c) Phased implementation of ACD without controls (except Indonesia)

On the political settlement of issues simultaneously with the adoption of ACD measures, the attitudes of countries having relatively large armies vary considerably, with Indonesia and South Korea favoring the measure and India, South Vietnam, and Taiwan opposing it.

7) Finally, special mention should be made of Indonesia's position on the sequence in which ACD measures are adopted. Indonesia opposes the idea of a control apparatus -- whether it is established prior to, simultaneous with, or following ACD. She also opposes phased implementation of ACD with controls, but favors the same without controls, again indicating an opposition to control itself. Although opposing political settlement after the adoption of

ACD measures, she does favor such settlement prior to, and simultaneous with, their adoption, perhaps with the assumption that she may be able to manipulate such settlements to her advantage.

Control Organization

Although the original matrix contained a number of detailed proposals, we have found it more meaningful to examine two aspects of the control organization. (1) Should the control organization be subject to a veto by any party to the ACD agreement? (2) What should the composition of the field staff and inspectorate be?

Countries favoring a control organization*	
Subject to veto	Not subject to veto
Australia - New Zealand	Burma
Burma	Cambodia
Cambodia	Ceylon
Ceylon	India
India	Japan
Japan	Laos
Pakistan	Malaysia
Taiwan	Pakistan
	Philippines
	South Korea
	South Vietnam
	Thailand

Indonesia's opposition to a control organization not subject to veto is most likely an opposition to the very idea of a control organization, rather than to the absence of a veto, for she also opposes a control organization subject to a veto.

In analyzing regional attitudes toward the composition of the field staff and inspectorate, three alternatives are considered: (1) field staff and inspectorate chosen on an international basis, (2) field staff and inspectorate chosen on a national basis only, and (3) field staff and inspectorate chosen on a neutral basis.

Field staff and inspectorate to be chosen on		
An international basis	A neutral basis	A national basis (to serve only in own country)
Australia - New Zealand	Burma	Burma
Burma	Cambodia	Cambodia
Cambodia	Ceylon	Ceylon
Ceylon	India	Pakistan
India	Japan	South Korea
Japan	Malaysia	South Vietnam
Malaysia	Pakistan	
Pakistan		
Philippines		
South Korea		
South Vietnam		
Taiwan		
Thailand		

All countries apparently favor a field staff and inspectorate chosen on an international basis.**

No outstanding or different patterns appear in considering field staffs chosen on a national or a neutral basis. In general, the two less effective methods for control are approved by those countries whose predisposition toward ACD measures is strong -- Burma, Cambodia, and Ceylon; India and

*A country may appear in more than one category, indicating that although favoring one particular aspect, it is willing to accept a less than perfect arrangement, if necessary.

**Indonesia and Laos are classified as having no predictable position.

Japan approve selection on an international basis also. Other nations approving these proposals seem to do so from national motives without any consistent pattern. South Korea and South Vietnam, two of the divided countries, seem to see an advantage in the exchange of neutral inspectors.

Having made the above comparisons, we may now draw the following conclusions regarding regional attitudes toward the control organization and the veto, and the composition of the field staff and inspectorate.

As might be expected, neutralist countries, with the exception of Laos, are willing to accept a control organization subject to a veto, even though they would probably prefer an organization not subject to a veto. Laos is again an exception as a result of her experiences with the International Control Commission (ICC). It is also worth noting that Pakistan seems willing to favor this measure and stands on common ground with India.

1) Pro-Western countries (Australia - New Zealand, Japan, Malaysia, the Philippines, South Korea, South Vietnam, Taiwan, and Thailand) favor:

a) Control organization not subject to a veto (except Australia - New Zealand and Taiwan)

b) Field staff and inspectorate chosen on an international basis (except Taiwan)

Pro-Western countries oppose:

a) Control organization subject to a veto (except Australia - New Zealand, Japan, and Taiwan)

b) Field staff and inspectorate chosen on a national basis (except South Korea and South Vietnam)

c) Field staff and inspectorate chosen on a neutral basis (except Japan and Malaysia)

2) Neutralist countries (Burma, Cambodia, Ceylon, India, and Laos) favor all alternatives considered with the exception of Laos, which opposes a control organization subject to a veto and has no predictable position concerning the basis on which a field staff and inspectorate should be chosen; and India, which opposes a field staff and inspectorate chosen on a national basis.

3) Countries perceiving a considerable threat from Communist China (India, South Korea, South Vietnam, Taiwan, and Thailand) and planning a military response to this threat favor:

a) Control organization not subject to a veto (except Taiwan)

b) Field staff and inspectorate chosen on an international basis (except Taiwan)

These countries oppose a control organization subject to a veto (except India). However, they are divided on the issue whether a field staff and inspectorate should be chosen on a national or neutral basis.

4) Countries perceiving almost no threat from Communist China (Ceylon) and countries perceiving a threat but planning to meet it with non-military means (Burma, Cambodia, and Laos) except Laos favor all alternatives considered. These are the same countries which, in general, have no confidence in their ability to defend themselves even with outside aid, which have relatively weak and (or) ineffective armies, and which, with the exception of Burma, are willing to consider an ACD arrangement even if it is not observed by Communist China.

Methods of Inspection and Verification

Two categories have been established for the analysis of methods of inspection and verification: methods applicable to nuclear weapons only and methods applicable to all types of weapons, nuclear and nonnuclear. For nuclear weapons, three alternatives are considered: (1) long-range methods of control from stations outside the country; (2) long-range methods of control with instruments stationed in the country and with inspection by outsiders; and (3) long-range methods of control with instruments stationed in the country without inspection by outsiders.

Each country considered favors long-range methods of control from stations outside its own territory. These favorable responses, however, are predicated on the assumption that such a method of control could, and would, be proved effective and on the belief that such a control would be better than no control at all.

Countries favoring long-range methods of control from stations				
Outside own country		Inside own country (Inspected by outsiders)		Inside own country (Not inspected by outsiders)
Australia -	New Zealand	Australia -	New Zealand	Cambodia
Burma	Malaysia	Burma	Malaysia	Ceylon
Cambodia	Pakistan	Cambodia	Pakistan	Indonesia
Ceylon	Philippines	Ceylon	Philippines	Japan
India	South Korea	India	South Korea	Laos
Indonesia	South Vietnam	Japan	South Vietnam	Pakistan
Japan	Taiwan	Laos	Taiwan	
Laos	Thailand		Thailand	

The question whether long-range instruments should be stationed outside one's own country elicits the first unanimous response in the survey. Countries approving long-range inspection methods stationed inside their own territory with no inspection by outsiders, the weakest of the methods proposed, fit a now familiar pattern. Pakistan's response may be based upon her lack of confidence in defending herself from the Soviet Union and Communist China, thus accepting any nuclear control measure as better than nothing. Indonesia's position may be explained by the fact that if she must agree to an inspection system at all, an inspection system outside her own country, or, if necessary, inside her country, but not inspected by outsiders would be relatively easy to circumvent.

In analyzing methods of inspection and verification applicable to all types of weapons systems, five alternatives are considered: (1) aerial inspection, (2) occasional or periodic on-site inspection, (3) continuous on-site inspection, (4) limited freedom of access to site by control teams, and (5) unlimited freedom of access to site by control teams.

Countries favoring control by				
Aerial inspection		Continuous on-site inspection		Periodic on-site inspection
Australia -	New Zealand	Australia -	New Zealand	Burma
Burma	Pakistan	Burma	Pakistan	Cambodia
Cambodia	Philippines	Cambodia	Philippines	Ceylon
Ceylon	South Korea	Ceylon	South Korea	Japan
India	South Vietnam	India	South Vietnam	Malaysia
Japan	Taiwan	Japan	Taiwan	Pakistan
Laos	Thailand	Laos	Thailand	
Malaysia		Malaysia		

Unlimited freedom of access		Limited freedom of access
Australia -	New Zealand	Burma
Burma	Pakistan	Cambodia
Cambodia	Philippines	Ceylon
Ceylon	South Korea	Japan
India	South Vietnam	Pakistan
Japan	Taiwan	
Laos	Thailand	
Malaysia		

Malaysia's attitude favoring periodic inspection is apparently based on the assumption that there would be unlimited freedom of access; otherwise Malaysia would probably not approve this measure, in view of the fact that Malaysia opposes limited freedom of access.

The following conclusions may thus be drawn:

1) Pro-Western countries take the following positions:

They favor

a) Long-range methods of control from stations outside one's own country
b) Long-range methods of control with instruments stationed in the country and controlled by inspection by outsiders
c) Aerial inspection (overflight)
d) Continuous on-site inspection
e) Unlimited freedom of access to inspection teams

They oppose

a) Long-range methods of control with instruments stationed in the country without inspection by outsiders (except Japan)
b) Occasional or periodic on-site inspection (except Japan and Malaysia)
c) Limited freedom of access (except Japan)

2) Neutralist countries, except India and Laos, favor all measures considered; India and Laos oppose periodic inspection and limited freedom of access, and in addition, India opposes long-range methods of control with instruments stationed in the country without inspection by outsiders.

3) Countries perceiving a threat from Communist China and planning to respond militarily; countries confident of defending themselves with outside aid, although some may not be wholly confident of it; countries having numerically large armies, and countries strongly opposing ACD arrangements not observed by Communist China take the following positions:

They favor

a) Long-range methods of control from stations outside one's own country
b) Long-range methods of control with instruments stationed in the country with inspection by outsiders (except Indonesia)
c) Aerial inspection (except Indonesia)
d) Continuous on-site inspection (except Indonesia)
e) Unlimited freedom of access (except Indonesia)

They oppose

a) Long-range methods of control with instruments stationed in the country without inspection by outsiders (except Indonesia, Japan, and Pakistan)
b) Periodic on-site inspection (except Japan, Malaysia, and Pakistan)
c) Limited freedom of access (except Japan and Pakistan)

4) Countries perceiving relatively little threat from Communist China or, perceiving it, do not plan to respond militarily; countries having ineffective and (or) insignificant armies; and countries willing to consider ACD arrangements even if they are not observed by Communist China -- except Laos and Burma -- favor all the alternatives considered. Laos opposes periodic or occasional on-site inspection and limited freedom of access, and Burma opposes long-range methods of control from stations inside one's own country, not inspected by outsiders.

International Police Force

Under this category, the following alternatives are considered: (1) an international police force established on a permanent basis, or (2) an international police force established occasionally when necessary, said force to be composed of (a) international troops, (b) troops from regional states only, or (c) troops solely from states neutral to the problem at hand. Again, regional attitudes toward these measures follow a rather predictable position.

Except Indonesia, all the states in the region favor an international police force established on a permanent basis; and as an alternative, all, without exception, favor an international police force established on an ad hoc basis.

Regional attitudes toward the composition of the international police force are not so uniform, however,

Countries favoring an international police force composed of

International troops		Regional states only	Neutral states only
Australia -	New Zealand	Burma	Burma
Burma	Pakistan	Cambodia	Cambodia
Cambodia	Philippines	Ceylon	Ceylon
Ceylon	South Korea	Indonesia	Indonesia
India	South Vietnam	Japan	Japan
Japan	Taiwan		Pakistan
Laos	Thailand		
Malaysia			

With the exception of Indonesia, all countries are willing to consider an international police force of international troops. Only a few -- the hard-core neutralists -- will consider a force composed of regional troops or troops from neutral states. Again, this lineup probably reflects the difficulty these states have in keeping peace in their own region.

The following conclusions may thus be drawn:

1) Pro-Western countries take these positions:

They favor

a) An international police force established on a permanent basis
b) An international police force established occasionally when necessary
c) An international police force composed of international troops

They oppose

a) An international police force composed of troops from regional states only (except Japan)
b) An international police force composed of troops from neutral states only (except Japan)

2) Neutralist countries favor all alternatives considered -- except India and Laos, which oppose an international police force composed of troops from regional or neutral states only.

3) Countries perceiving a threat from Communist China and planning to respond militarily; countries confident of defending themselves with outside aid, although some may not be wholly confident of doing so; countries having numerically large armies; and countries strongly opposing the consideration of ACD arrangements not also applied to Communist China take these positions:

They favor

a) An international police force established on a permanent basis (except Indonesia)
b) An international police force established when needed
c) An international police force composed of troops from international states (except Indonesia)

They oppose

a) An international police force composed of troops from regional states only (except Indonesia and Japan)
b) An international police force composed of troops from neutral states only (except Indonesia, Japan, and Pakistan)

4) Countries perceiving relatively little threat from Communist China or, perceiving it, do not plan to respond militarily; countries having no confidence in their ability to defend themselves, even with outside aid; countries having insignificant and (or) ineffective armies; and countries willing to consider ACD arrangements even if they are not observed by Communist China favor all the alternatives considered, with the exception of Laos, which opposes an international police force composed of troops from regional or neutral states only.

Obviously, the attitude of any nation toward the composition of a police force is closely tied in with its attitude toward a control organization and whether or not that control organization is subject to a veto by its members. Separate consideration is somewhat artificial, but it is unavoidable under the circumstances of the exercise.

Determination and Punishment of Violations

Regional attitudes toward the determination of violations of ACD arrangements focus on two points: (1) determination by an international authority without a veto and (2) determination by an international authority with a veto. With the exception of Indonesia and Taiwan, all regional states analyzed favor the determination of violations by an international authority without a veto. In general, the following countries favor having an international authority to determine violations.

Without a veto		With a veto
Burma	Malaysia	Australia - New Zealand
Cambodia	Pakistan	Burma
Ceylon	Philippines	Cambodia
India	South Korea	Ceylon
Japan	South Vietnam	Japan
Laos	Thailand	Pakistan
		Taiwan

The general pattern remains unchanged.

Except India, those countries favoring the determination of violations by an international authority with a veto are the same ones that favored a control organization subject to a veto, as earlier discussion showed. In most cases, however, the measures are apparently seen as "less-than-perfect" alternatives. Although India strongly favors a control organization not subject to a veto, she conditionally opposes the determination of violations by an international authority with a veto, probably because of her unresolved conflicts with Communist China and Pakistan as well as the more "sensitive" matter of actually determining if an ACD measure has been violated.

Finally, two alternatives have been considered with regard to the application of sanctions: (1) the application of sanctions by an international authority and (2) the application of sanctions by regional powers only.

Countries favoring international sanctions applied by

International authority		Regional powers
Australia - New Zealand		Burma
Burma	Laos	Cambodia
Cambodia	Malaysia	Ceylon
Ceylon	Philippines	Indonesia
India	South Korea	Japan
Japan	South Vietnam	Laos
	Thailand	Philippines

In both instances, Pakistan has been listed as having no predictable position. Again, except Indonesia and Taiwan, all countries considered favorably the application of sanctions by an international authority.

Regional attitudes toward the application of sanctions by regional powers follow the familiar pattern. Japan has already become a predictable exception, and the Philippines is willing to consider such a measure. Apart from these two, the pro-Western countries oppose the application of sanctions by regional powers only.

With the exception of India, whose regional conflict in this instance overrides neutralist considerations, the neutralist countries favor the application of sanctions by regional powers only.

Having made the above comparisons, the following conclusions may be drawn:

1) Pro-Western countries take these positions:

They favor

a) Determination of violations by an international authority without a veto (except Australia - New Zealand and Taiwan)

b) The application of sanctions by an international authority (except Taiwan)

They oppose

a) Determination of violations by an international authority with a veto (except Australia - New Zealand, Japan, and Taiwan)

b) The application of sanctions by regional powers only (except Japan and the Philippines)

2) Neutralist countries favor all alternatives analyzed with the exception of India and Laos which oppose the determination of violations by an international authority with a veto and of India which opposes the application of sanctions by regional powers only.

3) Countries perceiving a threat from Communist China and planning to respond militarily; countries confident of defending themselves with outside aid, although some may not be wholly confident of doing so; countries having numerically large armies; and countries strongly opposing the consideration of ACD arrangements not also applied to Communist China take these positions:

They favor

a) Determination of violations by an international authority without a veto (except Indonesia and Taiwan)

b) The application of sanctions by an international authority (except Indonesia and Taiwan)

They oppose

a) The determination of violations by an international authority with a veto (except Japan and Pakistan)

b) The application of sanctions by regional powers only (except Indonesia, Japan, and the Philippines)

4) Countries perceiving relatively little threat from Communist China or, perceiving it do not plan to respond militarily; countries having no confidence in their ability to defend themselves; and countries willing to consider ACD arrangements not applicable to Communist China, favor all alternatives considered -- with the exception of Laos, which opposes the determination of violations by an international agency with a veto.

5) Finally, it should be mentioned that except for Pakistan's unpredictable position on the application of sanctions, Japan and Pakistan favor all the alternatives analyzed. Also, Taiwan and Indonesia oppose most alternatives considered, except for Indonesia's attitude favoring sanctions

applied by regional powers only. The last consideration may be based on Indonesia's assumption that she would be able to play a dominating role among the regional powers and thus influence their actions to her advantage. Taiwan's position is based on her belief that sanctions would, in this instance, be more readily applied to her than to Communist China.

CONCLUSION

By comparing "test groupings" and answers given on the attitudinal matrix, we have found that considerations of ideological orientation, perception of threat, defense capability, and applicability of ACD to Communist China strongly influence regional attitudes toward various arms control and disarmament measures. This is not to say, however, that other "test groupings" do not influence regional attitudes. For example, although we have emphasized regional perception of the threat from Communist China, the perception of a threat either from an extraregional power other than Communist China or from a regional power (or both) also influences and reinforces regional positions toward ACD measures, but apparently not to the same extent that the perception of a threat from Communist China does.

Also, cultural and economic factors influence regional attitudes. In general, however, these factors are secondary to those analyzed above, and thus they reinforce or temper rather than determine the positions of regional states on ACD. The influence of Theravada Buddhism and Indian Hinduism show a particularly marked influence on matters pertaining to ACD. If their immediate threats and anxieties are removed, these countries will probably return to the ideals rooted in their cultural tradition.

On the basis of the above comparisons and conclusions, we have found that countries that are pro-Western, countries planning to respond militarily to perceived threats, countries confident of defending themselves with outside aid, countries having numerically large armies, and countries opposing the consideration of any ACD arrangements not also applied to Communist China insist upon a number of prerequisites concerning the type of control apparatus they are willing to accept. Neutralist countries (with the frequent exceptions of India and Laos, whose neutralist inclinations are overridden by considerations of practical reality and experience), countries perceiving virtually no threat from Communist China or, perceiving it, do not plan to respond militarily, countries having no confidence in their ability to defend themselves, even with outside aid, countries having insignificant and (or) ineffective armies, and countries willing to consider ACD arrangements even if not applied to Communist China, are less demanding about the type of control organization they are willing to accept, some of them realizing they have little to lose and possibly something to gain by following such a policy.

One point of paradox to add here is that as a result of the preceding considerations, the countries most favorable to the United States and her policies are the very ones that take the strongest stand in opposing the various ACD measures considered -- Taiwan, South Korea, South Vietnam, and Australia - New Zealand, for example. Conversely, the countries most favorably disposed toward ACD controls are by their very policies the most lenient in their view toward communism outside their own borders. Since the United States has consistently urged active resistance to Communist encroachment, they may have in the past taken a suspicious attitude toward our policies. They may extend this attitude to our ACD proposals because they mistrust United States' motives. Cambodia, Ceylon, and Burma are notable examples.

CHAPTER 2: LIMITATIONS AND POSSIBILITIES OF ARMS CONTROL AND DISARMAMENT IN THE FAR EAST

INTRODUCTION

The analysis in the preceding chapters points to six factors that govern the limitationsand possibilities of ACD in the Far East. First, the definite ranking of the acceptability of objectives that may be regulated by ACD agreements implies that certain regional ACD arrangements might be possible now.

Second, the measures that rank low are less acceptable because of certain basic underlying factors. One of these factors consists of the present and potential internal and external conflicts and tensions which the individual regional powers have with one another or with extraregional powers. These conflicts and tensions, as summarized in Part II, Chapter 3, can be divided into three categories: (a) those involving extraregional powers, such as Japan versus the Soviet Union or India versus Communist China and Pakistan; (b) those involving regional powers only; and (c) those involving internal forces only. Present or potential conflicts of the first category cannot be resolved without arrangements with the extraregional powers, particularly the Communist powers. Some conflicts of the second category, on the other hand, can be resolved through regional arrangements with regional powers only. Conflicts of the third category can only be resolved by the individual countries themselves although regional arrangements and extraregional cooperation may be helpful.

Third, to the extent that existing conflicts cannot be resolved now, attempts may be made to alter the underlying factors which make certain ACD arrangements untenable, inapplicable, unacceptable, or unattractive in the present international context. These arrangements could in turn be of two kinds: (a) those which would increase the sense of security felt by the regional powers from extraregional threats, thus making them more inclined to consider future ACD arrangements involving both themselves and the extraregional powers, and (b) those which would promote or create a habit of cooperation and a community of interest among some or all of the regional powers.

Fourth, various existing arrangements for cooperation among individual regional powers or within a combination of regional and extraregional powers -- such as SEATO -- have not always functioned effectively because *the participants are frequently interested parties without a common interest.* Attempts to alter the determining factors underlying national attitudes thoward ACD through the promotion of regional cooperation should therefore be based on a set of common interests which have to be identified and promoted or created.

Fifth, the analysis in the preceding chapters leads to the conclusion that ACD arrangements should not *ipso facto* seek universality in their coverage. Instead, *ad hoc* arrangements aimed at the needs of certain individual regional powers might often constitute a more practical and useful first step. In addition, ACD arrangements for specific regional powers might be accepted and implemented more rapidly if they were not tied to global arrangements. Although a great power arrangement would be extended to cover the regional countries, certain regional arrangements can be concluded without involving any or all of the extraregional powers. It is likely, in fact, that some such agreements could be more readily concluded if the Communist powers were bypassed.[1] A successful regional ACD arrangement could then be linked to other existing ACD arrangements or to any new arrangement which might arise later.

Finally, unless the same controls are applied to Communist China, many regional countries will not accept ACD measures regulating the weapons they believe necessary for safeguarding their national security. Since the acceptance of such controls by Communist China cannot be presumed, ACD measures that are feasible under present conditions are substantially circumscribed.

Therefore, many objects of control found in past ACD proposals, as well as other possible objects of control, cannot be considered at this time as general propositions for the region, although some of them might be relevant if their application were purely regional.

The preceding points form a logical basis from which the following discussion of feasible ACD measures, as understood in the broad sense, can be undertaken. To recapitulate, the basic concept underlying the approach advocated here is that one of the most important aspects of ACD is its initiation. Once an ACD arrangement has been implemented, it might lead to other ACD arrangements, and, if fortuitous circumstances prevail, it might even generate its own momentum. A beginning can be made more easily if the arrangements are limited in scope and do not seek universal participation, whether among the regional states alone or among both regional and extraregional powers. A limited proposal is more likely to find participants who have a common interest in making it effective, and common interest can be carefully nurtured once the beginning has been made. Nonetheless, to profit from any breakthrough, an array of desirable ACD measures should be held in reserve so that they can be applied whenever and wherever they become feasible.

In addition, the ACD measures chosen should not be confined to those that have been frequently considered in past ACD proposals, many of which have had no direct bearing on the regional countries themselves. No purely regional ACD measures have been suggested or attempted although there have been a number of security arrangements between regional countries and extra-regional nations as well as several ceasefire agreements and peacekeeping arrangements of varying effectiveness along some of the more sensitive border areas where fighting has taken place, e.g., in Korea, Laos, and Kashmir. All regional proposals, in addition to those advanced by the great powers, have included extraregional countries and have been limited to controls of nuclear weapons, such as nuclear-free zones. Since 68 of the 215 categories of ACD measures considered in Appendix I, Part C, have never been proposed by any nation and since 62 of these 68 could be directly applied to the regional military situation, the potential for action among the 15 regional countries would appear to be great. This conclusion is not to imply, however, that ACD arrangements with some of the extraregional powers would not be productive and therefore should not be considered. (The special case of Communist China is discussed more fully in a separate report entitled *Arms Control Implications of Communist China's Domestic and Foreign Policies*.)

Finally, in formulating ACD measures for implementation in the region, there are two *caveats*, one general, the other specific. The general *caveat* is that each individual ACD proposal must not create more tension and instability than it seeks to remove or reduce. Preferably, it should not generate any new tensions or instability. The particular *caveat* is that, from the point of view of the United States, the ACD proposal considered should promote the national interests of the United States, or at least be in accord with them.

ACCEPTABILITY OF ARMS CONTROL AND DISARMAMENT MEASURES

If we consider the total number of hypothetical responses elicited for the regulation of the use of outer space, various weapons systems, denuclearized zones, the armed forces, military expenditures, and deployment (the number of individual measures within the category multiplied by the number of countries responding -- 15), we find (Tables 1 and 2) that the highest percentage of favorable response occurs in regard to the regulation and control of the use of outer space (93.3%), followed by the regulation of nuclear and thermonuclear weapons, long-range unmanned delivery systems, and chemical, biological, and radiological weapons (89.1%), the establishment of denuclearized zones (80%), the regulation of military expenditures (71.1%), the regulation of heavy offensive weapons (49.1%), the regulation of deployment (47.8%), and the regulation of conventional weapons and the armed forces (both 33.3%).[2]

Implications of Above Percentages

These results show that most regional countries seem to be willing to agree to ACD regulation of weapons which they neither possess nor plan to acquire in the immediate future. The only opposition to the regulation of such weapons, as well as to the control of the use of outer space and the establishment of denuclearized zones, has come from Indonesia who has claimed to be developing a nuclear capability of her own; from Australia and New Zealand and the Republic of China who oppose denuclearized zones; and from several regional countries which, while agreeing in principle to these measures, oppose certain aspects of them, e.g., international monopoly of existing stockpiles of nuclear weapons, international control of research and development of nuclear weapons, and restrictions on the freedom to obtain nuclear weapons from allies, should the need arise.

One can only speculate as to whether or not it might be possible to alter these opposing positions. It is possible, however, that Indonesia, with her post-September 30, 1965 government, may be more amenable to ACD arrangements in this area -- even to the point of publicly abandoning the nuclear program she has claimed to be pursuing. On the other hand, should one of the regional countries undertake to acquire a nuclear capability, other regional countries might reconsider their previous positions and, if capable of doing so, also attempt to develop a nuclear capability. Should this occur, the percentage of regional response favoring the regulation of nuclear weapons would, of course, decrease. This is one good argument for regional agreements being made prior to and independent of the settlement of great power controversies over the control of nuclear weapons.

In general, however, the greatest potential for direct ACD arrangements in the immediate future lies in the regulation of nuclear weapons and the use of outer space. It may be argued that an ACD arrangement is of little or no value if it only covers weapons that the regional countries concerned do not possess, and that, therefore, do not directly affect their security. However, the successful conclusion of such an arrangement might prevent a number of issues from arising in the future (such as nuclear proliferation, if the issue had been faced before Communist China's nuclear tests). The partial test-ban treaty has, for instance, had no direct effect on the regional powers with no nuclear weapons program, but regional signatories to the treaty would have to denounce it in order to begin testing as part of a nuclear weapons development program.[3] It is also possible that the mere process of concluding an ACD arrangement may have a psychological impact great enough to alter other regional perceptions and perhaps make the governments of these countries more amenable to other ACD proposals. Finally, a regional declaration favoring the regulation of nuclear weapons and the use of outer space might discourage some regional countries from presenting future ACD proposals on issues that do not directly affect them or their security. This, in turn, would make future ACD discussions focus on the issues having an immediate bearing on regional security and conflicts.

SOURCES OF THREAT TO REGIONAL SECURITY AND THEIR EFFECTS ON THE FEASIBILITY OF ARMS CONTROL AND DISARMAMENT

If we consider the aspects of ACD that are more directly related to regional security -- regulation of military expenditures, armed forces, deployment, and heavy offensive and other conventional weapons -- the percentage of regional responses favoring such measures greatly decreases. As seen in the last chapter, the basic factors that appear to account for this response include perceived threats to national security, aggressive pursuit of national policies, ruling military governments, and confidence in present or developing defense capabilities. Since Ceylon is the only country within the region which perceives little or no threat to her security, the overriding factor influencing regional attitudes toward ACD would seem to be that of perceived threats to national security. However, as indicated in the last chapter, a greater ability to defend oneself against external threat may increase opposition to ACD as long as a threat exists or is perceived to exist. The real key, then, for successful and meaningful ACD arrangements in the region is to increase the sense of security by decreasing the perceived threat. The ideal ACD arrangement would be one that reduces both the possibility of armed conflict and the perceived threat.

Internal dissidence. The regulation of armed forces and conventional weapons is opposed by countries with a high level of actual or potential internal dissidence, as well as by countries which feel that their armed forces are not strong enough, or much above the level needed, to maintain internal security. Although many of these same countries also oppose the regulation of heavy offensive weapons, this opposition is in large part a result of factors other than that of actual or potential internal dissidence. However, the myth that modern or heavy weapons are of little use against a revolutionary insurgency may be changing. (This myth began with the Chinese Communist People's Liberation Army victories over the Nationalist armies in 1948-49, and was further enhanced by the Viet Minh victory over the French in the first Indochina War ending in 1954). If the United States demonstrates that heavy weapons can be used effectively in countering insurgency in South Vietnam, the spell of the myth could be broken. Should this happen, the regional powers could become more reluctant to control the weapons grouped as heavy offensive weapons.

If the threat of internal dissidence precludes a number of countries from favoring the regulation of armed forces and conventional weapons, the elimination or at least reduction of this threat might produce a change in attitude, provided no new large-scale insurgency makes these efforts impossible. Such a reduction could come as a result of several developments. For example, a regional arrangement designed to pool economic resources and technical skills might help remove one basic cause of internal disorder. This undertaking could consist of regional states only, of regional states plus one or more of the major extraregional powers, or of regional states working through an international organization such as the United Nations. The solution of economic problems would not in itself eliminate all sources of internal dissidence, but it would enable government officials to concentrate on other factors giving rise to internal conflicts.

It is also possible that a regional country may at times overestimate the defense level necessary to check actual or potential internal conflicts. If the regional countries concerned could be convinced of the possibility of this type of misjudgment, they might become more predisposed to consider ACD arrangements covering the armed forces and conventional weapons. If not, measures calling for the prohibition of external support for insurrections as well as for the prohibition of antiforeign and war propaganda would at least remain open for consideration.

Except when internal instability is instigated by external sources, the impetus for adopting certain principal means of promoting internal stability, and consequently increasing receptiveness to ACD measures, often lies outside the province of extranational efforts. For instance, the elimination of regional rivalry and of ethnic and religious animosity among groups within the same country depends on the efforts of the individual country itself. Although external assistance can greatly facilitate the economic development of some countries, thereby opening new horizons and allaying existing discontent, sustained development would not be possible without the will to undertake measures that would mobilize the nation's own resources.

Until and unless such efforts are initiated by the countries themselves, one cannot expect them to perceive any major benefit from ACD plans calling for the diversion of resources from the military effort to programs for peaceful development. This situation would seem to be particularly applicable to Indonesia prior to the September 1965 coup, as well as to Burma and even

India, in view of her domestic tensions. Therefore, an outside power -- such as the United States -- can do little to help resolve problems of internal tension and instability that are of domestic origin. Indeed, the initiative for such solutions must come from the country or countries concerned.

External threats from regional sources. Countries perceiving an external threat to their security -- whether the source be regional or extraregional -- and prepared to respond militarily, as well as countries aggressively pursuing their national policies, not only oppose the regulation of armed forces and conventional weapons, but also oppose that of heavy offensive weapons and most aspects controlling armed forces deployment. The most desirable solution for the first category of countries would be the removal of the cause of such perceptions. When the perceived threat originates within the region, means may be found to remove it without calling upon the support or concurrence of extraregional Communist powers. For the second category of countries -- Indonesia, the Republic of China, and to some extent, Pakistan -- a change in national goals (or a change of government or in government perception) may be required before ACD measures can become acceptable.

Some regional conflicts appear to be amenable to peaceful settlement although the prospects can vary sharply within short periods of time because of the unstable policies of some of the governments involved. Since Indonesia's aggressive pursuit of her foreign policy has been the immediate cause of these potential conflicts, the apparent change in approach signaled by her recognition of Singapore and the cessation of her confrontation with Malaysia may create a more favorable atmosphere in which ACD measures can be considered. The same prospect may exist for the potential dispute between Indonesia and Australia over New Guinea.

The instability caused by the aggressive pursuit of national policies on the part of some of the regional countries could be altered by developing their perception of alternative, peaceful goals. In such a country, a change in emphasis on the part of the decision-makers is not always possible without a change in government. Since a change in government is itself often destabilizing, it can hardly be advocated as a prerequisite to ACD. However, where a change in Government has occurred, any opportunity for ACD should be acted upon. For example, if the post-September 1965 Government of Indonesia should turn its efforts inward and earnestly attempt to solve some of the existing domestic problems, the prospects for ACD might improve as the possibilities of economic development and its benefits become better understood and more visible. The "return-to-the-mainland" policy of the Republic of China is also a destabilizing factor, but this might change if the prosperity and growth of Taiwan and the consequent viability of the island as a separate entity can be demonstrated.

Indonesia also offers an example where an initial relaxation of tension could conceivably be followed by other ACD measures. The cessation of the confrontation between Indonesia and Malaysia could be followed by other ACD arrangements, such as an agreement not to infiltrate each other's territory or engage in other hostile acts. Many of the measures not discussed in the ACD proposals of the major powers might well be tested here. (These items are preceded by the letter "N" in the matrix in Appendix I, Part C. The necessary condition for such follow-through is the existence of a common interest shared by the participants. How such a common interest might be developed will be discussed later.

Regional conflicts which have to be relegated to a different category are those between India and Pakistan and between Cambodia and Thailand and South Vietnam. The Kashmir and Rann of Kutch incidents and the 1965 border war between India and Pakistan were regrettable, but they were not without some relatively encouraging aspects. They showed that both Governments exercised restraint in an attempt to prevent an all out war; that both sides were susceptible to external pressures (as shown by the effect of withholding external aid and military supplies); and that both sides were acutely aware of the disastrous cost of any expansion of the conflict. On the other hand, the very fact that there were hostilities and that the terms of the Tashkent Agreement which followed were limited also point to the intransigence of both sides. The Indo-Pakistani dispute is further aggravated by the involvement of extraregional powers, the basic elements of which include (a) Pakistan's fear of the Soviet Union and India, (b) India's fear of Communist China and, to a lesser extent, Pakistan, (c) the United States' interest with which that of the United Kingdom generally coincides in supporting Pakistan vis-à-vis the Soviet Union and India vis-à-vis Communist China, and (d) India's role in the Sino-Soviet dispute. Resolution of the dispute, therefore, is difficult and cannot be expected without involving some or all of the extraregional powers, short of a change of attitude on the part of the disputants. Perhaps a promising approach would consist of an arrangement which would enhance the sense of security of both Pakistan and India without increasing the military capability under the direct control of either. Such an arrangement would have to involve external guarantees against attack. How it might be profitably explored will be discussed in a later section.

The conflict involving Cambodia, Thailand, and South Vietnam is of lesser significance, but it stands out because of Prince Sihanouk's perception of the policies of the United States and Communist China. If Sihanouk did not feel a need to placate China and North Vietnam by being intransigent toward the United States, his anxiety about invasion by Thailand and Vietnam might be less severe and he might be more amenable to either bilateral or multilateral ACD arrangements. Fear of Communist China and North Vietnam and of involvement in the Vietnam war has made consideration of any ACD overture sponsored by the United States difficult for Cambodia and unenforceable for the time being. The key would seem to lie in United States policy and its success in Vietnam and in other arrangements which would enhance the security of regional powers against extraregional threats.

The removal or lessening of certain regional conflicts would reduce the complexity of the outstanding problems of the region and thereby possibly increase the prospects for regional peace. This, in turn, would create a more favorable climate for the consideration of various ACD measures.

External threats from extraregional sources. The sources of extraregional threats are primarily Communist China and, to a lesser extent, North Korea and North Vietnam. In addition, the Soviet Union is a potential threat to Pakistan, Japan, and South Korea.

Existing treaty arrangements designed to meet such threats consist of (1) ANZUS (Australia, New Zealand, and the United States), (2) SEATO (Australia, France, New Zealand, Pakistan, the Philippines, Thailand, the United Kingdom, and the United States), and (3) bilateral defense treaties between the United States and Japan, the Philippines, the Republic of Korea, and the Republic of China. In addition, the United States has made a number of general defense aid arrangements with the various regional powers, and the United Kingdom has entered into agreements with Commonwealth members in the region -- Australia and New Zealand, Ceylon, India, Malaysia, Pakistan, and Singapore.

Of the defense treaties, SEATO has been tested implicitly in Vietnam and found not wholly satisfactory. Some SEATO members have not come to the aid of South Vietnam because of concern for their relations with Communist China and the Soviet Union. As pointed out before, the underlying cause of the failure of some of the signatories of SEATO to fulfill their obligations is that the agreement involves a number of powers interested in a specific area but not necessarily sharing a common interest. Only two bilateral treaties involving the United States and several of the regional countries have been tested -- Taiwan in 1958 and South Korea, by prior example, in 1953. The Mutual Security Treaty with Japan has not yet been tested, and problems surrounding its credibility will be discussed later.

It is significant that no mutual defense or aid arrangement involving regional powers only has come into existence thus far. One could speculate on the possibility of creating such an arrangement. As an ACD measure, such an arrangement should preferably involve no increase in the total number of the armed forces of the participating countries. The principal aim should be to reduce the military burden on the countries' resources while increasing their feeling of security by pooling their defense power. A series of ACD measures that would create such a regional defense apparatus could free some resources previously devoted to military functions for economic development programs. On the other hand, the use of these regional defense forces in nonmilitary functions could be accomplished without decreasing the total size of the forces, thus bypassing possible objections to an outright reduction on the part of some participants. For example, at any time a proportionally greater number of the national defense forces could be used for nondefense purposes, such as the employment of army teams in road building, rural aid projects, and other "country building" work. A program of this nature could be advocated as a typical example of combining security with peaceful construction.

Although security considerations are of more importance than potential economic benefits in determining the willingness of countries to allocate resources to defense, progress in economic development in the civilian sector of the economy cannot but in the long run make peaceful pursuits more attractive and thereby increase receptiveness to ACD.

POSSIBLE ARMS CONTROL AND DISARMAMENT ARRANGEMENTS FOR THE REGION

The preceding sections have established that internal, regional and extraregional threats to security prevent regional acceptance of ACD measures covering armed forces, heavy offensive and conventional weapons, military expenditures, and deployment. It is now possible to suggest some specific and more concrete methods for removing or altering these factors through various ACD measures, thereby creating a more favorable climate for the consideration of other ACD measures. Feasible ACD arrangements for the region can be divided into four categories: (1) measures which would involve extraregional Communist powers, (2) measures which would involve extraregional non-Communist powers, (3) measures which would involve extraregional Communist and non-Communist powers, and (4) measures which would involve only the regional countries. Since the feasibility of all ACD arrangements is greatly affected by the involvement of Communist powers, we may group categories (1) and (3) together and categories (2) and (4) together and consider only two groups of measures -- those involving one or more extraregional Communist powers and those involving only the regional and non-Communist extraregional powers.

Arms Control Measures Involving Extraregional Communist Powers

Nuclear nonproliferation measures: One of the most urgent issues in ACD discussions at Geneva in 1965-1966 has been the problem of nuclear proliferation. The issue commands great attention both in Europe and in Asia as a result of (1) the expressed intent of two additional nations to acquire a nuclear capability of their own, namely Communist China and France, and (2) the increasing technological capability of a number of other countries to develop at least token nuclear forces. Two aspects of the issue are examined in this study -- technological capability and the factors underlying the political decision to proceed with the development of nuclear weapons.

At the present, of the regional states only India and Japan are technologically capable of producing plutonium devices on their own within fairly short periods of time, once the decision to undertake weapons production is made. Compared with India, the time required by Japan to produce nuclear weapons is somewhat shorter. Furthermore, Japan has a far greater long-range missile delivery capability, although delivery by aircraft would be no great problem for India. The crucial issue, therefore, has to do with intent -- under what conditions would either country choose to produce nuclear weapons of its own?

In Japan, all the political parties are reluctant, for emotional and, to a lesser degree, economic reasons, to espouse a policy of nuclear armament. The perception of threat is still low. In particular, most of her scientists, whose support would be needed to undertake a nuclear weapons program, are opposed to such a course of action. Therefore, Japan would not be expected to decide in favor of a nuclear weapons program unless she became the direct object of nuclear blackmail or unless the credibility of the United States defense commitments to Japan against external attack by either conventional or nuclear weapons were seriously questioned.

Her rejection of a policy of nuclear armament was tested when the French General P. M. Gallois, the chief architect of de Gaulle's present independent nuclear policy, was interviewed by a major Japanese newspaper on January 30, 1964. In that interview, he told the Japanese that they, like France, could not continue to maintain complete independence or real security under the protection of the United States nuclear umbrella. The United States, he said, could not be depended on to aid Japan against a nuclear threat, for fear of becoming involved in a general world-wide nuclear conflagration. Therefore, he maintained, Japan must follow France in developing nuclear weapons of her own if she wished to maintain her security and independence in the face of a developing Chinese nuclear capability.[4]

The Gallois interview caused a furor. The Socialists welcomed the French support for their contention that Japan could not rely on the United States, but they found the Gallois idea of nuclear armament repugnant in the extreme. In the ensuing Diet interpellations, the Government reaffired its intention to continue the present Japan-United States Mutual Security Pact and not to develop nuclear weapons. All in all, this controversy probably had the net effect of strengthening the mutual security pact. It made the unarmed neutrality position of the Socialists seem less plausible than ever and confirmed the fact that almost no one advocated nuclear arms for Japan herself. The only sensible path left was to follow the United States and maintain that General Gallois was wrong.

Nevertheless, future changes in the world situation could give rise to new Japanese doubts about the credibility of the United States defense commitment to Japan. The Japanese still fear that the Japan-United States defense ties may be the ruin of Japan if the United States becomes embroiled in a war with either the Soviet Union or a nuclear-armed China. There is resentment against United States troops and bases, and the Japanese still fear the possibility of the introduction of nuclear weapons into Japan.

Japan perceives a threat to her security from the Soviet Union, but this concern is not particularly serious and is offset by the uneasy equilibrium which prevails between the United States and the Soviet Union. Japan does not perceive an equally serious threat from Communist China for the time being, nor does she see Communist China in a position to threaten United States interests seriously until the Chinese overall weapons and delivery capability is further developed. But the Chinese capability may change in a few years, possibly by 1970 when the Japan-United States Security Treaty can become an open issue. If crude conventional means of delivery, such as aircraft and merchant ships, are taken into account, the time may not be too distant when a change in Japanese perception will take place. Signs of change are now clearly discernible within the Japan Socialist Party, and a new split between right and left factions over the issue of disarmament seems to be in the making. Moreover, lack of interest among the general public for the Socialist Party's latest drives against the Japan-Republic of Korea Normalization Treaty and the visit of the United States nuclear submarines to Japanese ports possibly reflects a reduction in popular support for the Party's program. Although highly improbable at this writing, a Japanese decision to develop an independent nuclear weapons system should not be dismissed altogether.

The reluctance of India to develop nuclear weapons is also rooted in emotional and historical reasons. But in the face of Chinese nuclear development and against the background of an outright attack by China in 1962 and intermittent threats since then, the effect of these considerations may be wearing thin.[5] A more serious obstacle at present consists of India's economic plight. However, if Chinese threats appear to increase, India may decide to develop at least a token nuclear force. In view of this possibility, proliferation of nuclear weapons within the region is more likely to take place through India than through Japan. Should India decide to undertake such a course of action, Pakistan might try to acquire nuclear weapons of her own or, more likely, attempt to avail herself of the fledgling Communist Chinese nuclear arsenal. Japan might then in turn feel compelled to reconsider her own position.

If proliferation is to be averted, it is necessary, therefore, to increase India's sense of security against possible threats (nuclear or otherwise) from Communist China. To prevent Pakistan from expanding her military establishment, especially through the importation of Chinese arms, it is necessary that India gain a greater sense of security without increasing her military capability in being. These conditions could probably be fulfilled if India were given a guarantee of defense aid by one or more of the nuclear powers, excluding Communist China.

In October 1964, President Johnson referred to such an arrangement when, in a radio-television address, he remarked,

> The nations that do not seek national nuclear weapons can be assured that, if they need our strong support against some threat of nuclear blackmail, then they will have it.[6]

In May 1965, an appeal by the Indian delegate to the United Nations requested that the nuclear powers protect nonnuclear nations threatened by nuclear attack. On January 27, 1966, in his message to the Eighteen-Nation Disarmament Commission, President Johnson again made reference to the idea of a guarantee of retaliation against nuclear attack in what seemed to be a response to the Indian appeal:

> . . . so that those who foreswear nuclear weapons may forever refrain without fear from entering the nuclear arms race, let us strive to strengthen the United Nations and other international security arrangements. Meanwhile, the nations that do not seek the nuclear path can be sure that they will have our strong support against threats of nuclear blackmail.[7]

The Soviet response was to announce

> . . . its willingness to include in the draft treaty a clause on the prohibition of the use of nuclear weapons against non-nuclear States parties to the treaty which have no nuclear weapons in their territory.[8]

This response, however, was apparently directed toward the NATO countries in general -- and Germany in particular -- rather than toward India.

Since India has appealed for such a guarantee and since President Johnson has apparently given a positive response to this appeal, the practicability of such a guarantee should be given more serious consideration. Although the Indian appeal referred to a guarantee from the United Nations, President Johnson did not limit his suggestion to an international agreement. Therefore, a strictly bilateral approach between India and the United States could be possible.

A United States guarantee to India could and probably should be limited to situations arising from direct nuclear attack on India. Attack by nonnuclear powers or by nuclear powers with nonnuclear weapons would thus be placed outside the guarantee, thereby reducing the chance of involving the guarantors in occasional skirmishes between India and Communist China or India and Pakistan. The guarantee could also be given jointly by the United States and the Soviet Union. In either event, it should be given in return for a guarantee that India would not undertake a nuclear weapons program of her own, a guarantee which would free her from an onerous economic burden she can ill afford.[9] Furthermore, such a guarantee does not and should not necessarily bind the guarantor(s) to respond with nuclear weapons.

If India can be induced to forswear the development of an independent nuclear force, the credibility of external guarantees would, by necessity, be reinforced, and Japan's present reluctance to engage in nuclear armament would be given additional support. It is, therefore, entirely possible that nonproliferation may generate a momentum of its own.

On the basis of the analyses in earlier chapters, it appears that efforts to forestall nuclear proliferation within the region should be focused on India. The problem can be simplified by considering India per se, instead of relating it to any scheme of guarantees extended by all nuclear powers to all nonnuclear powers. This arrangement may not be acceptable to India indefinitely, or for that matter to the United States or the Soviet Union indefinitely or even concurrently; at this juncture, however, a pragmatic appeal and approach must be made to initiate some breakthroughs, however limited -- the increase from zero to one is an infinite increase.

Miscellaneous measures. The preceding section on nuclear nonproliferation deals with a principal matter of common concern to the regional powers as well as to most of the extraregional nations. In addition to the possibility of agreeing on a nonproliferation arrangement with India, the United States and the Soviet Union may also find other areas of agreement with some or all of the regional powers, for example, declaratory renunciations on the military use of outer space and the production and use of nuclear weapons.

For the present, the proposals and approaches discussed above appear to constitute the limits of feasible regional ACD arrangements involving the United States and the Soviet Union on the one hand and some or all of the regional powers on the other. Extension beyond these limits will depend on developments in Sino-Soviet, Sino-American, and Soviet-American relations, as well as on alterations in the regional milieu, some of which may be brought about by ACD measures suggested elsewhere in this chapter.

Insofar as Communist China is concerned, feasible ACD measures of regional importance that do not require her voluntary concurrence are best illustrated by the virtual ceasefire which has prevailed in the Taiwan Strait since 1958, as well as by the Korean armistice since 1953. One could envisage some eventual analogous arrangement in Vietnam. Other additional measures which might be feasible depend on Chinese attitudes and policies toward ACD, which are extensively discussed in the report on Communist China.

Arms Control and Disarmament Measurements Without the Concurrence of Extra-regional Communist Powers.

Several ACD programs might be acceptable to the regional countries even without the concurrence of the extraregional Communist powers. The following suggested plans include only the measures involving more than one regional state. The assumption is made that any independent action taken by an individual regional country will depend primarily on factors at work within the country itself rather than on proposals suggested from without.[10] In addition, many of the suggested measures are not ACD measures per se, but are instead programs which might alter factors working against regional ACD arrangements and thereby create a more favorable climate for the future consideration, adoption, and implementation of more specific ACD measures.

Declaratory and voluntary renunciations. Most regional powers are willing to accept a number of specific measures within the general area of

ACD. It _is_ therefore possible that these regional countries could join together in a series of declaratory and voluntary renunciations of certain uses of violence. These voluntary declarations by some or all of the regional powers could cover a number of issues: (1) regulation of the use of outer space; (2) prohibition, reduction, or international control of the production and use of nuclear and thermonuclear weapons, longrange unmanned delivery systems, and chemical, biological, and radiological weapons; (3) elimination, reduction, or international control of the existing stock of nuclear and thermonuclear weapons, longrange unmanned delivery systems, and chemical, biological, and radiological weapons; and (4) prohibition or international control of the development and testing of nuclear or thermonuclear weapons, longrange unmanned delivery systems, and chemical, biological, and radiological weapons. A similar regional declaration could call for the control of the international movement of, traffic in, and gift or sale of such weapons. The latter development, however, would probably require a series of strong guarantees from extraregional allies, particularly the United States.

In addition to the categories above, the renunciation of hostile acts directed against particular countries, such as infiltration and subversion, smuggling of arms, training of guerrillas, and distribution of hostile propaganda, could be covered by a series of regional declarations and possibly be included in other cooperative measures among regional powers.

As suggested earlier, these declarations need not require universal acceptance. A series of "open-end" agreements which could be joined by regional countries when they felt secure enough to participate with the original signatories could be devised for covering the ACD measures above and any other similar measures. The fact that they would be applicable to the regional countries is at present sufficient. This suggestion does not preclude the possibility of linking such arrangements to other extraregional proposals which already exist or which may be contemplated or proposed.

Regional mutual aid in defense and joint "Arms to Plowshare" arrangements. In an effort to increase security against extraregional threats and thereby create a more favorable atmosphere for the consideration of ACD, a regional arrangement involving mutual aid and joint defense planning could possibly be undertaken by some or all of the regional powers. This type of arrangement would call for the use of existing national military forces for developmental projects in the participating countries. The emphasis could perhaps be placed on engineering constructions through the creation of a joint armed forces engineering corps.

The armed forces of many underdeveloped countries have proved their value when their leadership, cohesion, and disciplined training are applied to the basic economic and social problems of developing states. The use of the military power for social and economic change does not necessarily have to be accompanied by the seizure of state power by the military forces themselves although the underdeveloped world abounds in examples of this. Within the region, Burma, Pakistan, Thailand, South Vietnam, South Korea, Taiwan and now Indonesia are controlled by their armed forces, directly or indirectly. Nonetheless, the relatively well-educated officers, the trained and disciplined manpower, the youthful energy, and the modern outlook embodied in these military forces often make the military one of the best overall tools for reform and progress available to the nation.

The possible role of the military is not confined merely to the obvious military skills with civilian application but can be expanded to include a wide range of educational and training functions completely beyond the scope of normal military activity. No attempt is made here to discuss all the paths open to the military in modernizing a nation, but the possibilities are about limitless in underdeveloped states where the level of education and knowledge of modern techniques is extremely low among the broad mass of the population. A nation willing to use a portion of its armed forces for this purpose, however, must be assured that the military can be spared its primary duty --

the defense of the nation. For this reason, regional defense arrangements might stimulate "country building" by the armed forces, while at the same time increase security and stability in the region.

The defense function of such a program would be inoperable in the long run without the active participation of several key countries that possess the economic and technical potential needed to maintain a viable joint defense establishment. India and Japan would be included in this category, as well as South Korea and Taiwan, which have relatively large armed forces despite their smaller potential. At the present, however, certain conditions might prevent these countries from working together. For example, an element of regional dislike and distrust still exists toward Japan and the Japanese. South Korea and Taiwan are too militant for most other nations. India is plagued with internal, regional, and extraregional problems and is in the process of reevaluating some of her basic national interests. In addition, other regional countries perceive a more immediate threat from within the region than from an extraregional power. They might, therefore, require the solution of the regional problem before entering into any kind of regional collective defense and mutual aid system calling for the pooling of national defense forces. By stressing the joint development aspect, the program could have a greater "demonstration effect" and become more attractive.

In view of these factors, a practical ACD plan of this nature would probably have to focus on the gradual and sequential expansion of a subregional arrangement. Should a subregional undertaking prove effective, other regional powers might gradually be willing to join if the subregional arrangement did not increase regional tensions or conflicts among the participants. One might, for example, envisage an *ad hoc* group initially involving only South Korea and Taiwan, and possibly the Philippines, and Japan. India, Thailand, and Japan (if not previously included) might be induced to join after the usefulness and nonaggressive nature of the arrangement has been established.

The role of the United States in promoting such an arrangement should perhaps be limited to technical and some economic assistance, and possibly open participation in joint defense planning should be eschewed. This role of tacit nonparticipation for the United States would not alter present commitments under the various bilateral arrangements she has with the participants of the proposed scheme, but it could possibly reduce the Communist Chinese feeling that such an arrangement would pose an added threat.

A regional police force. All the regional countries favor an international police force on an *ad hoc* basis, and all but Indonesia favor it on a permanent basis. At the same time, however, some of the regional countries are willing to participate in international defense forces only if the missions are relatively minor and under United Nations auspices. In contrast to the large number of regional countries favoring an international police force, only five countries -- Burma, Cambodia, Ceylon, Indonesia, and Japan[11] -- seem willing to agree to a police force composed of regional troops only. All except Japan are apparently willing to participate in such a force.[12] Indonesia's position was probably based on the calculated assumption that she would be able to dominate a police force composed of regional troops only. In view of this fact and the fact that the other three countries have small, ineffective, and generally insignificant armies in terms of resisting outside aggression, it is hardly likely that the four countries could provide the necessary power basis for an effective regional police force vis-à-vis external threats. However, it is possible that troops from these nations -- particularly from Burma and Ceylon -- could be effectively used for such tasks as supervising border armistices and troop withdrawals. The use of troops from nonaligned nations in such limited roles as observation of the armistice on the India-Pakistan border under United Nations command could serve a useful purpose not only in averting involvement of the major extraregional powers, but also in educating the regional powers in the practical tasks necessary for the implementation of ACD. For the time being, however, an effective regional police force will have to be considered in terms of joint participation between regional nations and certain extraregional powers, the participation of the latter depending on the nature of the envisaged force as well as its functions.

<u>Joint technical, scientific, and economic exchanges and programs.</u> The series of declaratory ACD measures suggested previously begs the question why any regional state would wish to renounce certain military postures or undertakings, apart from the peace-loving image such declarations may help create. <u>A more positive inducement is needed.</u> Such an inducement can be provided by joining the ACD measures with other cooperative undertakings so that each would serve to reinforce the other. Through the development of joint technical, scientific, and economic exchanges and programs, it might be possible to promote the habit of regional cooperation as well as to create a community of interest among regional states that would help to allay mutual suspicions. Because of the size and diversity of the region itself, these exchanges and programs should not attempt to cover the entire area initially, but rather they should be undertaken on a subregional or partial (e. g., cross-subregional) basis.

A program of this nature could be based on the following points, which only illustrate a few of many existing possibilities:

1) The development and use of specialized agricultural technical-aid teams from Taiwan and Japan and of demonstration farms for promoting agricultural development in such countries as India, Ceylon, and the Philippines. The work of the Food and Agriculture Organization (FAO) and the Rice Institute in the Philippines could be related to this effort.

2) A more intensive effort to promote cooperation among the members of organizations such as ASA and Maphilindo in an attempt to increase economic and cultural cooperation, as suggested by Thai Foreign Minister Thanat Khoman in June 1966.[13] Additional support might also be given the regional association proposed by Indonesian Vice Premier (and Foreign Minister) Malik which would initially include Thailand, the Philippines, Malaysia, Indonesia, and Singapore (in other words the combined membership of ASA and Maphilindo). Finally, support could also be given the new Asian and Pacific Council (ASPAC) formed in June 1966 by the delegates to the Asian-Pacific conference of foreign ministers (Thailand, South Korea, Japan, the Philippines, Malaysia, the Republic of China, South Vietnam, Australia, and New Zealand, with Laos as an observer).[14] Declaratory ACD measures could subsequently be associated with these regional efforts.

3) The encouragement of economic cooperation among Malaysia, Singapore, and Indonesia, with the possibility of creating joint marketing arrangements for certain primary commodities.

4) The encouragement of joint development schemes by several regional countries, such as the one between India and Pakistan for the Indus River headwaters. This example is felt to be especially relevant, inasmuch as the 1960 Delhi-Karachi settlement of this problem provides some encouragement for what appears to be an otherwise bleak situation.

5) The development of an Asian Development Bank and possibly an Asian Payments Union, both of which could be linked to programs for regional economic development and cooperation. The participation of Japan could be especially encouraged in these matters.

Despite the lesser significance of economic considerations in determining the willingness of countries to allocate resources to defense, it should be stressed that progress in economic development in the civilian sector of the economy cannot but in the long run make peaceful pursuits more attractive and thereby increase receptiveness to ACD.

<u>Informal but earnest discussions of regional arms control and disarmament problems.</u> To promote the measures suggested above and the serious consideration of ACD and its implications for the regional powers, a series of informal but earnest meetings could be held among the regional countries. To analyze the issue of regional security and the aspects of ACD which may or may not be

feasible, such discussions should not focus on unilateral and complete disarmament, but instead should emphasize the realities and problems of arms control in the Far East as a whole as well as in the individual countries of the region.

Since few, if any, of the regional countries possess the necessary understanding of ACD and its problems, an undertaking of this nature would probably have to be done in conjunction with either an international agency, such as the United Nations or an international, nongovernmental group. Again, the role of the United States should be one of indirection. The decision to call these discussions should be announced by the regional countries themselves; the United States could, however, use her array of official and unofficial contacts in the area, particularly Japan and the Philippines, to promote the discussions.

POSSIBLE REGIONAL AND EXTRAREGIONAL RESPONSE TO ARMS CONTROL AND DISARMAMENT IN THE FAR EAST

Current Milieu as a Conditioner of the Attitudes of the Extraregional Communist Powers Toward Arms Control and Disarmament in the Far East

In addition to historical factors that have helped to shape the policies of the extraregional powers toward ACD, the current milieu of conflicts is certain to condition the attitudes of regional and extraregional powers toward proposals dealing with arms control in the Far East.

As the revolution of rising expectations fails to produce desired and, in some cases, anticipated results, the growing gap between expectation and realization becomes a powerful lever for Communist activity in a number of regional states. On the basis of this gap the Communists claim that the forces of history are on their side and find the motivation for creating anti-Western feelings and promoting revolutionary activities. Therefore, the Communists can hardly be expected to renounce subversive activities or support for indigenous insurgency movements in the Far East for the altruistic reason of reducing tensions. The Communists are more likely to support with arms the leaders, parties, and movements that show favor to their cause, particularly in countries with "unfriendly" governments and where they perceive little danger of a hard (and, once committed, inescapable) confrontation with the United States.

The Soviet Union is not afraid that her grants of military aid might eventually be turned against her in this regard. Communist China, on the other hand, is more concerned. The Soviet Union has a preponderance of military strength over every possible opponent in Asia, save the United States, and she therefore desires to build up the power of her friends. Communist China's preponderance of power is less vis-à-vis her neighbors. However, the two Communist countries agree in that they demand the termination of all military alliances or collective security arrangements which might be used against them.

The Soviet Union stands ready to support friendly states if she can avoid exposing herself to unusual risks or danger. Communist regimes must be kept in power lest they be swept away by regimes less amenable to Communist influence. In such countries -- including North Vietnam and possibly Laos, Cambodia, and Burma -- the Soviet Union can be counted on to resist ACD measures which would prevent the continued supplying of military assistance.[15]

The Soviet Union is not disposed to antagonize India, and she may incline to favor India in the Sino-Indian dispute. The Soviet Union is without great influence in Asian countries that are on the side of the West, such as Japan, South Korea, the Philippines, Thailand, and Malaysia, but she would undoubtedly approve any measure which would make it more difficult for regional nations to obtain Western assistance. She is adamantly opposed to SEATO and the bilateral agreements between the United States and Japan, the Republic of Korea, the Republic of China, the Philippines, and the ANZUS powers. For example, she provided great quantities of arms to Indonesia in the latter's confrontation with Malaysia. Finally, the Soviet Union is uneasy about the extension of Communist Chinese power and influence over neighboring states or Communist powers anywhere in Asia.

Communist China's foreign policy toward selected nations of Asia has followed divergent courses depending on the categories to which the countries belong. This is discussed more fully in the Hoover Institution's report on China. Suffice it to note that the tactics and strategies vary and that Communist China still believes that "to struggle against imperialism and against new and old colonialism remains the cardinal and most urgent task of the oppressed nations and people in the vast regions of Asia, Africa, and Latin America." The Chinese posture has, however, improved Peking's relations with certain nations in the Far East, but, in the minds of some people, it has left a question as to the sincerity of Communist China's desire to live in peaceful coexistence,[16] expecially after the dispute with India.

The question of Chinese dynamism or historic expansionism must still be answered. When China has been strong, she has tended to extend her influence if not her territory. For the first time, an aggressive ideology has been wedded to a strong sense of national destiny in Peking, and it must be assumed that Communist China will correlate her policies and attitudes toward ACD with the fulfillment of her stifled ambitions, constrained only by her capability and her perception of her best interest and appropriate strategy. This adds new dimensions to the tasks of deterrence, which have been assumed by the United States and her partners in the free world, and to the feasibility of regional ACD measures.

A main difference in the attitudes of Russia and China toward ACD may derive from the fact that the former is a great nuclear power, while the latter is a mere neophyte in the nuclear club. It is conceivable that Chinese attitudes might change as her nuclear power expands. In this respect, Communist China today is where the Soviet Union was under Stalin.

Both North Korea and North Vietnam have suffered from wars that have ravaged their territories. They may be bellicose in their pronouncements and echo the sentiments of their stronger Communist allies, but neither would welcome a new war on her own territory which would wipe out what progress she has made in rehabilitation.

Possible Regional and Extraregional Reaction to the Suggested Arms Control Measures

The ACD measures considered in an earlier section were divided into two categories: (1) those involving extraregional Communist powers and (2) those involving only the regional and (or) extraregional non-Communist powers. In the first category, attention focussed around the problem of nuclear proliferation. The outstanding question is whether or not the Soviet Union would join the United States in giving a nuclear guarantee to nonnuclear powers. As mentioned earlier, the Soviet Union refrained from making any direct reference to the Indian appeal of 1965. Although a joint Soviet-United States guarantee would be the ultimate assurance for India, short of Communist Chinese nuclear disarmament, the United States could give India a unilateral guarantee without concurrent Soviet action.

In the second category of possible measures -- those not requiring the concurrence of extraregional powers -- none of the suggested measures should give offense to any nonparticipating extraregional country, with the possible exception of the suggested mutual defense and development arrangement. Even a subregional defense and aid arrangement to which the United States is not an open participant should not be construed by Communist China as adding significantly to a United States effort to contain her. The Soviet Union may object to Japanese participation in any defense arrangement with other countries, however small her role may be. If Japan's participation is accompanied by a continued determination not to develop a nuclear force of her own, the Soviet Union may have fewer qualms.

Although both the Soviet Union and Communist China can probably be expected to give some verbal opposition to several of the suggested measures, most of this opposition will come under the heading of political expediency rather than actual perceived threat. In any event, since these proposals are designed to be feasible without Communist concurrence, extraregional Communist opposition need not preclude the acceptance and implementation of all these measures.

No nonparticipating regional country should perceive any of the suggested measures as contributions to regional insecurity or threats. Again, the suggested mutual defense and aid arrangement could prove to be an exception,[17] but as long as such an arrangement emphasizes the developmental aspect and the aim of not weakening security rather than increasing collective military capability, there should be no regional opposition to it. The other measures designed to promote regional cooperation and economic development, which in turn would create a more favorable climate for the consideration of ACD, can only work to the advantage of the region itself.

IMPLEMENTATION -- SEQUENCE AND PRIORITY

The previous discussion has dealt with conditions influencing the possibilities for arms control in the region, with ACD measures which might be feasible in the near future, and with arrangements which might alter present regional opposition to the regulation of such objects as military expenditures, "heavy offensive" weapons, "other conventional" weapons, and armed forces. Although a large part of the regional attitudinal matrix contained in Appendix II, analyzes regional attitude toward control organizations, methods of inspection and verification, nature of field staff and inspectorate, and determination and punishment of violations of ACD measures, we have not focused on this aspect of ACD since regional attention is more directly focused on the conditions underlying the consideration of ACD and the direct objects of ACD. Once these have been clearly established, more attention can be given to the nature of the organizational apparatus itself.

We can, however, give some consideration to the problems of implementation which might arise in the region. For example, of the underlying factors which give rise to resistance to ACD, which factors could be altered in the shortest possible time? Would the removal of one factor have any effect on the removal of a second factor? In short, should there be a preferred sequence for dealing with such problems? These points become even more relevant when several of the regional countries are affected by more than one of the factors mentioned above.

The following observations are advanced on the specific ACD suggestions discussed:

First, in terms of ACD measures that could be undertaken without the concurrence of the extraregional powers, a program calling for joint technical, scientific, and economic exchanges and planning could be implemented independently of all other suggested plans. Therefore, the sooner such arrangements are made, the better.

Second, a series of voluntary declarations covering ACD measures that enjoy the widest acceptance by the regional powers could be implemented after informal discussion. It would probably be best not to call a formal international conference since such a conference would raise the question of Soviet and Chinese participation and thus snarl the proceedings and weigh down the feasible ACD measures with the impractical, the irrelevant, and the unacceptable. Instead, these declarations could be made unilaterally or jointly after a series of informal discussions with the individual countries and with the

United States. If necessary, the applicability of these declarations could be restricted to the regional powers.

Third, while preparations are made for the groups of measures listed above, the United States can probably best advance the cause of ACD in the region by entering into serious discussions with India on some form of a nuclear guarantee and by sponsoring informal but earnest discussions of regional ACD problems.

Lastly, subregional mutual defense and development arrangements involving mutual economic aid and joint defense planning seem to be the only feasible way to increase the regional sense of security against extraregional threats without increasing the level of armament _per se_. If such arrangements can be successfully made, the establishment of an expanded regional defense and aid apparatus may eventually result. The exact organizational nature of such an arrangement is a matter of speculation although some indication can be obtained from the regional attitudinal matrix and the analysis contained in the preceding chapter.

CONCLUSION

Several basic conclusions can be drawn from the analysis in this chapter. There are a number of possibilities for ACD in the Far East, including concrete ACD measures themselves and auxiliary activities indirectly bearing on or leading to ACD. Because the region has been virtually untouched by any ACD measure, the first steps in ACD might best focus attention on arms control problems which have a direct bearing on the region, but which regional nations would feel no insecurity in accepting. Instead of attacking the most difficult ACD problems, either regional ones or problems involving extraregional powers such as China, it might be better to work for the acceptance and implementation of ACD arrangements that would be relatively simple to achieve. These would mainly consist of previously mentioned controls on nuclear weapons and the use of outer space even though a few regional nations such as Japan and Burma might accept certain measures regulating "heavy offensive" weapons.

The easy steps should be taken first. Once a spirit of participation and cooperation has been established for what may appear to be only minor measures, a more positive attitude may emerge for facing the more serious regional ACD problems which for many regional countries lie in the category of "other conventional" weapons.

Although caution would have to be exercised in applying this principle, it would not be unfeasible to make "open-end" ACD agreements that could be joined by regional countries whenever they felt secure enough to participate with the original signatories. In this way, regional group pressures might be brought to bear on recalcitrant countries.

Finally, even though all these suggested arrangements are designed to be feasible even without the concurrence of the extraregional Communist powers, it is possible that once such plans are undertaken, they can be linked to previous and future United States-Soviet agreements. Such a development will depend on the nature and timing of ACD agreements involving the major powers. A notable example is the suggested guarantee to India in return for her promise not to develop her own nuclear force, which could be incorporated into a nonproliferation treaty if and when United States-Soviet agreement is reached. Because of the dynamic nature of the area concerned and because of changes which might result as the plans above begin to be implemented, it is practically impossible to formulate any firm long-range plans. Instead, emphasis might better be placed on the successful implementation of some or all of the measures as well as on the development of an educational program designed to analyze the resolution of conflict through ACD, with specific reference to the regional powers.

TABLE 1

REGIONAL RESPONSE TOWARD THE REGULATION OF THE USE OF OUTER SPACE AND OTHER ACD MEASURES

Subject of Regulation	Regional Response (%)	
	Favorable	Opposed
Outer space	93.3%	6.7%
Nuclear Weapons *	89.1	10.9
Denuclearized Zones	80.0	20.0
Military Expenditures	71.1	28.9
Heavy Offensive Weapons	49.1	50.9
Deployment[a]	47.0	15.6
Conventional Weapons	33.3	66.7
Armed Forces[b]	33.3	64.5

* These same percentages also apply to chemical, biological, and radiological weapons and to long range unmanned delivery systems.

[a] 6.6% not predictable

[b] 2.2% not predictable

TABLE 2

RESPONSE OF INDIVIDUAL COUNTRIES TO THE ACD MEASURES BY MAJOR CATEGORIES

Country	Favorable Response (%) to Indicated Subject of Regulation						
	* Nuclear Weapons	Denuclear-ized Zones	Military Expenditure	Heavy Offensive Weapons	Deployment	Conventional Weapons	Armed Forces
Australia & New Zealand	72.7	0	100.0	0	16.7	0	33.3
Burma	100.0	100.0	100.0	82.8	100.0	10.0	16.7
Cambodia	100.0	100.0	100.0	100.0	100.0	100.0	66.7
Ceylon	100.0	100.0	100.0	100.0	100.0	100.0	100.0
India	100.0	100.0	100.0	0	33.3	0	0
Indonesia	0	0	0	0	83.3	0	0
Japan	100.0	100.0	100.0	100.0	66.7	100.0	100.0
Laos	100.0	100.0	100.0	100.0	16.7[a]	70.0	16.7[a]
Malaysia	81.8	100.0	100.0	54.5	33.3	60.0	16.7
Pakistan	100.0	100.0	100.0	9.1	16.7[b]	0	16.7
Philippines	90.9	100.0	100.0	81.8	50.0	60.0	83.3
South Korea	100.0	100.0	66.7	0	33.3	20.0	0
South Vietnam	100.0	100.0	0	36.4	16.7	0	16.7
Taiwan	90.9	0	0	0	16.7	0	0
Thailand	100.0	100.0	0	72.7	33.3	10.0	33.3

*These same percentages also apply to chemical, biological, and radiological weapons and to long range unmanned delivery systems.

[a]33.33% not predictable

[b]50.00% not predictable

FOOTNOTES

[1]Indeed, some arrangements may be more readily acceptable if all extraregional powers were bypassed. It is not argued that such arrangements would necessarily be effective or that they would be in the national interest of the United States. Such a possibility, however, should not be overlooked.

[2]Some countries were listed as having no predictable position; however, the percentage of no predictable position responses is not great enough to alter the general trend of regional attitudes significantly (2.2% of regional response toward regulation of armed forces and 6.6% of regional response toward regulation of deployment of armed forces fell into this category). For a more detailed country-by-country analysis, see Table 2 at the end of this chapter.

[3]With the exception of Cambodia, Pakistan, and South Vietnam, all regional countries signed the partial Nuclear Test Ban Treaty.

[4]Mainichi Shimbun, January 30, 1964.

[5]For an Indian argument for Indian development of a tactical nuclear capability, see Raj Krishna, "India and the Bomb," India Quarterly, Vol. 21, No. 2, April-June 1965, pp. 119-137 passim., but esp. pp. 128, 130-131.

[6]United States Arms Control and Disarmament Agency, Documents on Disarmament: 1964, (Washington, D. C.: U.S. Government Printing Office, 1964) p. 468.

[7]"Message from President Johnson to the Conference of the Eighteen-Nation Committee on Disarmament," Conference of the Eighteen-Nation Committee on Disarmanent, ENDC/165 (27 January 1966).

[8]"Message from the Chairman of the Council of Ministers of the Union of Soviet Socialists Republics to the Conference of the Eighteen-Nation Committee on Disarmament," Conference of the Eighteen-Nation Committee on Disarmament, ENDC/167 (3 February 1966).

[9]See reference 5 in which Raj Krishna (an economist in the Indian government) concludes that the investment could not only be afforded but would have a salutary effect on the Indian economy.

[10]The current, oft-heard argument that any freedom of action on the part of pro-Western (or, more correctly pro-U.S.) states in the region is impossible (because they are mere puppets) is considered untenable and unsupportable by the authors of this report.

[11]See matrix analysing regional positions.

[12]Japan is precluded from participation by virtue of her Constitution. (Article Nine). She even declined a United Nations request to furnish military observers during the Lebanon crisis of 1958 because the Government wished to avoid opposition and criticism on the ground that the Constitution prohibited dispatch of troops overseas.

[13]See the section on Thailand in the preceding chapter.

[14]The New York Times, June 17, 1966, p. 8.

[15]The Vietnam conflict may be a separate and distinct case, for the Soviet Union would gladly abstain from supplying further materiel and see a negotiated settlement.

[16]For a contrasting view, see Chang Hsin-hai, America and China, (New York: Simon and Schuster, 1966), p. 72. "The whole of China's foreign policy is basically quite simple. She is trying to set her own house in order; she has no desire to spread communism to other parts of the world."

[17]For example, Cambodia might perceive a threat in a defense arrangement directed against Communist China in that it might seem to give Thailand and South Vietnam some opportunity to move against Cambodia.

CHAPTER 3: IMPLICATIONS FOR THE NATIONAL INTERESTS OF THE UNITED STATES

INTRODUCTION

The preceding chapter analyzed the limitations and possibilities for Arms Control and Disarmament (ACD) in the Far East. In the course of this analysis, six major categories of ACD proposals that might be possible in the Pacific-Asian region were suggested, and the problems that might arise from them were discussed. The six proposals are the following:

1) A guarantee of defense aid to India by one or more of the nuclear powers, excluding Communist China. This guarantee would be in exchange for India's promise not to develop or acquire nuclear weapons of her own and would be limited to situations arising from direct nuclear attack on India; thus attack either by nonnuclear powers or by nuclear powers using nonnuclear weapons would be outside the guarantee, and the chance of involving the guarantor(s) in occasional skirmishes between India and Communist China or India and Pakistan would thereby be reduced. This guarantee could be a unilateral one by the United States, or it could be made jointly by one or more of the nuclear powers. Further, the guarantee does not necessarily require retaliation with nuclear weapons.

2) A series of voluntary declaratory renunciations by the regional countries. These renunciations or declarations could cover a number of issues, such as the regulation of the use of outer space; the regulation of nuclear-weapons production (including the elimination of existing stock); and the regulation of the international traffic in nuclear weapons, long-range unmanned delivery systems, chemical, biological, and radiological weapons; and so forth. These declarations could also cover such issues as infiltration and subversion, training of guerrillas, distribution of hostile propaganda, etc. Further, these declarations could be open-ended, so that additional regional countries could participate later.

3) A regional or subregional joint-defense and mutual-aid arrangement, with the primary emphasis on the economic and developmental aspects of such an arrangement.

4) A regional police force to undertake observation of border armistices and so forth.

5) A series of joint regional or subregional technical, economic, and scientific programs.

6) A series of informal but earnest discussions and educational programs on the problems of ACD in the region.

The question whether or not these proposals would be in the national interest of the United States now arises. In an attempt to determine the answer, we have established six basic criteria against which each of the proposals has been judged. These six criteria (in no particular order or priority) are the following:

1) "Communist Power Criterion"

Will the proposed measure increase the power of the Communist countries in relation to that of the United States?

2) "United States Commitment Criterion"

Will the proposed measure increase the commitments of the United States more than it would enhance the relative capability of the United States to meet the commitments?

3) "Regional Power-Bloc Criterion"

Will the proposed measure encourage the growth of the power of regional states as individuals and (or) groups, whether nonaligned or aligned with non-Communist countries, to the extent that it would create one or more new centers of power with which the United States must contend in the future?

4) "Alliance Criterion"

Will the proposed measure add to the future difficulties of United States diplomacy by discouraging her present allies and (or) by alienating neutral powers?

5) "Flexibility Criterion"

Will the proposed measure reduce the flexibility of response which United States policy should continue to enjoy?

6) "Freedom Criterion"

Will the proposed measure be contrary to the basic United States ideology of preserving freedom for her own citizens and for all other peoples who enjoy or aspire to enjoy the same freedom?

We shall now turn to the individual proposals, considering each one against the six criteria. The numbered paragraphs below each proposal refer to our evaluation of the particular proposal by each criterion.

PROPOSAL I: A GUARANTEE OF DEFENSE AID TO INDIA BY ONE OR MORE OF THE NUCLEAR POWERS, EXCLUDING COMMUNIST CHINA

1) "Communist Power Criterion"

Should such an arrangement be acceptable to India, it would preclude her from becoming a nuclear power. While this would eliminate one nuclear power with which the Communists might have to contend in the future, it would in itself have little or no effect upon further development by the Communist powers in the field of nuclear weapons. It would not noticeably affect the nuclear balance between the Communist powers and the United States. Therefore, on the basis of this criterion, such a guarantee would not be detrimental to the national interest of the United States.

2) "United States Commitment Criterion"

By agreeing to come to India's defense in the event of a nuclear attack, the United States would have to make provisions for the deployment of weapons and forces. If this guarantee should prove effective, other regional states may wish to conclude a similar arrangement. While the guarantee to India and this possible subsequent development would seem to put additional burdens upon the United States, the Communist country, or countries, targeted for retaliatory response would remain the same even if the United States were considering only her own defense. Therefore, the magnitude of any military build-up required by such guarantees would be more apparent than real.

3) "Regional Power-Bloc Criterion"

The answer based upon the third criterion is obvious -- a guarantee of defense aid to India would not result in the creation of any independent regional power bloc.

4) "Alliance Criterion"

Such a guarantee on the part of the United States (and possibly the Soviet Union) should meet with no real objection either from allies of the United States or from neutral nations, inasmuch as it would be a voluntary bilateral or tripartite arrangement involving no significant increase of existing military forces. Those regional nations with which the United States already has mutual-defense arrangements may desire a similar guarantee of aid in the event of nuclear attack. This would seem to involve no additional commitment on the part of the United States. Of course, it is always possible that Communist China, for example, may at some future time seek to test the credibility of such guarantees by making a nuclear attack on one of the smaller powers allied with the United States.

However, the point to be noted here is that the United States would retaliate in any event, but, most important, the retaliation need not ipso facto be with nuclear weapons.

In order to keep our regional allies from having any feeling that the United States is discriminating against them in favor of India, the United States may offer to make explicit what are now possibly considered to be implied guarantees. The credibility of United States commitments would thereby be enhanced.

5) "Flexibility Criterion"

Such a guarantee might appear to reduce the degree of flexibility of United States policy to some extent. However, we have placed certain restrictions on such a guarantee: It would apply only in the event of a nuclear attack and does not necessarily require a nuclear response. In addition, the salutary effect of preventing nuclear proliferation in the South Asian subregion will work to the benefit of the United States in the long run. It should be remembered that total flexibility is impossible if commitments are to be at all credible.

6) "Freedom Criterion"

Such a guarantee would in no way conflict with the American ideal of freedom.

PROPOSAL II: A SERIES OF VOLUNTARY RENUNCIATIONS ON THE PART OF THE REGIONAL COUNTRIES

1) "Communist Power Criterion"

It is assumed that any voluntary renunciation on the part of the regional countries would always take cognizance of the world as it exists. Our analysis of the individual countries in the region contains ample evidence to support this assumption. Such renunciations may apply to some or all of the regional countries without necessarily involving any extraregional power. If any specific renunciation or declaration should also involve an extraregional power, the latter's concurrence would have to be obtained for the renunciation or declaration to have any meaning at all. Therefore, such concurrence, or lack of it, could only be determined on the basis of the content of the proposed renunciation or declaration. Unless the act of renunciation or declaration marked a sharp reversal of position toward an extraregional power, it would not be likely to alter presently held perceptions. Although an increase in flexibility arising out of specific regional renunciations or declarations could result in an increase in the relative power of extraregional Communist nations, it is highly improbable.

2) " United States Commitment Criterion"

If a serious threat to regional security should arise as the result of a renunciation, or series of renunciations, the threatened countries might seek United States aid, thereby increasing United States commitments. As noted in the last point, however, the considerations and constraints of the real world would preclude any patently utopian renunciation or declaration detrimental to the national security of the countries involved. It is highly unlikely that any particular renunciation or declaration would be predicated upon the vague and undefined hope that United States aid would be forthcoming should the renunciation or declaration invite aggression.

3) "Regional Power-Bloc Criterion"

Because these voluntary declarations can be made unilaterally, intraregional consultation is not an absolute precondition for a country's advancing them. Should intraregional consultation take place, it could add to regional cohesion but would not per se lead to the creation of a regional power bloc.

4) "Alliance Criterion"

Inasmuch as this proposal deals with renunciations or declarations by regional states without necessarily involving the United States, this criterion does not apply. Allies of the United States might register concern, however, if the effectiveness of United States assistance to them were adversely affected by such renunciations or declarations.

5) "Flexibility Criterion"

It is conceivable that certain declarations or renunciations, whether immediately relevant to ACD or not, might adversely affect United States flexibility in implementing present or future security measures. For example, the regional countries might decide to declare the Far East, or part of it, a nuclear-free zone and thus limit the freedom of the United States in deploying her forces in the Far East, should she accede to the declaration to which she was not a party. Conceivably, such a declaration could even cover United States territories in the Pacific like Guam, Midway, and Wake, thus in turn forcing the United States to declare that these territories would not be bound by the regional declaration. A similar problem would arise if certain regional states declared that foreign bases were not allowed in their territories. These dangers are quite real, and the degree of United States flexibility could indeed be restricted. There is no solution to this problem except insofar as the regional countries assess security requirements and ACD implications realistically and understand the motives underlying United States involvement in the Far East. This is precisely the purpose of the sixth proposal (discussed below) on the sponsorship of regional informal discussions and educational programs.

6) "Freedom Criterion"

The encouragement of regional ACD declarations or renunciations is a recognition of the right of regional states to exercise their freedom.

PROPOSAL III: THE FORMATION OF A REGIONAL OR SUBREGIONAL JOINT DEFENSE AND MUTUAL ASSISTANCE ARRANGEMENT

1) "Communist Power Criterion"

This proposal aims at the pooling of the meager resources of the participating countries for their mutual advantage and development without sacrificing individual or regional security. It could not therefore increase Communist power. By employing the present military forces of the participating countries constructively in nonmilitary endeavors, this proposal, if carried out, would serve to reduce inequities and enhance stability, thereby increasing the political and economic health of the participating countries. Such an arrangement could not therefore be inimical to the interests of the United States.

2) "United States Commitment Criterion"

The proposal specifically recommends that the United States not be an open participant and that any United States assistance be limited to economic and technical aid. No additional United States commitments are involved or envisaged under this proposal.

3) "Regional Power-Bloc Criterion"

The type of regional mutual aid and joint-defense arrangement envisaged as feasible in this proposal should not result in the creation of an independent regional power bloc hostile to the United States. The United States can attempt to prevent such a hostile group from developing by indirectly influencing the programs and actions of the regional arrangement.

4) "Alliance Criterion"

This proposal should in no way discourage United States allies or alienate neutrals because the United States would not be a signatory to any such regional agreement.

5) "Flexibility Criterion"

The suggested arrangement should not significantly reduce United States flexibility, in view of the fact that bilateral agreements between the United States and certain regional countries will remain in force. No additional loss of United States flexibility is entailed under this proposal.

6) "Freedom Criterion"

There is obviously no conflict in this regard.

PROPOSAL IV: REGIONAL POLICE FORCE FOR LIMITED PEACE-KEEPING FUNCTIONS SUCH AS OBSERVATION OF BORDER ARMISTICES AND SO FORTH

1) "Communist Power Criterion"

There is no way in which the creation of a regional police force could increase Communist power.

2) "United States Commitment Criterion"

The United States may be required to provide training and equipment for such a police force. However, the point here is that the potential benefits of such a regional police force would far outweigh the minimal costs and commitments that the United States might be called upon to bear.

3) "Regional Power-Bloc Criterion"

Countries that would be included in such a regional police force, like Burma, Ceylon, and Thailand, would not constitute a power bloc as the term is usually understood. In addition, it should be remembered that this proposal envisages only limited peace-keeping functions for this force.

4) "Alliance Criterion"

The proposal will not alienate neutrals if forces from countries such as Burma and Ceylon are participants. Besides, one of the purposes of this proposal is to reduce extraregional involvement where it is not necessary. By reducing such unnecessary involvement, the United States would be better able to concentrate attention on her alliances and commitments.

5) "Flexibility Criterion"

The creation of a regional police force would reduce the occasions on which the United States would have to intervene directly in a regional dispute. In order to be effective, a regional police force may have to be formed under the auspices of the United Nations or a regional agency. As a member of the United Nations, SEATO, ANZUS, and other organizations the United States is not of course precluded from becoming involved in regional disputes, should such involvement be required. Therefore, the United States would not sacrifice any flexibility of action under this proposal.

6) "Freedom Criterion"

The creation of a regional police force would in no way conflict with the American ideal of freedom.

PROPOSAL V: A SERIES OF JOINT TECHNICAL, ECONOMIC, AND SCIENTIFIC PROGRAMS

1) "Communist Power Criterion"

The arrangements suggested under this proposal aim at the promotion of regional cooperation, joint benefit, and common interest. If successful, they should reduce the opportunities for Communist agitation, infiltration, and exploitation of present inequities. They would not therefore increase the relative power of the extraregional Communist countries.

2) "United States Commitment Criterion"
The degree of United States commitment depends upon the nature of the program and the extent and manner of her participation or support. Because the proposed programs are of a nonmilitary nature, no increase in the American military commitment would be required. The extent of nonmilitary commitment on the part of the United States should be considered in conjunction with the next criterion.

3) "Regional Power-Bloc Criterion"
The emergence of a self-sufficient regional bloc which might eventually attempt to exclude or "freeze out" the United States, possibly economically at first, must be recognized as a possibility, however remote. If the United States desires to preclude this development, she might participate in such programs in a manner and to the extent that their success will depend upon United States participation. The United States should not therefore encourage the growth of regionalism <u>per se</u>, but should rather encourage regional growth within a multilateral framework. Because the long-term participation of the United States is required to make these arrangements work, her participation should be so structured as to maintain the long-term support of the Congress as well as of the American public.

4) "Alliance Criterion"
That an ally of the United States could be excluded from such regional arrangements is a possibility which in turn reinforces the argument that United States participation and insistence upon nondiscrimination are vital. If this can be assured, then the benefits that accrue to the participants in such arrangements would not be won at the expense of nonparticipants. If this cannot be assured, then the arrangement should not be initiated.

5) "Flexibility Criterion"
If the conceptualization and implementation of the proposal meet the preceding two criteria, then it would not adversely affect United States flexibility. On the contrary, it would allow the United States to commit less of her resources to any individual country.

6) "Freedom Criterion"
There is no conflict in this regard.

PROPOSAL VI: SPONSORSHIP OF REGIONAL INFORMAL DISCUSSIONS AND EDUCATIONAL PROGRAMS WITH REGARD TO ACD PROBLEMS

1) "Communist Power Criterion"
Such a program must focus attention on the realities of regional security and ACD problems and <u>not</u> on general and complete disarmament, unilateral disarmament, and other goals that are unrealizable at present, however attractive they may be in abstract. If the program is so conceived and executed, no adverse effect is foreseen.

2) "United States Commitment Criterion"
Under the same assumptions as in the preceding point (concerning the realistic focus of the programs), this criterion involves no United States commitment beyond the informal discussions and educational programs envisaged.

To be effective, the United States should participate and offer guidance where desired, but only as one of a number of interested parties, that is, she should not attempt to take credit for such programs or to preempt the "idea market." Possibly, the United States should concentrate on encouraging certain regional countries to call for such discussions.

3) "Regional Power-Bloc Criterion"

Inasmuch as informal discussions and educational programs constitute the sum and substance of the proposal, they could not per se lead to the formation of a regional power bloc. To the extent that these discussions should lead to a change of attitude in favor of regionalism, such a long-term result is conceivable. However, this development would have to arise from concrete regional arrangements of the kind discussed under the fifth proposal.

4) "Alliance Criterion"

The present proposal would not adversely affect United States' allies if the discussions are informal and realistic and if they take cognizance of the interests of our allies. It is understood that these latter regional states would be parties to the discussions and programs.

5) "Flexibility Criterion"

Flexibility would not be affected by the discussions and programs envisaged in this proposal.

6) "Freedom Criterion"

Such programs and discussions would indeed be consonant with the ideal of free exchange of ideas.

The preceding review of the six categories of proposals has been summarized in the following chart, which shows that (1) Proposals I, IV, and VI, are in total harmony with the national interest of the United States as determined by the six criteria set forth. (2) The merits of Proposals III and V, from the point of view of the United States, depend upon their conceptualization and implementation, inasmuch as these proposals cannot be evaluated in the abstract; (3) Proposal II contains one possibly negative element which, it is hoped, would be removed by the implementation of Proposal VI. (See chart on following page.)

The reader may wonder why we have not included a single proposal that would require an actual reduction of arms or armed forces from their present levels. The answer may be found if we examine the regional attitudinal matrix and the discussion in Part III, Chapter 1. Cambodia and Ceylon are the two countries willing to accept almost any ACD measure in the abstract. In our opinion, this position is essentially a result of their impotence in altering the realities confronting them, together with the fact that Ceylon has no serious problems of security.

We do not wish to advocate either for ourselves or for others a position in which we have "peace" simply because we cannot defend ourselves and must accept the declarations or fiat of others if we wish to survive. Therefore, we cannot advocate a reduction of arms where the threat to the whole region is such that no regional state is completely free from fear. On the other hand, we do not advocate an increase in arms; instead we advocate an increased sense of regional security. The preceding proposals are designed to promote this end and to effect a breakthrough in realistic arms control. In our view, these proposals will best serve the long-term interest of the United States as well as that of the region.

SUGGESTED ACD PROPOSALS

UNITED STATES NATIONAL INTERESTS

PROPOSALS	I Nuclear Guarantee To India	II Regional Voluntary Declarations and Renunciations	III Regional Mutual Aid and Joint Defense Arrangements	IV Regional Police Force	V Series of Joint Economic, Technical, Etc. Programs	VI Regional Discussions and Educational Program
1. Communist Power Criterion	X	X	X	X	X	X
2. U.S. Commitment Criterion	X	X	X	X	X	X
3. Regional Power-Bloc Criterion	X	X	?	X	?	X
4. Alliance Criterion	X	X	X	X	?	X
5. Flexibility Criterion	X	O	X	X	?	X
6. Freedom Criterion	X	X	X	X	X	X

X - In consonance with U.S. interests

O - Contrary to U.S. interests

? - Effect of criterion debatable

APPENDIX I

PART A: MAJOR NONREGIONAL ACD PROPOSALS
PART B: REGIONAL ACD PROPOSALS
PART C: THE MATRIX

APPENDIX I, PART A

MAJOR NONREGIONAL ACD PROPOSALS (EXCLUDING COMMUNIST CHINA)

Number on Matrix			
U-1	USA	Baruch Plan	14 June 1946
R-2	USSR	Ban the Bomb	19 June 1946
R-3	USSR	Periodic Inspection	11 June 1947
R-4	USSR	Armed Forces Reduction	25 September 1948
R-5	USSR	Prohibition and Control Simultaneously	2 October 1948
R-6	USSR	Peace Pact	12 January 1952
U-7	USA	Disclosure and Verification	5 April 1952
U-8	USA	Anti-Germ Warfare	15 August 1952
U-9	USA	Eliminate Bacterial Weapons	4 September 1952
U-10	USA	Atoms for Peace	8 December 1953
R-11	USSR	Anti-Atoms for Peace	21 December 1953
U-12	USA	Implementation and Enforcement of Disarmament	25 May 1954
13	UK-France	Ban Atomic Weapons and Arms Reduction	11 June 1954
R-14	USSR	Unconditional Prohibition	11 June 1954
R-15	USSR	Int'l Treaty to Ban Atomic Weapons and Reduce Arms	19 March 1955
16	UK France	Reduce Armed Forces of Great Powers	29 March 1955
17	UK-France	Prohibit and Eliminate Nuclear Weapons	19 April 1955
R-18	USSR	End Cold War	10 May 1955
R-19	USSR (Geneva)	Reduction of Arms and Prohibition of Atomic Weapons	21 July 1955
U-20	USA (Geneva)	Aerial Inspection and Blueprint Exchange	21 July 1955
21	UK (Geneva)	Joint Inspection of European Armed Forces	21 July 1955
U-22	USA	Implementation of Aerial Inspection	30 August 1955
U-23	UK	Methods, Objects, and Rights of Control Organ	13 September 1955
U-24	USA	Conventional Force Levels	22 March 1956
R-25	USSR	Reduction of Conventional Arms and Armed Forces	27 March 1956
U-26	USA	Comprehensive Agreement for Disarmament	3 April 1956
R-27	USSR	Nonintervention in Middle East	11 February 1957
R-28	USSR	Reduction and Prohibition	18 March 1957
U-29	UK-USA	Self-Imposed Restraint	24 March 1957
R-30	USSR	Implementation of Disarmament	30 April 1957
R-31	USSR	Cease Atomic and Hydrogen Tests	14 June 1957
U-32	UK, USA, France, Canada	Partial Disarmament	29 August 1957
33	Poland	Rapacki Plan	2 October 1957

R-34	USSR	Bulganin's Letter	10 December 1957
U-35	USA	Eisenhower's Letter	12 January 1958
U-36	USA	Dulles on Outer Space	16 January 1958
R-37	USSR	Atom-Free Zone in Middle East	21 January 1958
R-38	USSR	Arms Shipments to Middle East	31 January 1958
39	Poland	Rapacki Memorandum	14 February 1958
R-40	USSR	International Cooperation in Space	15 March 1958
R-41	USSR	End US Bomb Flights Toward USSR	21 April 1958
R-42	USSR	Khrushchev's Letter	22 April 1958
U-43	USA	Arctic Inspection Zone	29 April 1958
R-44	USSR	Khrushchev's Letter	7 September 1958
R-45	USSR	Memorandum on Measures for Disarmament	18 September 1958
46	Poland	Atom-Free Zone in Central Europe	4 November 1958
R-47	USSR	Discontinue Nuclear Tests	7 February 1959
U-48	USA	Discontinue Nuclear Tests	25 March 1959
U-49	USA	Eisenhower's Letter	13 April 1959
R-50	USSR	Khrushchev's Letter	14 May 1959
51	12 Nations	Antarctic Treaty	1 December 1959
U-52	USA	Discontinue Nuclear Tests	11 February 1960
R-53	USSR	Discontinue Nuclear Tests	16 February 1960
R-54	USSR	Discontinue Nuclear Tests	19 March 1960
U-55	USA-UK	Coordinate Research Programs	29 March 1960
R-56	USSR	Discontinue Nuclear Tests	3 May 1960
R-57	USSR	Universal and Total Disarmament	2 June 1960
U-58	USA	General and Complete Disarmament	27 June 1960
U-59	USA	Detection and Identification System	20 July 1960
R-60	USSR	Discontinue Nuclear Tests	26 July 1960
61	Poland	Gomulka's Address	27 September 1960
R-62	USSR	Discontinue Nuclear Tests	21 March 1961
U-63	USA	Discontinue Nuclear Tests	21 March 1961
U-64	USA	Discontinue Nuclear Tests	28 April 1961
U-65	USA-UK	Sliding Scale of On-Site Inspections	29 May 1961
U-66	USA	Discontinue Nuclear Tests	30 August 1961
U-67	USA	General and Complete Disarmament in a Peaceful World	25 September 1961
R-68	USSR	General and Complete Disarmament	26 September 1961
R-69	USSR	Denuclearized Zone in Africa and Prohibition of Nuclear Weapons	8 November 1961
70	General Assembly	Denuclearized Zone of Africa	24 November 1961
R-71	USSR	Discontinue Nuclear Tests	28 November 1961
72	General Assembly	Prevent Wider Dissemination of Nuclear Weapons	4 December 1961
R-73	USSR	General and Complete Disarmament under Strict Int'l Control	22 March 1962
U-74	USA	Treaty on General and Complete Disarmament in a Peaceful World	18 April 1962
75	NUCLEAR TEST BAN TREATY		25 July 1963

SOME MAJOR NONREGIONAL ACD PROPOSALS SINCE 25 JULY 1963

R-76	USSR	Gromyko Proposals	19 September 1963
U-77	USA	Johnson Letter on Control and Non-Proliferation of Nuclear Weapons	21 January 1964
R-78	USSR	Proposal to Slow Down Armaments and Relax Tensions	28 January 1964
U-79	USA	Draft Treaty on the Non-Proliferation of Nuclear Weapons	17 August 1965
R-80	USSR	Draft Treaty on the Non-Proliferation of Nuclear Weapons	24 September 1965
U-81	USA	Johnson Seven Point Message to ENDC	27 January 1966
R-82	USSR	Kosygin Proposal on No First Use	3 February 1966

APPENDIX I, PART B

REGIONAL ACD PROPOSALS (COMMUNIST CHINA ADDED)

1.		Baguio Conference Declaration	30 May 1950
2.	India	Nehru's Speech to Parliament	2 April 1954
3.		Bandung Conference Declaration	24 April 1955
4.	Communist China	"Pact for Peace"	30 July 1955
5.	India	Suspend Tests and Establish Arms Truce	6 December 1955
6.	India	Cease Nuclear Tests	12 July 1956
7.	Japan	Registration of Nuclear Tests with UN	18 January 1957
8.	Japan	Diet Resolution	20 March 1957
9.	Japan	Suspend Nuclear Test Explosions	23 September 1957
10.	India	Scientific Commission for Inspection	1 November 1957
11.	India	Refrain from Use of Nuclear Weapons	1 November 1957
12.	India	Nehru's Appeal to Stop Testing	28 November 1957
13.		Afro-Asian Peoples' Solidarity Conference Declaration	26 December 1957
14.	India	Immediate Halt to Nuclear Testing	14 October 1958
15.	Communist China	Universal Disarmament	21 January 1960
16.		Afro-Asian Peoples' Solidarity Conference Declaration	15 April 1960
17.	Communist China	No Negotiation without Recognition	8 May 1960
18.	Communist China	No Disarmament While Imperialism Exists	8 June 1960
19.	Communist China	Asian-Pacific Mutual Nonaggression Pact	30 July 1960
20.	12-nation resolution	General & Complete Disarmament with Inspection	15 November 1960
21.	19-nation resolution	General & Complete Disarmament with Control	8 December 1960
22.	Pakistan	Economic & Social Consequences of Disarmament	15 December 1960
23.	Commonwealth Prime Ministers	Declaration on Disarmament	17 March 1961
24.	Japan	Note to US to Stop Testing	6 September 1961
25.		Belgrade Conference Statement	6 September 1961
26.	India	Nehru on Soviet Testing	31 October 1961
27.	India-USA	Urgent Need for Test Ban Treaty	9 November 1961
28.	Communist China	National Independence Before Disarmament	18 December 1961
29.	8 Neutrals	Compromise Detection System	16 April 1962
30.	India	One-Year Quota of Inspections	30 November 1962
31.		Afro-Asian Peoples' Solidarity Conference Declaration	11 February 1963
32.	Communist China	Complete Prohibition & Thorough Destruction of Nuclear Weapons	31 July 1963
33.	India-Ceylon	Extend Nuclear-Free Zones to the Seas	14 September 1964
34.	Communist China	Message to the Heads of State after their First Nuclear Explosion	17 October 1964
35.	Communist China	No First Use Proposal to the US at Warsaw	17 October 1964
36.	India-Canada	Int'l Guarantees for Nonnuclear Countries Threatened with Nuclear Attack	4 & 5 May 1965

ACD PROPOSALS - SOURCES OF DATA IN MATRIX

Department of State, Historical Offices, Bureau of Public Affairs, Documents on Disarmament, (series), 1945-1960, Washington, D. C.

Jack, Homer A., Cairo: The Afro-Asian Peoples' Solidarity Conference, A Toward Freedom pamphlet (Chicago, Ill., 1958).

Mendlovitz, Saul H., Legal and Political Problems of World Order (New York: The Fund For Education Concerning World Peace Through World Law, 1962).

On Record (Disarmament and The Nuclear Test Ban Treaty) Vol. 1, No. 6, (New York: Keynote Publications, Inc., 1963).

Permanent Secretariet of Afro-Asian Peoples' Solidarity Political-Organizational Report to The Second Afro-Asian Peoples' Solidarity Conference (Conakry 11-15 April 1960), (Cairo, U. A. R.: Dar el Hana Press, n. d. (1960?)).

United Nations, Yearbook of the United Nations (series) (New York: Columbia University Press, 1946 ff.).

United States Arms Control and Disarmament Agency, Documents on Disarmament, (series) 1961-1964, Washington, D. C.

The New York Times, various dates, 1965.

APPENDIX I, PART C

THE MATRIX

The matrix itself was constructed in two ways: (1) chronologically, taking the entire sample of nonregional proposals, including British, French, and Polish proposals as well as those advanced by the United States and the Soviet Union, and casting them over time; and (2) comparatively, taking United States proposals as one group and Soviet proposals as another, excluding all other nonregional proposals.[1]

The matrix is composed of five major parts, with detailed categories and subcategories in each part. The first part (I) deals with the "objects of control" -- i. e., what should be controlled. The objects of control are divided into six broad categories: (A) weapons systems, (B) armed forces, (C) military expenditures, (D) outer space, (E) zonal arrangements, and (F) hostile acts. Each category is further broken down into analytically useful subcategories. For example, in regard to the control of weapons systems, specific types of weapons systems as well as their "locus of regulation" are considered.[2]

The second part of the matrix (II) is concerned with the sequence of ACD -- i. e., how ACD should be carried out. More specifically, it deals with the sequential implementation of ACD in relation to the development of control machinery, time schedule, and political settlement.

The third part (III) deals with the actual implementation of ACD through various types of control organizations.

The fourth and fifth parts of the matrix (IV and V) are concerned with the territories included in ACD agreements and punishments for violators, respectively.

The matrix was developed through both a synthesis of past ACD proposals and the insights gained from discussions in the research group. The matrix has been developed logically, and many of the subcategories were added to the broader categories contained in or suggested by previous ACD proposals. The addition of these subcategories strengthens the thoroughness and meaning of the matrix, increases its utility and (it is believed) adds to its precision.

THE ATTITUDES OF THE MAJOR POWERS

Before undertaking a comparison and contrast of United States and Soviet ACD proposals, a variant representation of the categories and subcategories in the matrix seems appropriate.

Of the 215 categories and subcategories that compose the matrix, 68 are not mentioned in any proposal in the representative sample. In addition, 36 other categories or subcategories are dealt with in United States proposals but not in Soviet proposals, and another 37 are included in Soviet proposals but absent from those advanced by the United States. This means that, even though certain subcategories are reverse formulations of other subcategories, 141 components (i. e., 66 percent of the total universe) were not included in the proposals advanced by either one or both of the major powers.

It was also determined that the United States and the Soviet Union, on the basis of volume count, are in "substantial agreement" on 23 points and "substantial disagreement" on 22 points. Eight (8) earlier disagreements were reduced because of a shift by one of the two powers (5 shifts by the United States, 3 shifts by the Soviet Union).

Finally, there were two (2) cases in which earlier agreement was lost due to a change in attitude on the part of the Soviet Union with the United States standing firm. The reverse -- i.e., earlier agreement being lost due to a change in attitude on the part of the United States with the Soviet Union standing firm -- did not occur.

In the following representation, these cases are coded as follows:

N	Not in any proposal (68)
U	In U.S. proposals only (36)
S	In Soviet proposals only (37)
SA	"substantial agreement" (28)
SDUF	"substantial disagreement, U.S. favors" (8)
SDSF	"substantial disagreement, Soviet Union favors" (14)
EDRU	Earlier disagreements now reduced due to the U.S. shift to Soviet position (5)
EDRS	Earlier disagreements now reduced due to Soviet shift to U.S. position (3)
ADUC	Earlier agreement lost due to U.S. change and Soviet standing firm (none)
ADSC	Earlier agreement lost due to Soviet change and U.S. standing firm (2).

Uncoded entries indicate that no clear code determination was considered possible from the study of the proposals. (Note also that, in the following representation, the numbers 1 to 215 inclusive indicate the categories or subcategories. Major headings were not numbered to avoid double counting.)

OBJECTS OF CONTROL

ACD Item	Letter Code	Matrix Outline	
		A	Weapons systems
		1	Types of weapons systems to be controlled
1	SA	a	nuclear weapons, general
2	SA	b	long-range, unmanned delivery systems (e.g., ICBM's and orbitting carriers)
3	SA	c	other delivery systems for nuclear warheads (e.g., cannon, bombers, missile submarines)
4	SA	d	heavy offensive weapons (e.g., capital ships, heavy artillery, conventionally armed bombers and submarines)
5	SA	e	other conventional weapons
6	EDRS	f	chemical, biological, and/or radiological weapons
7	SA	g	general or unspecified weapons
		2	Locus of regulation
		a	production of raw materials and other inputs used in producing the above
8	N	1)	limitation and/or prohibition

9	N		2)	international control
			b	production of end-products
10	EDRU		1)	prohibition
11			2)	reduction
12	SA		3)	limitation
13	N		4)	internationalization
14	S		5)	surveillance (supervision)
15	U		6)	international control
			c	international movement of and traffic in fissionable materials or weapons
16	SDSF	S	1)	prohibition of movement or stationing outside one's own country
17		N	2)	regulation of movement or stationing outside one's own country
18			3)	prohibition of gift or sale of weapons, information, or blueprints for developing such weapons (non-proliferation)
19		N	4)	regulation of gift or sale of weapons, information, or blueprints for developing such weapons
20		U	5)	international control
			d	disposition of existing stock
21	SDUF	U	1)	transferring stock to national depots for inspection
22		U	2)	transferring stock to international agency
23		U	3)	international monopoly of stock
24		SA	4)	destruction
25		SA	5)	conversion to peaceful uses
26		SA	6)	reduction
27		N	7)	ceiling
28	SDSF	S	8)	percentage
29		U	9)	ratio
			e	use
30	S		1)	unconditional renunciation
31	S		2)	conditional renunciation (includes no first use and guarantees for nonnuclear powers)
32	EDRU		3)	unconditional prohibition
33			4)	conditional prohibition
34	U		5)	international monopoly of use
35	S		6)	international control
			f	weapons development and research
36	S		1)	prohibition of research and development
37	U		2)	international monopoly of research and development
38	SDSF	S	3)	exchange of information
39	EDRS		4)	registration of tests
40	SDUF	U	5)	limitation of tests
41	SA		6)	internationalization of tests
42	EDRU		7)	prohibition of tests
43	SA		8)	prohibition of tests in specified environment
			9)	moratorium on tests in specified environment

44	SDUF		a)	short-term
45	SDSF	S	b)	long-term
			B	Armed Forces
			1	Categories
			a	military
46			1)	army
47			2)	navy
48			3)	air force
49	N		4)	special forces
50	N		5)	volunteers (as Chinese in Korean War)
51	N		6)	foreign military advisors
52			7)	not specified
			b	paramilitary
53	N		1)	militia
54	N		2)	security forces
55	N		3)	police
56	N		4)	intelligence collection agencies
57			5)	not specified
58			c	general or unspecified
			2	Locus of regulation:
			a	recruitment
59			1)	prohibition of conscription
60	N		2)	limitation on volunteers
61	N		3)	specification as to length of service
			b	preparation and training
62	N		1)	prohibition of inculcation of military spirit
63	S		2)	prohibition of all training
64	N		3)	prohibition of specified forms of training (to include training and schooling in foreign country)
65	S		4)	abolition of general staff and all military agencies
			c	deployment
66	SDSF	S	1)	prohibition of foreign bases
67	SDUF	U	2)	limitation of foreign bases
68		N	3)	limitation on number of troops stationed in specified foreign bases or countries
69		S	4)	prohibition of movement of troops outside one's own frontiers
70		N	5)	limitation on movement of troops outside one's own frontiers
71		S	6)	withdrawal of forces from specified areas
			d	size
72	SA		1)	numerical ceiling on troops
73	S		2)	percentage cut

74	N		3)	national ratio
75	N		4)	internationalization of troops
76	U		5)	reduction
77			6)	elimination of all military and paramilitary organizations beyond those required to maintain internal order
			C	Military Expenditures
78	SA		1	prohibition of military expenditures
79	SA		2	reduction of military expenditures
80			3	limitation of military expenditures
			D	Outer Space
81	SA		1	prohibition of the use of outer space for military purposes
			E	Zonal Arrangements
82	SDSF	S	1	denuclearized
83		S	2	demilitarized
84			3	demonstrative (pilot) ACD zone
			F	Hostile Acts
85		S	1	prohibition of military provocation
86		S	2	prohibition of formation of military alliances or blocs
87			3	prohibition of support for insurrections and revolts in other countries
88		S	4	prohibition of economic discriminations against other countries (embargo, sanctions, blockade, etc.)
89	SDSF	S	5	prohibition of war propaganda or anti-foreign propaganda
90		S	6	prohibition of war
91			7	prohibition of violations of the U.N. Declaration of Human Rights
92		S	8	others (specified)

II SEQUENCE OF ACD

93		U	A	establishment of control machinery before proceeding with ACD
94		S	B	proceeding with ACD before establishment of control machinery
95	SDSF		C	ACD simultaneously with control
96	SDSF		D	phased implementation of ACD with control
97		S	E	phased implementation of ACD without controls
98	SDUF	U	F	phased implementation of ACD depending upon satisfaction at each phase
99		N	G	phased implementation of ACD with controls for some specific phases
100	EDRU		H	definite time schedule for ACD
101	EDRS		I	no definite time schedule for ACD
102	U		J	political settlement prior to ACD
103	N		K	ACD prior to political settlement
104			L	ACD simultaneous with political settlement

III CONTROL ORGANIZATION

A Structure and Composition

105	SA		1	Control commission
106			a	number (specified)
			b	selection
107		N	1)	unanimous agreement of all ACD parties
108		U	2)	majority of ACD parties with unanimous approval of all major powers participating in ACD
109		N	3)	Security Council
110		N	4)	General Assembly
111		S	5)	other
			2	Secretariat
			a	central administration (selection of)
112	SDUF		1)	one administrator (director) (chosen by)
113		N	a)	unanimous agreement of all ACD parties
114		U	b)	majority of ACD parties with unanimous approval of all major powers participating in ACD
115		N	c)	Security Council
116		N	d)	General Assembly
117			e)	control commission
118		S	2)	Administrative Council (troika) (chosen by)
119		N	a)	unanimous agreement of all ACD parties
120		N	b)	majority of ACD parties with unanimous approval of all major powers participating in ACD
121		N	c)	Security Council
122		N	d)	General Assembly
123		N	e)	control commission
			b	administrative staff (selection of)
124		U	1)	Secretariat
125		N	2)	Secretariat with control commission approval
126		S	3)	other
127	SDSF	S	4)	international basis (unspecified)
			5)	international basis (specified)
128		N	a)	quota or fixed ratio
129		N	b)	national ratio
130		U	c)	technical competence
131		U	d)	other
			c	field staff (selection of)
132		U	1)	Secretariat
133		N	2)	Secretariat with control commission approval
134		S	3)	other
135		S	4)	international basis (unspecified)
			5)	international basis (specified)

136 a) quota or fixed ratio
137 N b) national ratio
138 U c) technical competence
139 U d) other

3 Regional Substructure

140 N a regions specified

b permanent

141 N 1) responsible to Secretariat
142 N 2) responsible to control commission
143 U 3) not specified

c ad hoc

144 N 1) responsible to Secretariat
145 N 2) responsible to control commission
146 S 3) not specified

4 Inspectorate

147 a number specified

b selection

148 U 1) by Secretariat(s)
149 N 2) Secretariat with control commission approval
150 S 3) other
151 U 4) non-national basis (no national to serve in own country)
152 N 5) national basis (nationals to serve only in their own country)
153 N 6) only "neutrals" to serve
154 SDSF S 7) international basis (unspecified)
8) international basis (specified)

155 S a) quota or fixed ratio
156 N b) national ratio
157 U c) technical competence
158 N d) other

B Functions

159 1 development of procedures for control and inspection
160 ADSC 2 implementation of control and inspection
161 ADSC 3 verification
162 SDUF U 4 determination and reporting of violations
163 SA 5 other (specified)

C Methods of Control

1 Without inspection

164 a long-range scientific methods from stations outside one's own country
165 N b stationing scientific instruments in foreign country without inspection

166			c	exchange of scientific, technical, and/or budgetary information
167			d	exchange of military blueprints
168			e	other (specified)
			2	With inspection
			a	on-site
169	SA		1)	quota of on-site
170	U		2)	specific percentage of on-site
171			3)	occasional or periodic
172	SA		4)	continuous
173	SA		b	control posts
174			c	mobile inspection teams
175	SA		d	definite routes or specified areas of inspection
176			e	aerial inspection
177	SDSF	S	f	limited freedom of access
178		U	g	complete freedom of access
179			h	other (specified)
180	EDRU		3	international police force
			D	Authority of Control Organization over Control Measures
181		U	1	authority not subject to veto
182			2	authority in certain specified areas not subject to veto
			3	authority subject to veto of:
183	SDSF		a	Security Council
184		U	b	control commission
185		S	c	directorate
186		N	4	authority in certain specified areas subject to veto
187		N	a	Security Council
188			b	control commission
189		N	c	directorate

IV TERRITORIES COVERED BY ACD

190	SA		A	signatories only
191			B	signatories plus other specified territories
192			C	certain specified territories only
193	SA		D	all countries[3]

V PUNISHMENTS FOR VIOLATORS

			A	Determined By
194		N	1	Security Council (with veto)
195		U	2	International authority (without veto)
196		N	3	International authority (with veto)
197		N	4	General Assembly

198	N	5	International Court of Justice
199		6	not specified
		B	Executed by
200	N	1	Security Council (with veto)
201	N	2	International authority (without veto)
202	N	3	International authority (with veto)
203	N	4	General Assembly
204	N	5	International Court of Justice
205		6	not specified
		C	Nature of Sanctions
		1	international sanctions against nation
206	N	a	political
207	N	b	economic
208	N	c	military
209	U	d	not specified
		2	international sanctions against individuals or groups
210	N	a	political
211	N	b	economic
212	N	c	military
213	U	d	not specified
214	U	3	national sanctions against individuals or groups
215	S	4	not specified

(AREAS OF AGREEMENT & DISAGREEMENT, WITH COUNT)

Note: the number indicates the category or subcategory. The figures in parentheses indicate US/USSR proposals; for example, 1(21/26) means that on point 1, there were 21 U. S. proposals and 26 Soviet proposals.

<u>Substantial Agreement</u>: 1(21/26), 2(4/5), 3(3/5), 4(2/2), 5(2/2), 7(7/11), 12(4/4), 24(6/6), 25(4/6), 26(5/6), 41(6/6), 43(8/5), 71(5/8), 78(4/6), 80(4/4), 104(16/15), 162(3/3), 168(5/5), 171(5/5), 172(12/10), 174(4/4), 189(16/17), 192(9/8).

<u>Substantial Disagreement, U. S. Favors</u>: 21(4/0), 22(6/0), 40(5/0), 44(5/1), 66(2/0), 97(11/0), 111(10/2), 161(7/0).

<u>Substantial Disagreement, U. S. S. R. Favors</u>: 16(0/6), 28(0/6), 38(0/5), 45(0/5), 65(0/10), 70(0/10), 81(0/6), 88(0/6), 94(1/6), 95(3/13), 126(0/7), 153(0/6), 176(0/5), 182(1/7).

FOOTNOTES

[1]If a joint proposal had either the United States or the Soviet Union as one of its authors, it is in the "comparative" matrix.

[2]The term "locus of regulation," as used in this analysis, includes: the regulation of various components in the production, international movement of and traffic in, weapons or material; disposition of existing stock; use of weapons; and weapons research and development.

[3]This appears to be contradictory to 190; however, the proposals were made on different occasions and refer to separate spheres.

75 SELECTED NON-REGIONAL A

Chronology: *page 1*

		US 1	R 2	R 3	R 4	R 5	R 6	US 7	US 8	US 9	US10	R 11	US12	13	R 14	R 15	16	17	R 18	R 19	US20	21	US22
	I. OBJECTS OF CONTROL																						
	A. WEAPONS SYSTEMS																						
	1. Types of weapons systems to be controlled																						
1	*a. Nuclear weapons (general)*	■	■	■	■	■	■	■	■	■	■	■		■	■	■		■	■	■			
2	*b. Long-range delivery systems (e.g., ICBM's and carriers in orbit)*																						
3	*c. Other delivery systems for nuclear warheads (e.g., cannon and bombers)*																						
4	*d. Heavy offensive weapons (capital ships, heavy artillery, etc.)*																						
5	*e. Other conventional weapons*																						
6	*f. Chemical, biological, and/or radiological weapons*								■	■													
7	*g. General or unspecified weapons*				■		■	■	■	■				■	■	■		■	■	■			
	2. Locus of regulation																						
	a. Production of raw materials and other inputs used in producing the above																						
8	1) Limitation and/or prohibition																						
9	2) International control																						
	b. Production of end-products																						
10	1) Prohibition		■	■			■							[a]	■	■		[a]	■	■			
11	2) Reduction																						
12	3) Limitation	■												■		■		■					
13	4) Internationalization																						
14	5) Surveillance (supervision)																						
15	6) International control	■																					
	c. Int. movement of and traffic in fissionable materials or weapons																						
16	1) Prohibition of movement or stationing outside one's own country																						
17	2) Regulation of movement or stationing outside one's own country																						
18	3) Prohibition of gift or sale of weapons or information for developing such weapons (nonprofit)																						
19	4) Regulation of gift or sale of weapons or information for developing such weapons (nonprofit)																						
20	5) International control	■																					
	d. Disposition of existing stock																						
21	1) Transfer of stock to national depots for inspection purposes																						
22	2) Transfer of stock to international agency	■									■												
23	3) International monopoly of stock	■																					
24	4) Destruction	■	■						[f]	[f]				[a]		[a]		[a]		[a]			
25	5) Conversion to peaceful uses	■												[a]		[a]		[a]	[a]	[a]			
26	6) Reduction													[g]				[g]	[g]	[g]			
27	*a) Ceiling*																						
28	*b) Percentage*				[g]		[g]								[g]	[g]							
29	*c) Ratio*										■												
	e. Use																						
30	1) Unconditional renunciation																						
31	2) Conditional renunciation (incl. first use and guarantees for non-nuclear state)																						
32	3) Unconditional prohibition		■		[a]	■	[a]		[f]	□		■		[a]	[a]	[a]		[a]	[a]	[a]			
33	4) Conditional prohibition													[a]				[a]					
34	5) International monopoly of use																						
35	6) International control	■																					

Where lower case letters have been substituted for a ■, they refer to control of the weapons listed IA1 a thru g above.

…POSALS TO 25 JULY 1963

7 MAJOR NON-REGIONAL ACD PROPOSALS AFTER 25 JULY 1963

	[illegible]	R 30	R 31	US32	33	R 34	US35	US36	R 37	R 38	39	R 40	R 41	R 42	US43	R 44	R 45	46	R 47	US48	US49	R 50	51	US52	R 53	R 54	US55	R 56	R 57	US58	US59	R 60	61	R 62	US63	US64	US65	US66	US67	R 68	R 69	70	R 71	72	R 73	US74	75	R 76	US77	R 78	US79	R 80	US81	R 82
1		■	■	■			■										■		■	■	■	■		■	■	■	■	■	■	■	■	■	■	■	■	■	■	■	■	■	■		■	■	■	■	■	■	■	■	■	■	■	■	■
2								■				■		■															■	■									■						■	■		■					■	
3												■	■																■	■									■						■	■				■			■	
4																													■	■															■	■								
5																													■	■															■	■								
6																													■	■									■						■	■								
7		■		■			■										■																						■														■	
8																																																	■				■	
9																																																						
10																													■	[a]									[a]						[illegible]	[af]								
11																													■	■									■						■	■							■	
12																													■	■									■						[illegible]	■								
13																																																						
14																													■																[b]									
15																																																						
16												■		■			[a]												■																■					■				
17																																																						
18																																																						
																													■			■							[a]	■					■	[a]	[a]	■	■	■	■	■	■	■
19																																																						
20																																																					■	
21				□																										■									■							■								
22				[a]			[a]																																[a]															
23																																																						
24																													■	■									■						■	■							■	
25																													■	■									■						■	■			■				■	
26							[g]																						■	■									■						■	■							■	
27																																																	■				■	
28		[g]															[g]																																					
29				[a]																																																		
30																																								■														
31																																																						
		[a]															[a]																																				■	■
32																													[af]										■															
33				[a]																																										■								
34																																																						
35																																																						

Chronology: *page 2*

No.	Item	US 1	R 2	R 3	R 4	R 5	R 6	US 7	US 8	US 9	US10	R 11	US12	13	R 14	R 15	16	17	R 18	R 19	US20	21	US22
	f. Weapons research and development																						
36	1) Prohibition of research and development																						
37	2) International monopoly of research and development	■																					
38	3) Exchange of information		■																[a]				
39	4) Registration of tests																						
40	5) Limitation of tests																						
41	6) Internationalization of tests																						
42	7) Prohibition of tests																		[a]	[a]			
43	8) Prohibition of tests in specified environment																						
	9) Moratorium on tests in specified environment																						
44	*a) Short-term*																						
45	*b) Long-term*																						
	B. ARMED FORCES																						
	1. Categories																						
	a. Military																						
46	1) Army				■																		
47	2) Navy				■																		
48	3) Air Force				■																		
49	4) Special forces-type units																						
50	5) Volunteers																						
51	6) Foreign military advisers																						
52	7) Not specified							■	■	■				■		■	■	■	■	■			
	b. Para-military																						
53	1) Militia																						
54	2) Security forces																						
55	3) Police																						
56	4) Intelligence collection agencies																						
57	5) Not specified								■														
58	*c. General or unspecified*																						
	2. Locus of regulation																						
	a. Recruitment																						
59	1) Prohibition of conscription																						
60	2) Limitation on volunteers																						
61	3) Specification as to length of service																						
	b. Preparation and training																						
62	1) Prohibition of inculcation of military spirit																						
63	2) Prohibition of all training																						
64	3) Prohibition of specific forms of training																						
65	4) Abolition of general staff and all military agencies																						
	c. Deployment																						
66	1) Prohibition of foreign bases						■							■					■				
67	2) Limitation on foreign bases																						
68	3) Limitation on number of troops stationed in specified foreign bases / countries																						
69	4) Prohibition of movement of troops outside one's own frontiers																						
70	5) Limitation on movement of troops outside one's own frontiers																						
71	6) Withdrawal of forces from specified areas						■												■				

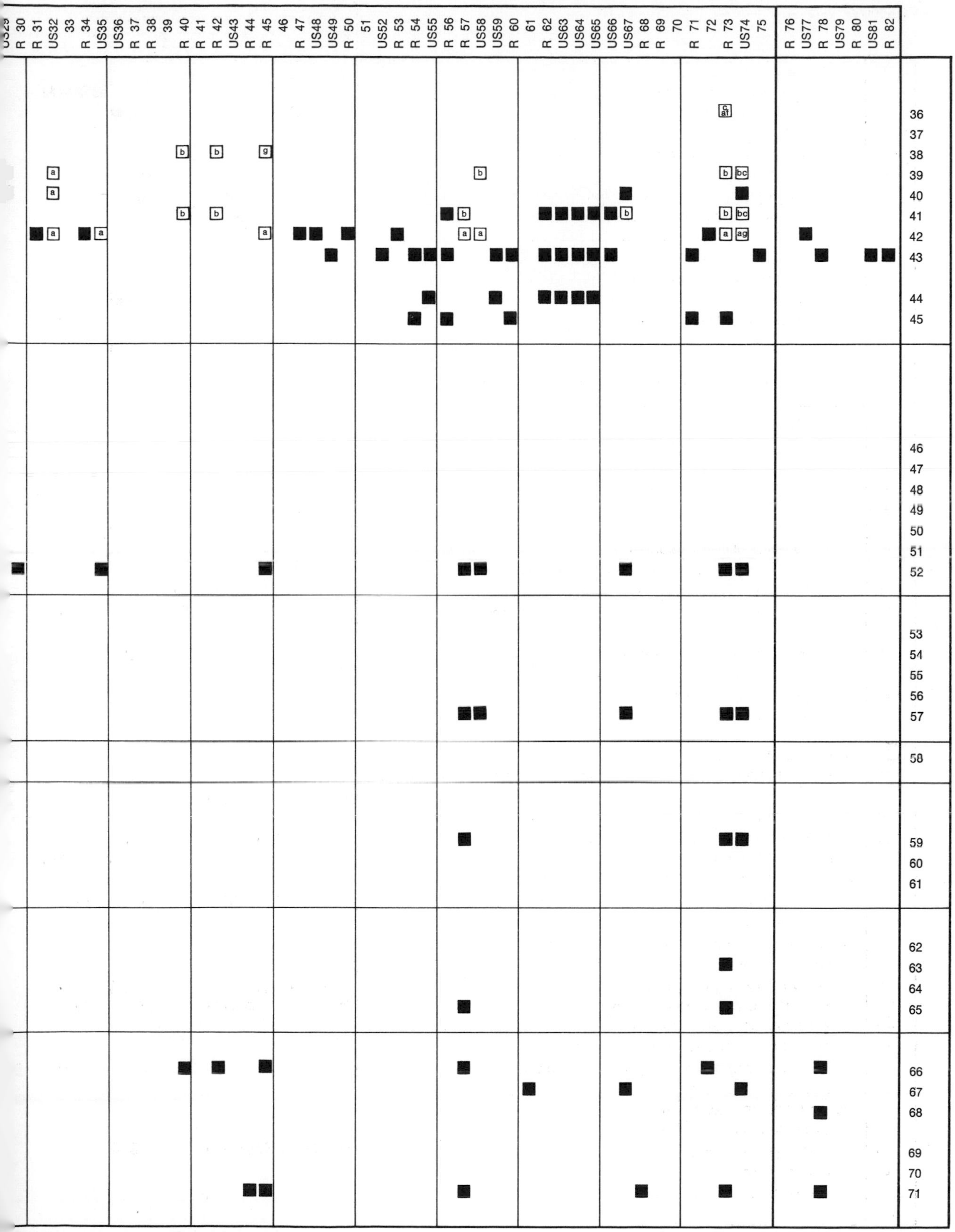

US29	R 30	R 31	US32	33	R 34	US35	US36	R 37	R 38	39	R 40	R 41	R 42	US43	R 44	R 45	46	R 47	US48	US49	R 50	51	US52	R 53	R 54	US55	R 56	R 57	US58	US59	R 60	61	R 62	US63	US64	US65	US66	US67	R 68	R 69	70	R 71	72	R 73	US74	75	R 76	US77	R 78	US79	R 80	US81	R 82

36
37
38
39
40
41
42
43
44
45

46
47
48
49
50
51
52

53
54
55
56
57

58

59
60
61

62
63
64
65

66
67
68
69
70
71

		US 1	R 2	R 3	R 4	R 5	R 6	US 7	US 8	US 9	US10	R 11	US12	13	R 14	R 15	16	17	R 18	R 19	US20	21
	d. Size																					
72	1) Numerical ceiling on troops																■	■	■	■		
73	2) Percentage cut				■										■	■						
74	3) National ratio																					
75	4) Internationalization of troops																					
76	5) Reduction													■								
77	6) Elimination of all military and para-military organizations beyond those required to maintain internal order								■													
	C. MILITARY EXPENDITURES																					
78	1. Prohibition of military expenditures																					
79	2. Reduction of military expenditures														■	■						
80	3. Limitation on military expenditures													■		■		■	■			
	D. OUTER SPACE																					
81	1. Prohibition of the use of outer space for military purposes																					
	E. ZONAL ARRANGEMENTS																					
82	1. De-nuclearized																					
83	2. De-militarized																					
84	3. Demonstrative (pilot) ACD zone																					
	F. HOSTILE ACTS																					
85	1. Prohibition of military provocation																					
86	2. Prohibition of formation of military alliances or blocs																					
87	3. Prohibitions of support for insurrections and revolts in other countries											■										
88	4. Prohibition of economic discriminations against other countries (embargo, sanction, etc.)											■							■			
89	5. Prohibition of war propaganda or anti-foreign propaganda														■				■			
90	6. Prohibition of war																					
91	7. Prohibition of violations of the U.N. Declaration of Human Rights																					
92	8. Other (specified)																					
	II. SEQUENCE OF ACD																					
93	A. ESTABLISHMENT OF CONTROL MACHINERY BEFORE PROCEEDING WITH ACD	■							■	■												
94	B. PROCEEDING WITH ACD BEFORE ESTABLISHMENT OF CONTROL		■																			
95	C. ACD SIMULTANEOUSLY WITH CONTROL					■	■								■							
96	D. PHASED IMPLEMENTATION OF ACD WITH CONTROLS															■			■	■		
97	E. PHASED IMPLEMENTATION OF ACD WITHOUT CONTROLS																					
98	F. PHASED IMPLEMENTATION OF ACD DEPENDING UPON SATISFACTION EACH PHASE								■					■				■				
99	G. PHASED IMPLEMENTATION OF ACD WITH CONTROLS FOR SOME SPECIFIC PHASES																					
100	H. DEFINITE TIME SCHEDULE FOR ACD		■		■		■								■	■			■			
101	I. NO DEFINITE TIME SCHEDULE FOR ACD	■						■	■	■				■				■				
102	J. POLITICAL SETTLEMENT PRIOR TO ACD																					
103	K. ACD PRIOR TO POLITICAL SETTLEMENT																					
104	L. ACD SIMULTANEOUS WITH POLITICAL SETTLEMENT																		■			■
	III. CONTROL ORGANIZATION																					
	A. STRUCTURE AND COMPOSITION																					
105	1. Control commission	■		■	■	■	■	■	■	■					■	■						
106	*a. Number (specified)*																					
	b. Selection																					

R 30	R 31	US32	33	R 34	US35	US36	R 37	R 38	39	R 40	R 41	R 42	US43	R 44	R 45	46	R 47	US48	US49	R 50	51	US52	R 53	R 54	US55	R 56	R 57	US58	US59	R 60	61	R 62	US63	US64	US65	US66	US67	R 68	R 69	70	R 71	72	R 73	US74	75	R 76	US77	R 78	US79	R 80	US81	R 82	
■															■												■	■									■						■	■									72
																																																					73
																																																					74
																																																					75
					■																																											■					76
																											■	■									■						■	■									77
																												■															■										78
■															■													■	■														■	■				■			■		79
																																						■													■		80
					■					■		■			■													■	■														■	■									81
			■	■			■		■						■	■					■										■							■	■	■						■		■				■	82
																					■																																83
		■											■															■																									84
														■																																	■						85
																																																					86
																																					■							■			■						87
																																																					88
■				■											■																							■									■						89
																																															■						90
																																					■						■	■									91
				■			■																																								■	■					92
																																																					93
																																																					94
	■																■	■		■																																	95
■															■	■			■			■	■	■	■	■	■			■	■	■											■										96
																																									■												97
		■																										■	■				■	■	■		■							■									98
																																																					99
																											■		■								■																100
																																											■										101
					■																																																102
																																																					103
						■																																															104
	■																■	■	■	■		■	■	■	■	■	■	■				■	■	■	■	■	■						■	■									105
																																■	■			■																	106

No.	Item	US 1	R 2	R 3	R 4	R 5	R 6	US 7	US 8	US 9	US10	R 11	US12	13	R 14	R 15	16	17	R 18	R 19	US20	21
107	1) Unanimous agreement of all ACD parties																					
108	2) Majority of ACD parties with unanimous approval of all major powers participating in ACD																					
109	3) Security Council																					
110	4) General Assembly																					
111	5) Other			■																		
	2. Secretariat																					
	a. Central administration (selection of)																					
112	1) One administrator (director)												■									
113	*a) Unanimous agreement of all ACD parties*																					
114	*b) Majority of ACD parties with unanimous approval of all major powers participating in ACD*																					
115	*c) Security Council*																					
116	*d) General Assembly*																					
117	*e) Control Commission*												■									
118	2) Administrative council or troika (selection of)																					
119	*a) Unanimous agreement of all ACD parties*																					
120	*b) Majority of ACD parties with unanimous approval of all major powers participating in ACD*																					
121	*c) Security Council*																					
122	*d) General Assembly*																					
123	*e) Control Commission*																					
	b. Administrative staff (selection of)																					
124	1) Secretariat												■									
125	2) Secretariat with Control Commission approval																					
126	3) Other																					
127	4) International basis (unspecified)														■	■			■			
	5) International basis (specified)			■																		
128	*a) Quota or fixed ratio*																					
129	*b) National ratio*																					
130	*c) Technical competence*	■																				
131	*d) Other*												■									
	c. Field staff (selection of)																					
132	1) Secretariat												■									
133	2) Secretariat with Control Commission approval																					
134	3) Other																					
135	4) International basis (unspecified)															■						
	5) International basis (specified)																					
136	*a) Quota or fixed ratio*																					
137	*b) National ratio*																					
138	*c) Technical competence*	■																				
139	*d) Other*												■									
	3. Regional sub-structure																					
140	*a. Region specified*																					
	b. Permanent																					
141	1) Responsible to Secretariat																					
142	2) Responsible to Control Commission																					
143	3) Not specified																					

US29	R 30	R 31	US32	33	R 34	US35	US36	R 37	R 38	39	R 40	R 41	R 42	US43	R 44	R 45	46	R 47	US48	US49	R 50	51	US52	R 53	R 54	US55	R 56	R 57	US58	US59	R 60	61	R 62	US63	US64	US65	US66	US67	R 68	R 69	70	R 71	72	R 73	US74	75	R 76	US77	R 78	US79	R 80	US81	R 82	
																																																						107
																			■																										■									108
																																																						109
																																																						110
																																																						111
																			■		■				■				■	■					■	■	■	■							■									112
																																																						113
																																					■																	114
																																																						115
																																																						116
																					■				■																				■									117
																																	■																					118
																																																						119
																																																						120
																																																						121
																																																						122
																																																						123
																																																						124
																																																						125
																					■				■																													126
		■																										■																■										127
																																																						128
																																																						129
																																																						130
																																																						131
																																																						132
																																																						133
																					■				■																													134
																												■																										135
																			■														■				■																	136
																																																						137
																																																						138
																																																						139
																																																						140
																																																						141
																																																						142
																			■											■																								143

No.	Item	US 1	R 2	R 3	R 4	R 5	R 6	US 7	US 8	US 9	US10	R 11	US12	13	R 14	R 15	16	17	R 18	R 19	US20	21
144	*c. Ad hoc*																					
145	1) Responsible to Secretariat																					
146	2) Responsible to Control Commission																					
147	3) Not specified																					
	4. Inspectorate																					
	a. Number (specified)																					
	b. Selection																					
148	1) By Secretariat(s)												■									
149	2) Secretariat with Control Commission approval																					
150	3) Other																					
151	4) Non-national basis (no national to serve in own country)												■									
152	5) National basis (nationals to serve *only* in their own countries)																					
153	6) Only "neutrals" to serve																					
154	7) International basis (unspecified)															■			■			
	8) International basis (specified)																					
155	*a) Quota or fixed ratio*																					
156	*b) National ratio*																					
157	*c) Technical competence*	■																				
158	*d) Other*																					
	B. FUNCTIONS																					
159	1. Development of procedures for control and inspection	■		■									■									
160	2. Implementation of control and inspection	■			■		■	■	■	■			■		■							
161	3. Verification	■					■	■	■	■			■		■							
162	4. Determination and reporting of violation	■						■	■	■			■									
163	5. Other (specified)	■		■									■									
	C. METHODS OF CONTROL																					
	1. Without inspection																					
164	*a. Long-range scientific methods from stations outside one's own country*																					
165	*b. Stationing scientific instruments in foreign country without inspection*																					
166	*c. Exchange of scientific, technical, and/or budgetary information*			■				■	■	■												
167	*d. Exchange of military blueprints*						■	■	■	■											■	
168	*e. Other (specified)*							■	■	■			■			■			■			
	2. With inspection																					
	a. On-site																					
169	1) Quota of on-site																					
170	2) Specific percentage of on-site																					
171	3) Occasional or periodic			■																		
172	4) Continuous	■					■	■	■	■					■	■			■			
173	*b. Control posts*																		■			
174	*c. Mobile inspection teams*												■									
175	*d. Definite routes or specified areas of inspection*																					
176	*e. Aerial inspection*							■	■	■			■								■	
177	*f. Limited freedom of access*						■								■	■			■			
178	*g. Complete freedom of access*	■						■	■	■												
179	*h. Other (specified)*							■	■	■									■			

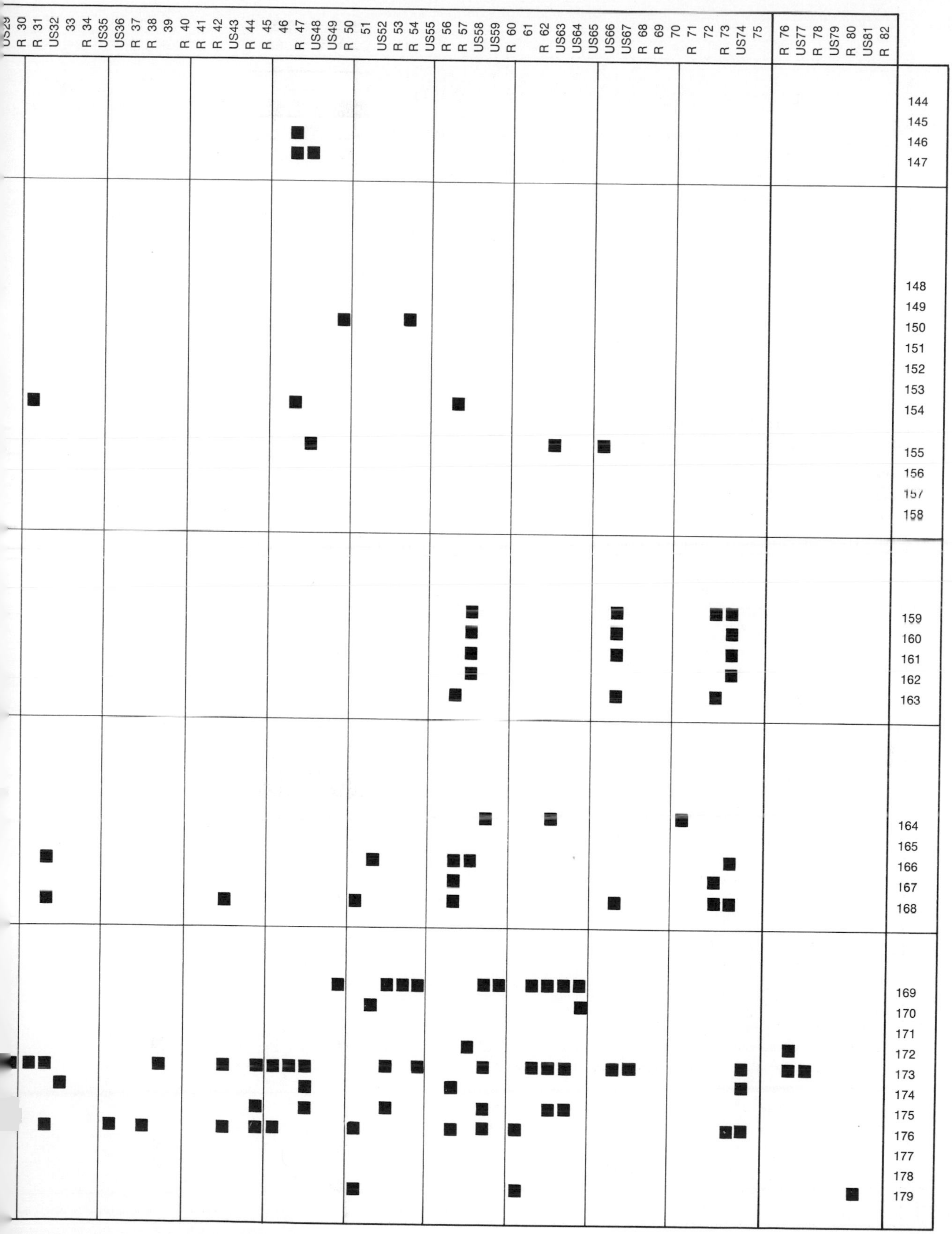

	US29	R 30	R 31	US32	33	R 34	US35	US36	R 37	R 38	39	R 40	R 41	R 42	US43	R 44	R 45	46	R 47	US48	US49	R 50	51	US52	R 53	R 54	US55
144																											
145																											
146																			■								
147																			■	■							
148																											
149																											
150																						■				■	
151																											
152																											
153																											
154			■																■								
155																				■							
156																											
157																											
158																											
159																											
160																											
161																											
162																											
163																											
164																											
165																											
166				■																				■			
167																											
168				■											■								■				
169																						■			■	■	■
170																								■			
171																											
172																											
173		■	■	■							■				■		■	■	■	■					■		■
174					■															■							
175																	■			■					■		
176				■				■		■					■		■	■					■				
177																											
178																											
179																							■				

	R 56	R 57	US58	US59	R 60	61	R 62	US63	US64	US65	US66	US67	R 68	R 69	70	R 71	72	R 73	US74	75	R 76	US77	R 78	US79	R 80	US81	R 82
144																											
145																											
146																											
147																											
148																											
149																											
150																											
151																											
152																											
153																											
154		■																									
155								■			■																
156																											
157																											
158																											
159			■									■						■	■								
160			■									■							■								
161			■									■							■								
162			■																■								
163		■										■						■									
164				■				■								■											
165																											
166		■	■																■								
167		■																■									
168		■										■						■	■								
169				■	■		■	■	■	■																	
170										■																	
171																											
172			■																			■					
173				■			■	■	■			■	■							■		■	■				
174		■																		■							
175				■				■	■																		
176		■		■		■													■	■							
177																											
178																											
179						■																				■	

No.	Item	US 1	R 2	R 3	R 4	R 5	R 6	US 7	US 8	US 9	US10	R 11	US12	13	R 14	R 15	16	17	R 18	R 19	US20	21	US22
180	3. International police force																		■				
	D. AUTHORITY OF CONTROL ORGANIZATION OVER CONTROL MEASURES																						
181	1. Authority not subject to veto	■																					
182	2. Authority in certain specified areas not subject to veto																						
	3. Authority subject to veto																						
183	*a. Security Council*		■		■		■								■	■							
184	*b. Control Commission*																						
185	*c. Directorate*																						
186	4. Authority in certain specified areas subject to veto																						
187	*a. Security Council*																						
188	*b. Control Commission*																						
189	*c. Directorate*																						
	IV. TERRITORIES COVERED BY ACD																						
190	A. SIGNATORIES ONLY			■	■	■	■				■				■				■		■		
191	B. SIGNATORIES PLUS OTHER SPECIFIED TERRITORIES ONLY											■											
192	C. CERTAIN SPECIFIED TERRITORIES ONLY																					■	
193	D. ALL COUNTRIES	■	■					■	■	■			■	■		■	■	■		■			
	V. PUNISHMENTS FOR VIOLATORS																						
	A. DETERMINED BY:																						
194	1. Security Council (with veto)																						
195	2. International Authority (without veto)	■																					
196	3. International Authority (with veto)																						
197	4. General Assembly																						
198	5. International Court of Justice																						
199	6. Not specified		■										■										
	B. EXECUTED BY:																						
200	1. Security Council (with veto)																						
201	2. International Authority (without veto)																						
202	3. International Authority (with veto)																						
203	4. General Assembly																						
204	5. International Court of Justice																						
205	6. Not specified	■	■										■										
	C. NATURE OF SANCTIONS																						
	1. International sanctions against nation																						
206	*a. Political*																						
207	*b. Economic*																						
208	*c. Military*																						
209	*d. Not specified*	■											■										
	2. International sanctions against individuals or groups																						
210	*a. Political*																						
211	*b. Economic*																						
212	*c. Military*																						
213	*d. Not specified*	■											■										
214	3. National sanctions against individuals or groups												■										
215	4. Not specified	■																					

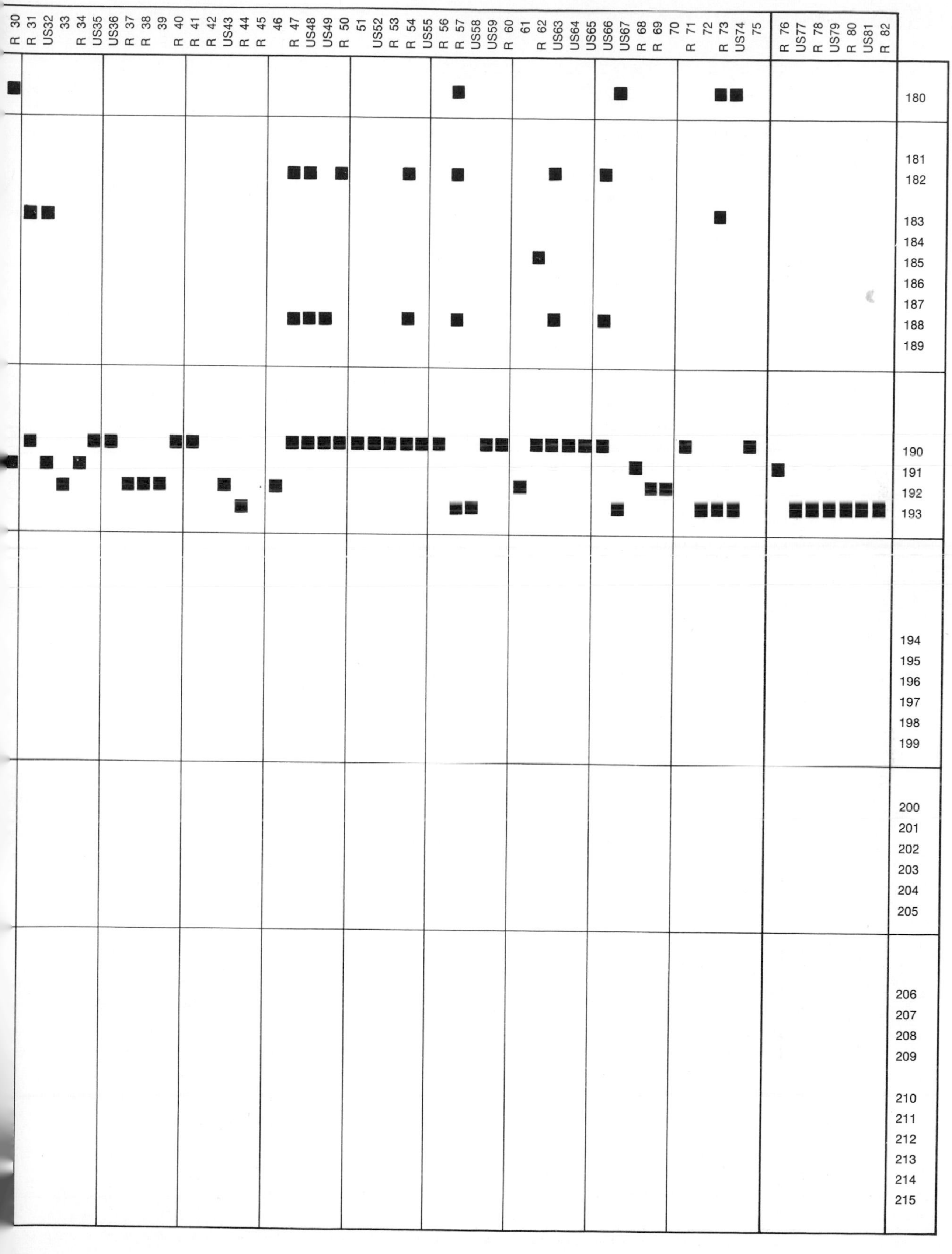

	R 30	R 31	US32	33	R 34	US35	US36	R 37	R 38	39	R 40	R 41	R 42	US43	R 44	R 45	46	R 47	US48	US49	R 50	51	US52	R 53	R 54	US55	R 56	R 57	US58	US59	R 60	61	R 62	US63	US64	US65	US66	US67	R 68	R 69	70	R 71	72	R 73	US74	75	R 76	US77	R 78	US79	R 80	US81	R 82
180	■																											■										■						■	■								
181																																																					
182																		■	■		■				■			■						■			■																
183		■	■																																									■									
184																																																					
185																																	■																				
186																																																					
187																																																					
188																		■	■	■					■			■						■			■																
189																																																					
190		■				■	■				■	■						■	■	■	■	■	■	■	■	■	■			■	■		■	■	■	■	■					■				■							
191	■		■		■																																		■								■						
192				■				■	■	■				■			■															■								■	■												
193															■													■	■									■					■	■	■			■	■	■	■	■	■
194																																																					
195																																																					
196																																																					
197																																																					
198																																																					
199																																																					
200																																																					
201																																																					
202																																																					
203																																																					
204																																																					
205																																																					
206																																																					
207																																																					
208																																																					
209																																																					
210																																																					
211																																																					
212																																																					
213																																																					
214																																																					
215																																																					

Comparison: *page 1*

		US 1	US 7	US 8	US 9	US10	US12	US20	US22	US24	US26	US29	US32	US35	US36	US43
	I. OBJECTS OF CONTROL															
	A. WEAPONS SYSTEMS															
	1. Types of weapons to be controlled															
1	*a. Nuclear weapons systems (general)*	■	■	■	■	■					■	■	■	■		
2	*b. Long-range delivery systems (e.g., ICBM's and carriers in orbit)*														■	
3	*c. Other delivery systems for nuclear warheads (e.g., cannon and bombers)*															
4	*d. Heavy offensive weapons (capital ships, heavy artillery, etc.)*															
5	*e. Other conventional weapons*															
6	*f. Chemical, biological, and/or radiological weapons*			■	■											
7	*g. General or unspecified weapons*		■	■	■					■			■	■		
	2. Locus of regulation															
	a. Production of raw materials and other inputs used in producing the above															
8	1) Limitation and/or prohibition															
9	2) International control															
	b. Production of end-products															
10	1) Prohibition															
11	2) Reduction															
12	3) Limitation	■														
13	4) Internationalization															
14	5) Surveillance (supervision)															
15	6) International control	■														
	c. Int. movement of and traffic in fissionable materials or weapons															
16	1) Prohibition of movement or stationing outside one's own country															
17	2) Regulation of movement or stationing outside one's own country															
18	3) Prohibition of gift or sale of weapons or information for developing such weapons (nonprofit)															
19	4) Regulation of gift or sale of weapons or information for developing such weapons (nonprofit)															
20	5) International control	■														
	d. Disposition of existing stock															
21	1) Transfer of stock to national depots for inspection purposes												g			
22	2) Transfer of stock to international agency	■				■					■		a	a		
23	3) International monopoly of stock	■														
24	4) Destruction	■		f	f											
25	5) Conversion to peaceful uses	■														
26	6) Reduction									■						
27	*a) Ceiling*															
28	*b) Percentage*															
29	*c) Ratio*					■					■		a			
	e. Use															
30	1) Unconditional renunciation															
31	2) Conditional renunciation (incl. no-first-use and guarantees for non-nuclear states)															
32	3) Unconditional prohibition			f	f											
33	4) Conditional prohibition												a			
34	5) International monopoly of use	■														
35	6) International control															

Where lower case letters have been substituted for a ■, they refer to control of the weapons listed IA1 a thru g above.

US64	US65	US66	US67	US74	R 2	R 3	R 4	R 5	R 6	R 11	R 14	R 15	R 18	R 19	R 25	R 27	R 28	R 30	R 31	R 34	R 37	R 38	R 40	R 41	R 42	R 44	R 45	R 47	R 50	R 53	R 54	R 56	R 57	R 60	R 62	R 68	R 69	R 71	R 73	US/USSR	
■	■	■	■	■	■	■	■	■	■	■	■	■	■	■	■		■	■	■								■	■	■	■	■	■	■	■	■	■		■	■	21/26	1
			■	■													■						■		■								■						■	4/5	2
			■	■													■						■		■								■						■	3/5	3
				■																													■						■	2/2	4
				■																													■						■	2/2	5
			■	■																													■						■	5/2	6
			■				■		■		■	■	■	■	■	■	■	■									■													7/11	7
																																									8
																																									9
			[a]	[ag]	■	■			■		■	■	■	■	[a]		[a]																■						[ag df]	3/11	10
			■	■																													■						■	3/2	11
			■	■								■					[g]																■						[be]	4/4	12
																																									13
																																	■						[b']	0/2	14
																																								1/0	15
																	[a]						■		■		[a]						■						■	0/6	16
			[a]	[a]																																					17
																■																	■				■		[a]	2/4	18
																																									19
																																								1/0	20
			■	■																																				4/0	21
			[a]																																					6/0	22
																																								1/0	23
			■	■	■							[a]		[a]			[a]																■						■	6/6	24
			■	■								[a]	[a]	[a]			[a]																■						■	4/6	25
			■	■									[g]	[g]	[g]		[g]																■						■	5/6	26
																																									27
							[g]		[g]		[g]	[g]						[g]									[g]													0/6	28
																																								3/0	29
																																				■				0/1	30
																			[a]								[a]													0/2	31
			■		■		[a]	■	[a]	■	[a]	[a]	[a]	[a]																			[af]							3/10	32
			■														[a]																							2/1	33
																																								1/0	34
																	[bc]																							0/1	35

No.	Item	US 1	US 7	US 8	US 9	US10	US12	US20	US22	US24	US26	US29	US32	US35	US36	US43	US48
	f. Weapons research and development																
36	1) Prohibition of research and development																
37	2) International monopoly of research and development	■															
38	3) Exchange of information																
39	4) Registration of tests											■	[a]				
40	5) Limitation of tests										■	■	[a]				
41	6) Internationalization of tests																
42	7) Prohibition of tests												[a]	[a]			■
43	8) Prohibition of tests in specified environment																
	9) Moratorium on tests in specified environment																
44	*a) Short-term*																
45	*b) Long-term*																
	B. ARMED FORCES																
	1. Categories																
	a. Military																
46	1) Army									■							
47	2) Navy									■							
48	3) Air Force									■							
49	4) Special forces-type units																
50	5) Volunteers																
51	6) Foreign military advisers																
52	7) Not specified		■	■	■						■			■			
	b. Para-military																
53	1) Militia																
54	2) Security forces																
55	3) Police																
56	4) Intelligence collection agencies																
57	5) Not specified			■													
58	*c. General or unspecified*																
	2. Locus of regulation																
	a. Recruitment																
59	1) Prohibition of conscription																
60	2) Limitation on volunteers																
61	3) Specification as to length of service																
	b. Preparation and training																
62	1) Prohibition of inculcation of military spirit																
63	2) Prohibition of all training																
64	3) Prohibition of specific forms of training																
65	4) Abolition of general staff and all military agencies																
	c. Deployment																
66	1) Prohibition of foreign bases																
67	2) Limitation on foreign bases																
68	3) Limitation on number of troops stationed in specified foreign bases /countries																
69	4) Prohibition of movement of troops outside one's own frontiers																
70	5) Limitation on movement of troops outside one's own frontiers																
71	6) Withdrawal of forces from specified areas																

US64	US65	US66	US67	US74	R 2	R 3	R 4	R 5	R 6	R 11	R 14	R 15	R 18	R 19	R 25	R 27	R 28	R 30	R 31	R 34	R 37	R 38	R 40	R 41	R 42	R 44	R 45	R 47	R 50	R 53	R 54	R 56	R 57	R 60	R 62	R 68	R 69	R 71	R 73	US/USSR	
																																							[ac df]	0/1	36
																																								1/0	37
					■								[a]										[b]		[b]		[g]													0/5	38
				[bc]																																			[b]	4/1	39
			■	■																																				5/0	40
■	■	■	[b]	[bc]																			[b]		[b]							■	[b]		■				[b]	6/6	41
				[af]									[a]	[a]	[a]				■	■							[a]	■	■	■			[a]						[a]	5/11	42
■	■	■																													■	■		■	■			■		8/5	43
■	■																																		■					5/1	44
																															■	■			■			■	■	0/5	45
							■																																	1/1	46
							■																																	1/1	47
							■																																	1/1	48
																																									49
																																									50
																																									51
			■	■								■	■	■	■		■	■									■						■						■	8/9	52
																																									53
																																									54
																																									55
																																									56
			■	■																													■						■	4/2	57
																																									58
				■																													■						■	1/2	59
																																									60
																																									61
																																									62
																																							■	0/1	63
																																									64
																																	■						■	0/2	65
									■		■		■			■	■						■		■			■					■						■	0/10	66
			■	■																																				2/0	67
																																									68
															■																									0/1	69
																																									70
									■				■			■	■	■								■	■						■			■			■	0/10	71

No.	Item	US 1	US 7	US 8	US 9	US10	US12	US20	US22	US24	US26	US29	US32	US35	US36	US43	US48	US49	US52	US55	US58	US59
	d. Size																					
72	1) Numerical ceiling on troops									■	■										■	
73	2) Percentage cut																					
74	3) National ratio																					
75	4) Internationalization of troops																					
76	5) Reduction													■								
77	6) Elimination of all military and para-military organizations beyond those required to maintain internal order			■																	■	
	C. MILITARY EXPENDITURES																					
78	1. Prohibition of military expenditures																				■	
79	2. Reduction of military expenditures									■											■	■
80	3. Limitation on military expenditures										■											
	D. OUTER SPACE																					
81	1. Prohibition of the use of outer space for military purposes													■							■	
	E. ZONAL ARRANGEMENTS																					
82	1. De-nuclearized																					
83	2. De-militarized																					
84	3. Demonstrative (pilot) ACD zone								■				■			■					■	
	F. HOSTILE ACTS																					
85	1. Prohibition of military provocation																					
86	2. Prohibition of formation of military alliances or blocs																					
87	3. Prohibition of support for insurrections and revolts in other countries																					
88	4. Prohibition of economic discriminations against other countries (embargo, sanction, etc.)																					
89	5. Prohibition of war propaganda or anti-foreign propaganda																					
90	6. Prohibition of war																					
91	7. Prohibition of violations of the U.N. Declaration of Human Rights																					
92	8. Other (specified)																					
	II. SEQUENCE OF ACD																					
93	A. ESTABLISHMENT OF CONTROL MACHINERY BEFORE PROCEEDING WITH ACD	■		■	■																	
94	B. PROCEEDING WITH ACD BEFORE ESTABLISHMENT OF CONTROL																					
95	C. ACD SIMULTANEOUSLY WITH CONTROL																■					
96	D. PHASED IMPLEMENTATION OF ACD WITH CONTROLS																	■	■	■		
97	E. PHASED IMPLEMENTATION OF ACD WITHOUT CONTROLS																					
98	F. PHASED IMPLEMENTATION OF ACD DEPENDING UPON SATISFACTION AT EACH PHASE		■							■	■		■								■	
99	G. PHASED IMPLEMENTATION OF ACD WITH CONTROLS FOR SOME SPECIFIC PHASES																					
100	H. DEFINITE TIME SCHEDULE FOR ACD																					
101	I. NO DEFINITE TIME SCHEDULE FOR ACD	■	■	■	■						■											
102	J. POLITICAL SETTLEMENT PRIOR TO ACD													■								
103	K. ACD PRIOR TO POLITICAL SETTLEMENT																					
104	L. ACD SIMULTANEOUS WITH POLITICAL SETTLEMENT														■							
	III. CONTROL ORGANIZATION																					
	A. STRUCTURE AND COMPOSITION																					
105	1. Control commission	■	■	■	■						■						■	■	■	■	■	
106	*a. Number (specified)*																					
	b. Selection																					

R 2	R 3	R 4	R 5	R 6	R 11	R 14	R 15	R 18	R 19	R 25	R 27	R 28	R 30	R 31	R 34	R 37	R 38	R 40	R 41	R 42	R 44	R 45	R 47	R 50	R 53	R 54	R 56	R 57	R 60	R 62	R 68	R 69	R 71	R 73	US/USSR	
								■	■	■		■	■									■						■						■	5/8	72
		■				■	■																												0/3	73
																																				74
																																				75
																																			1/0	76
																												■						■	4/2	77
										■																								■	1/2	78
						■	■					■	■									■												■	4/6	79
							■	■		■																					■				1/4	80
																		■		■		■												■	4/4	81
										■					■	■						■									■	■			0/6	82
												■																							0/1	83
										■		■																							4/2	84
																					■														0/1	85
											■																								0/1	86
					■			■																											2/2	87
					■			■																											0/2	88
						■		■					■		■							■									■				0/6	89
												■																							0/1	90
																																		■	2/1	91
											■				■		■																		0/3	92
																																			3/0	93
■																																			0/1	94
			■	■		■								■									■	■											1/6	95
							■	■	■			■	■									■			■	■	■	■	■	■				■	3/13	96
																																	■		0/1	97
																																			11/0	98
																																				99
■		■		■		■	■	■				■																■							2/8	100
																																		■	5/1	101
																																			1/0	102
																																				103
								■																											1/1	104
	■	■	■	■		■	■							■									■	■	■	■	■	■		■				■	16/15	105
																														■					2/1	106

Comparison: *page 4*

		US 1	US 7	US 8	US 9	US10	US12	US20	US22	US24	US26	US29	US32	US35	US36	US43	US48
107	1) Unanimous agreement of all ACD parties																
108	2) Majority of ACD parties with unanimous approval of all major powers participating in ACD																■
109	3) Security Council																
110	4) General Assembly																
111	5) Other																
	2. Secretariat																
	a. Central administration (selection of)																
112	1) One administrator (director)						■				■						■
113	*a) Unanimous agreement of all ACD parties*																
114	*b) Majority of ACD parties with unanimous approval of all major powers participating in ACD*																
115	*c) Security Council*																
116	*d) General Assembly*																
117	*e) Control Commission*						■										
118	2) Administrative council or troika (selection of)																
119	*a) Unanimous agreement of all ACD parties*																
120	*b) Majority of ACD parties with unanimous approval of all major powers participating in ACD*																
121	*c) Security Council*																
122	*d) General Assembly*																
123	*e) Control Commission*																
	b. Administrative staff (selection of)																
124	1) Secretariat						■										
125	2) Secretariat with Control Commission approval																
126	3) Other																
127	4) International basis (unspecified)																
	5) International basis (specified)																
128	*a) Quota or fixed ratio*																
129	*b) National ratio*																
130	*c) Technical competence*	■															
131	*d) Other*						■										
	c. Field staff (selection of)																
132	1) Secretariat						■										
133	2) Secretariat with Control Commission approval																
134	3) Other																
135	4) International basis (unspecified)																
	5) International basis (specified)																
136	*a) Quota or fixed ratio*																■
137	*b) National ratio*																
138	*c) Technical competence*	■															
139	*d) Other*						■										
	3. Regional sub-structure																
140	*a. Region specified*																
	b. Permanent																
141	1) Responsible to Secretariat																
142	2) Responsible to Control Commission																
143	3) Not specified																■

US64	US65	US66	US67	US74	R 2	R 3	R 4	R 5	R 6	R 11	R 14	R 15	R 18	R 19	R 25	R 27	R 28	R 30	R 31	R 34	R 37	R 38	R 40	R 41	R 42	R 44	R 45	R 47	R 50	R 53	R 54	R 56	R 57	R 60	R 62	R 68	R 69	R 71	R 73	US/USSR	
																																									107
				■																																				2/0	108
																																									109
																																									110
						■																																		0/1	111
■	■	■	■	■																									■		■									10/2	112
																																									113
		■																																						1/0	114
																																									115
																																									116
				■																									■		■									2/2	117
																																			■					0/1	118
																																									119
																																									120
																																									121
																																									122
																																									123
																																								1/0	124
																																									125
																													■		■									0/2	126
							■				■	■	■						■														■						■	0/7	127
																																									128
																																									129
																																								1/0	130
																																								1/0	131
																																								1/0	132
																																									133
																													■		■									0/2	134
												■																					■							0/2	135
		■																																	■					2/1	136
																																									137
																																								1/0	138
																																								1/0	139
																																									140
																																									141
																																									142
																																								2/0	143

No.	Item	US 1	US 7	US 8	US 9	US10	US12	US20	US22	US24	US26	US29	US32	US35	US36	US43	US48
	c. Ad hoc																
144	1) Responsible to Secretariat																
145	2) Responsible to Control Commission																
146	3) Not specified																
	4. Inspectorate																
147	*a. Number (specified)*																■
	b. Selection																
148	1) By Secretariat(s)						■										
149	2) Secretariat with Control Commission approval																
150	3) Other																
151	4) Non-national basis (no national to serve in own country)						■										
152	5) National basis (nationals to serve *only* in their own countries)																
153	6) Only "neutrals" to serve																
154	7) International basis (unspecified)																
	8) International basis (specified)																
155	*a) Quota or fixed ratio*																
156	*b) National ratio*																
157	*c) Technical competence*	■															
158	*d) Other*																
	B. FUNCTIONS																
159	1. Development of procedures for control and inspection	■					■										
160	2. Implementation of control and inspection	■	■	■	■		■										
161	3. Verification	■	■	■	■		■										
162	4. Determination and reporting of violation	■	■	■	■		■										
163	5. Other (specified)	■					■										
	C. METHODS OF CONTROL																
	1. Without inspection																
164	*a. Long-range scientific methods from stations outside one's own country*																
165	*b. Stationing scientific instruments in foreign country without inspection*																
166	*c. Exchange of scientific, technical, and/or budgetary information*		■	■	■						■		■				
167	*d. Exchange of military blueprints*		■	■	■			■	■		■						
168	*e. Other (specified)*		■	■	■		■				■		■			■	
	2. With inspection																
	a. On-site																
169	1) Quota of on-site																
170	2) Specific percentage of on-site																
171	3) Occasional or periodic								■								
172	4) Continuous	■	■	■	■												
173	*b. Control posts*								■	■	■		■			■	
174	*c. Mobile inspection teams*						■				■		■				■
175	*d. Definite routes or specified areas of inspection*																
176	*e. Aerial inspection*		■	■	■		■	■	■	■	■		■		■	■	
177	*f. Limited freedom of access*																
178	*g. Complete freedom of access*	■	■	■	■												
179	*h. Other (specified)*		■	■	■												

US64	US65	US66	US67	US74	R 2	R 3	R 4	R 5	R 6	R 11	R 14	R 15	R 18	R 19	R 25	R 27	R 28	R 30	R 31	R 34	R 37	R 38	R 40	R 41	R 42	R 44	R 45	R 47	R 50	R 53	R 54	R 56	R 57	R 60	R 62	R 68	R 69	R 71	R 73	US/USSR	
																																									144
																																									145
																												■												0/1	146
																												■												1/1	147
																																								1/0	148
																																									149
																													■		■									0/2	150
																																								1/0	151
																																									152
																																									153
													■	■		■				■									■					■							0/6	154
		■																																						3/0	155
																																									156
																																								1/0	157
																																									158
			■	■		■																																	■	5/2	159
			■	■			■		■		■																													8/3	160
			■	■					■		■																													8/2	161
				■																																				7/0	162
			■			■																										■							■	3/3	163
																																						■		2/1	164
																																									165
				■		■									■																	■							8/3	166
									■																							■						■	6/3	167
			■	■								■	■		■																	■						■	0/5	168
	■																											■	■	■			■	■					5/5	169
	■																																						2/0	170
						■																																	1/1	171
									■		■	■	■		■																									5/5	172
			■	■									■		■		■	■	■								■	■		■					■	■				12/10	173
				■																											■							5/1	174
																■	■									■			■										4/4	175
				■												■	■				■					■					■						■	13/6	176
									■		■	■	■		■																								0/5	177
																																							4/0	178
													■		■			■																					3/3	179

Comparison: *page 6*

No.	Item	US 1	US 7	US 8	US 9	US10	US12	US20	US22	US24	US26	US29	US32	US35	US36	US43	US4[illegible]
180	3. International police force																
	D. AUTHORITY OF CONTROL ORGANIZATION OVER CONTROL MEASURES																
181	1. Authority not subject to veto	■															
182	2. Authority in certain specified areas not subject to veto																
	3. Authority subject to veto																
183	*a. Security Council*												■				
184	*b. Control Commission*										■						
185	*c. Directorate*																
186	4. Authority in certain specified areas subject to veto																
187	*a. Security Council*																
188	*b. Control Commission*																■
189	*c. Directorate*																
	IV. TERRITORIES COVERED BY ACD																
190	A. SIGNATORIES ONLY					■		■	■	■		■		■	■		
191	B. SIGNATORIES PLUS OTHER SPECIFIED TERRITORIES ONLY												■				
192	C. CERTAIN SPECIFIED TERRITORIES ONLY															■	
193	D. ALL COUNTRIES	■	■	■	■		■				■						
	V. PUNISHMENTS FOR VIOLATORS																
	A. DETERMINED BY:																
194	1. Security Council (with veto)																
195	2. International Authority (without veto)	■															
196	3. International Authority (with veto)																
197	4. General Assembly																
198	5. International Court of Justice																
199	6. Not specified						■										
	B. EXECUTED BY:																
200	1. Security Council (with veto)																
201	2. International Authority (without veto)																
202	3. International Authority (with veto)																
203	4. General Assembly																
204	5. International Court of Justice																
205	6. Not specified	■					■										
	C. NATURE OF SANCTIONS																
	1. International sanctions against nation																
206	*a. Political*																
207	*b. Economic*																
208	*c. Military*																
209	*d. Not specified*	■					■										
	2. International sanctions against individuals or groups																
210	*a. Political*																
211	*b. Economic*																
212	*c. Military*																
213	*d. Not specified*	■					■										
214	3. National sanctions against individuals or groups						■										
215	4. Not specified																

US64	US65	US66	US67	US74	R 2	R 3	R 4	R 5	R 6	R 11	R 14	R 15	R 18	R 19	R 25	R 27	R 28	R 30	R 31	R 34	R 37	R 38	R 40	R 41	R 42	R 44	R 45	R 47	R 50	R 53	R 54	R 56	R 57	R 60	R 62	R 68	R 69	R 71	R 73	US/USSR	
			■	■									■		■			■															■						■	2/5	180
																																								1/0	181
		■																										■	■		■		■							3/4	182
					■		■		■		■	■							■																				■	1/7	183
																																								1/0	184
																																			■					0/1	185
																																									186
																																									187
		■																										■			■		■							4/3	188
																																									189
■	■	■				■	■	■	■		■		■						■				■	■				■	■	■	■	■	■		■			■		16/17	190
										■								■		■																■				1/4	191
																■					■	■															■			1/4	192
			■	■	■							■		■	■		■									■								■					■	9/8	193
																																									194
																																								1/0	195
																																									196
																																									197
																																									198
					■																																			1/1	199
																																									200
																																									201
																																									202
																																									203
																																									204
					■																																			2/1	205
																																									206
																																									207
																																									208
																																								2/0	209
																																									210
																																									211
																																									212
																																								2/0	213
																																								1/0	214
					■																																			0/1	215

APPENDIX II

REGIONAL ATTITUDINAL MATRIX

LOCUS OF REGULATION	AUSTRALIA NEW ZEALAND	BURMA	CAMBODIA	CEYLON	INDIA
I. TYPE OF WEAPONS SYSTEMS TO BE CONTROLLED					
A. Nuclear weapons, long-range unmanned delivery systems, chemical, biological, and radiological weapons					
1. Production					
a. Prohibition of production					
strongly favor		■	■	□	
conditionally favor	■				
strongly oppose					
conditionally oppose					
b. Reduction of production					
strongly favor		■	■	□	
conditionally favor	■				
strongly oppose					
conditionally oppose					
c. International control of production					
strongly favor		■	■	□	
conditionally favor	■				
strongly oppose					
conditionally oppose					
2. Existing stock					
a. Elimination of existing stock					
strongly favor			■	□	
conditionally favor	■	■			
strongly oppose					
conditionally oppose					
b. Reduction of existing stock					
strongly favor		■	■	□	
conditionally favor	■				
strongly oppose					
conditionally oppose					
c. International monopoly of existing stock					
strongly favor		■	■	■	
conditionally favor	■				
strongly oppose					
conditionally oppose					
3. Use					
a. Prohibition of use					
strongly favor		■	■	□	
conditionally favor					
strongly oppose					
conditionally oppose	■				
b. International control of use					
strongly favor		■	■	□	
conditionally favor	■				
strongly oppose					
conditionally oppose					

INDONESIA	JAPAN	LAOS	MALAYSIA	PAKISTAN	PHILIPPINES	SOUTH KOREA	SOUTH VIETNAM	TAIWAN	THAILAND
	■	■		■					
			■		■	■	■	■	■
■									
	■	■		■				■	
			■		■	■	■		■
■									
	■	■		■				■	
			■		■	■	■		■
■									
	■	■		■				■	
			■		■	■	■		■
■									
	■	■		■				■	
			■		■	■	■		■
■									
	■	■		■					
						■	■	■	■
■			■						
					■				
	■	■	■	■				■	
					■	■	■		■
■									
	■	■	■	■				■	
					■	■	■		■
■									

	AUSTRALIA NEW ZEALAND	BURMA	CAMBODIA	CEYLON	INDIA
4. Control of international movement of, traffic in, and gift or sale of weapons					
strongly favor		■	■		
conditionally favor					
strongly oppose					
conditionally oppose	■				
5. Developing and testing such weapons					
a. Prohibition of above					
strongly favor		■	■		
conditionally favor	■				
strongly oppose					
conditionally oppose					
b. International control of above					
strongly favor		■	■		
conditionally favor					
strongly oppose					
conditionally oppose	■				
B. Heavy offensive weapons					
1. Production					
a. Prohibition of production					
strongly favor		■	■		
conditionally favor					
strongly oppose					
conditionally oppose	■				
b. Reduction of production					
strongly favor		■	■		
conditionally favor					
strongly oppose					
conditionally oppose	■				
c. International control of production					
strongly favor		■	■		
conditionally favor					
strongly oppose					
conditionally oppose	■				
2. Existing stock					
a. Elimination of existing stock					
strongly favor			■		
conditionally favor		■			
strongly oppose					
conditionally oppose	■				
b. Reduction of existing stock					
strongly favor			■		
conditionally favor		■			
strongly oppose					
conditionally oppose	■				

INDONESIA	JAPAN	LAOS	MALAYSIA	PAKISTAN	PHILIPPINES	SOUTH KOREA	SOUTH VIETNAM	TAIWAN	THAILAND
	■	■							
			■	■	■	■	■		■
■								■	
	■	■						■	
			■	■	■	■	■		■
■									
	■	■		■					
					■	■	■	■	■
■			■						
		■							
	■		■						■
					■	■		■	
■				■			■		
	■	■	■		■	■			■
								■	
■				■			■		
	■	■							
			■	■	■	■			■
■								■	
							■		
	■	■	■		■				■
						■		■	
■				■			■		
	■	■	■		■	■			■
								■	
■				■			■		

	AUSTRALIA NEW ZEALAND	BURMA	CAMBODIA	CEYLON	INDIA
c. International monopoly of existing stock					
strongly favor					
conditionally favor		■	■	□	
strongly oppose					
conditionally oppose	■				
3. Use					
a. Prohibition of use					
strongly favor		■	■	□	
conditionally favor					
strongly oppose					
conditionally oppose	■				
b. International control of use					
strongly favor			■	□	
conditionally favor					
strongly oppose		■			
conditionally oppose	■				
4. Control of international movement of, traffic in, and gift or sale of					
strongly favor			■	□	
conditionally favor					
strongly oppose					
conditionally oppose	■	■			
5. Developing and testing such weapons and materials					
a. Prohibition of above					
strongly favor			■	□	
conditionally favor		■			
strongly oppose					
conditionally oppose	■				
b. International control of above					
strongly favor			■	□	
conditionally favor		■			
strongly oppose	■				
conditionally oppose					
C. Other conventional weapons					
1. Production					
a. Prohibition of production					
strongly favor				□	
conditionally favor			■		
strongly oppose					
conditionally oppose	■	■			
b. Reduction of production					
strongly favor				□	
conditionally favor			■		
strongly oppose					
conditionally oppose	■	■			

	INDONESIA	JAPAN	LAOS	MALAYSIA	PAKISTAN	PHILIPPINES	SOUTH KOREA	SOUTH VIETNAM	TAIWAN	THAILAND
			■							
		■								■
	■			■					■	
					■	■	■	■		
		■	■							■
						■				
	■						■	■	■	
				■	■					
		■	■			■				
	■						■	■	■	
				■	■					■
		■	■							
						■				
	■							■	■	
				■	■		■			■
			■							
		■		■		■				
	■								■	
					■		■	■		■
		■	■			■	■			■
	■			■	■			■	■	
		■	■							
	■			■		■	■	■	■	
					■					■
		■	■			■	■			
	■			■				■	■	
					■					■

	AUSTRALIA NEW ZEALAND	BURMA	CAMBODIA	CEYLON	INDIA
c. International control of production					
strongly favor					
conditionally favor			■		
strongly oppose					
conditionally oppose	■	■			
2. Existing stock					
a. Elimination of existing stock*					
strongly favor					
conditionally favor					
strongly oppose					
conditionally oppose					
b. Reduction of existing stock					
strongly favor					
conditionally favor			■		
strongly oppose		■			
conditionally oppose	■				
c. International monopoly of existing stock					
strongly favor					
conditionally favor			■		
strongly oppose		■			
conditionally oppose	■				
3. Use					
a. Prohibition of use					
strongly favor					
conditionally favor			■		
strongly oppose	■	■			
conditionally oppose					
b. International control of use					
strongly favor			■		
conditionally favor					
strongly oppose		■			
conditionally oppose	■				
4. Control of international movement of, traffic in, and gift or sale of					
strongly favor			■		
conditionally favor					
strongly oppose					
conditionally oppose	■	■			
5. Developing and testing such weapons and materials					
a. Prohibition of above					
strongly favor			■		
conditionally favor					
strongly oppose					
conditionally oppose	■	■			

* Although some regional countries might consider regulations on conventional weapons, it is our assumption that no country w

INDONESIA	JAPAN	LAOS	MALAYSIA	PAKISTAN	PHILIPPINES	SOUTH KOREA	SOUTH VIETNAM	TAIWAN	THAILAND

NOT APPLICABLE*

consider the elimination of existing stock of such weapons.

	AUSTRALIA NEW ZEALAND	BURMA	CAMBODIA	CEYLON	INDIA
b. International control of above					
strongly favor			■		
conditionally favor		■			
strongly oppose	■				
conditionally oppose					
II. ARMED FORCES					
A. Regulation of size of armed forces by:					
1. Numerical ceilings					
strongly favor			■		
conditionally favor	■	■			
strongly oppose					
conditionally oppose					
no predictable position					
2. Percentage cut					
strongly favor					
conditionally favor					
strongly oppose					
conditionally oppose	■	■	■		
no predictable position					
3. National ratio					
strongly favor					
conditionally favor	■				
strongly oppose		■			
conditionally oppose			■		
no predictable position					
4. Regulation or prohibition of conscription					
strongly favor					
conditionally favor			■		
strongly oppose					
conditionally oppose	■	■			
no predictable position					
5. Regulation of length of service					
strongly favor					
conditionally favor			■		
strongly oppose					
conditionally oppose	■	■			
no predictable position					
6. Regulation or prohibition of para-military formations					
strongly favor					
conditionally favor			■		
strongly oppose					
conditionally oppose	■	■			
no predictable position					

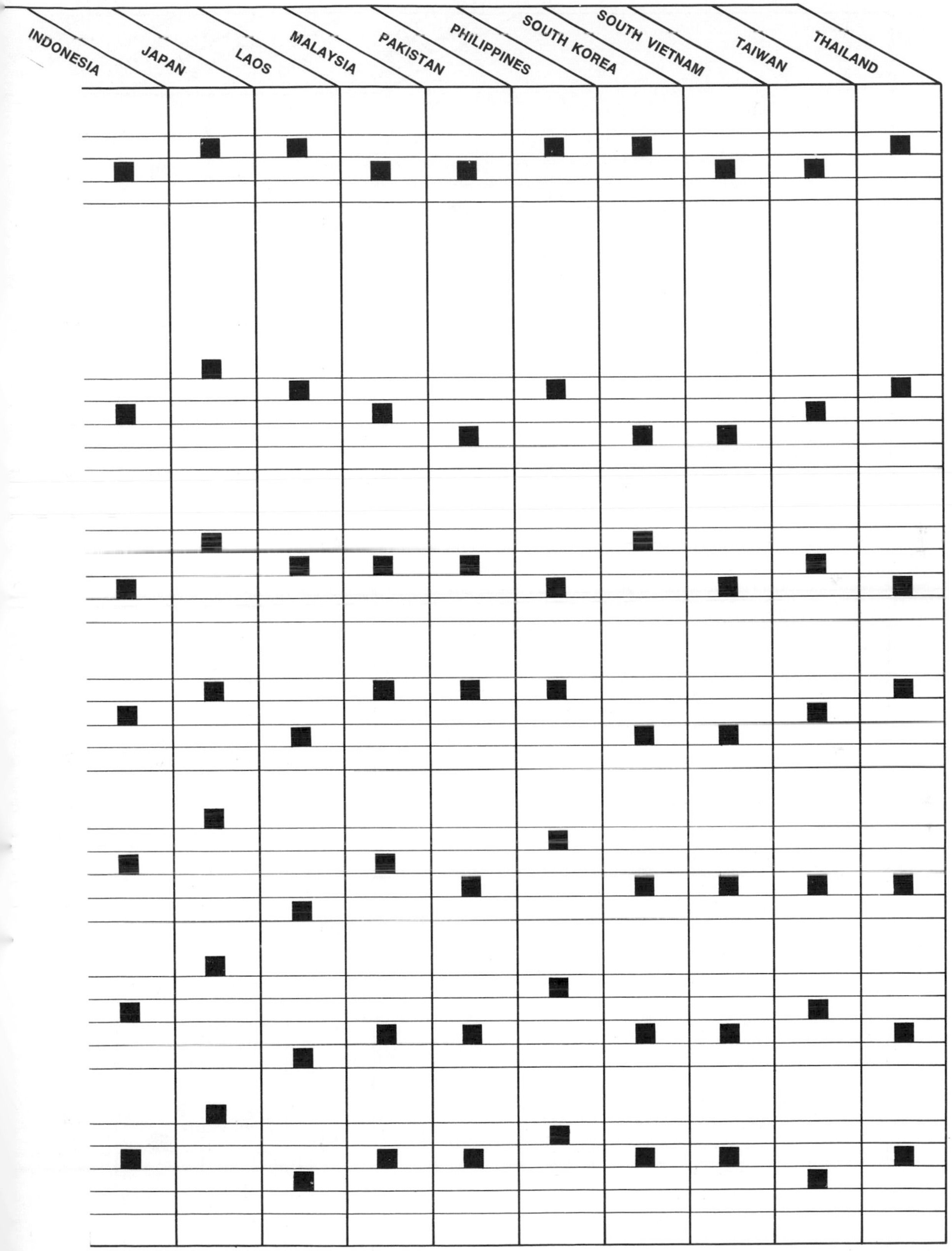

	INDONESIA	JAPAN	LAOS	MALAYSIA	PAKISTAN	PHILIPPINES	SOUTH KOREA	SOUTH VIETNAM	TAIWAN	THAILAND
		■	■			■	■			■
	■			■	■			■	■	
		■								
			■			■				■
	■			■					■	
					■		■	■		
		■					■			
			■	■	■				■	
	■					■		■		■
		■		■	■	■				■
	■								■	
			■				■	■		
		■								
						■				
	■			■						
					■		■	■	■	■
			■							
		■								
						■				
	■								■	
				■	■		■	■		■
			■							
		■								
						■				
	■			■	■		■	■		■
			■						■	

	AUSTRALIA NEW ZEALAND	BURMA	CAMBODIA	CEYLON	INDIA
III. DEPLOYMENT					
A. Foreign bases					
1. Prohibition of foreign bases					
strongly favor		■	■	■	
conditionally favor					
strongly oppose	■				
conditionally oppose					
no predictable position					
2. Limitations on foreign bases					
strongly favor		■	■	■	
conditionally favor					
strongly oppose	■				
conditionally oppose					
no predictable position					
3. Regulation of number of troops stationed in foreign bases					
strongly favor		■	■	■	
conditionally favor					
strongly oppose					
conditionally oppose	■				
no predictable position					
B. Military alliances					
1. Prohibition of military alliances with regional powers					
strongly favor					
conditionally favor		■	■	■	
strongly oppose					
conditionally oppose	■				
no predictable position					
2. Prohibition of military alliances with extraregional powers					
strongly favor					
conditionally favor		■	■	■	
strongly oppose	■				
conditionally oppose					
no predictable position					
C. De-militarized zones					
strongly favor		■		■	
conditionally favor	■		■		
strongly oppose					
conditionally oppose					
no predictable position					

INDONESIA	JAPAN	LAOS	MALAYSIA	PAKISTAN	PHILIPPINES	SOUTH KOREA	SOUTH VIETNAM	TAIWAN	THAILAND
■									
			■		■	■	■	■	■
	■	■							
				■					
■			■						
	■				■	■		■	■
							■		
		■							
				■					
■									
	■				■	■			
			■				■	■	■
		■							
				■					
■	■			■					
			■		■			■	
						■	■		■
		■							
■									
			■		■	■	■	■	■
	■			■					
		■							
			■						
	■	■		■	■				■
■								■	
				■					
							■		

	AUSTRALIA NEW ZEALAND	BURMA	CAMBODIA	CEYLON	INDIA
IV. MILITARY EXPENDITURES					
A. Exchange of information concerning expenditures for military purposes					
strongly favor			■	■	
conditionally favor	■	■			
strongly oppose					
conditionally oppose					
no predictable position					
B. Agreed regulation of expenditures for military purposes					
strongly favor			■		
conditionally favor	■	■		■	
strongly oppose					
conditionally oppose					
no predictable position					
C. Standardization of listing of expenditures for military purposes					
strongly favor			■		
conditionally favor	■	■		■	
strongly oppose					
conditionally oppose					
no predictable position					
V. OUTER SPACE					
A. Prohibition of its use for military purposes					
strongly favor		■	■	■	
conditionally favor	■				
strongly oppose					
conditionally oppose					
no predictable position					
B. Its use only under international control					
strongly favor		■	■	■	
conditionally favor	■				
strongly oppose					
conditionally oppose					
no predictable position					
VI. DE-NUCLEARIZED ZONES AND NON-PROLIFERATION					
A. No country within a specified zone to have, develop, or furnish nuclear weapons					
strongly favor		■	■	■	
conditionally favor					
strongly oppose					
conditionally oppose	■				
no predictable position					
B. No country to sell, detonate, or furnish such weapons to others in the zone					
strongly favor		■	■	■	
conditionally favor					
strongly oppose					
conditionally oppose	■				
no predictable position					

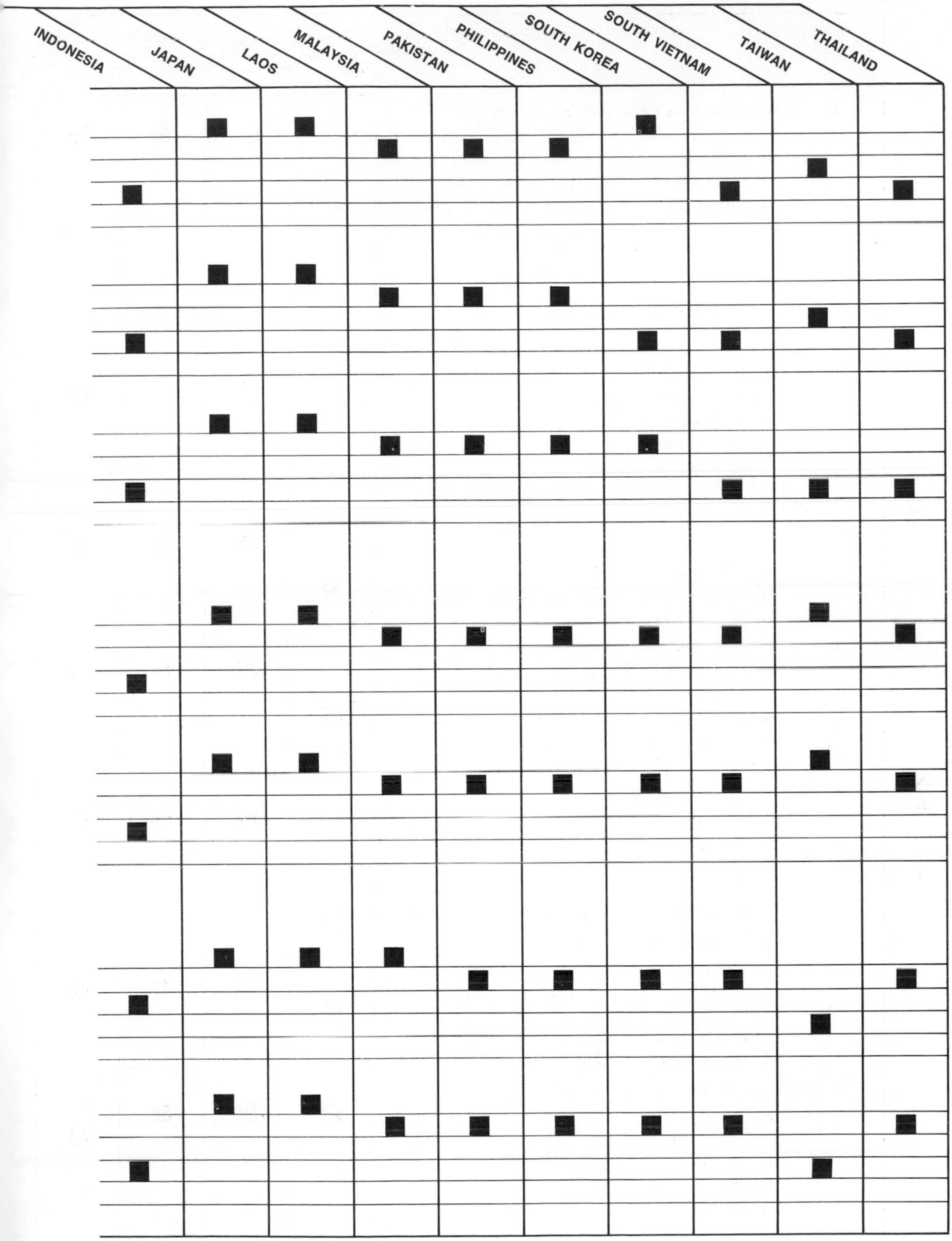

	INDONESIA	JAPAN	LAOS	MALAYSIA	PAKISTAN	PHILIPPINES	SOUTH KOREA	SOUTH VIETNAM	TAIWAN	THAILAND
		■	■				■			
				■	■	■				
									■	
	■							■		■
		■	■							
				■	■	■				
									■	
	■						■	■		■
		■	■							
				■	■	■	■			
	■							■	■	■
		■	■						■	
				■	■	■	■	■		■
	■									
		■	■						■	
				■	■	■	■	■		■
	■									
		■	■	■						
					■	■	■	■		■
	■									
									■	
		■	■							
				■	■	■	■	■		■
	■								■	

	AUSTRALIA NEW ZEALAND	BURMA	CAMBODIA	CEYLON	INDIA
C. No country to help others in the zone develop such weapons					
strongly favor		■	■	■	
conditionally favor					
strongly oppose					
conditionally oppose	■				
no predictable position					
CONTROL ASPECT OF ACD					
I. SEQUENCE OF ACD					
A. Establishment of control machinery before proceeding with ACD					
strongly favor	■	■	■		
conditionally favor				■	
strongly oppose					
conditionally oppose					
no predictable position					
B. Proceeding with ACD before establishment of control machinery					
strongly favor					
conditionally favor		■	■	■	
strongly oppose					
conditionally oppose	■				
no predictable position					
C. ACD simultaneous with control machinery					
strongly favor		■	■	■	
conditionally favor					
strongly oppose	■				
conditionally oppose					
no predictable position					
D. Phased implementation of ACD with controls					
strongly favor		■	■	■	
conditionally favor	■				
strongly oppose					
conditionally oppose					
no predictable position					
E. Phased implementation of ACD without controls					
strongly favor					
conditionally favor		■	■	■	
strongly oppose	■				
conditionally oppose					
no predictable position					
F. Political settlement prior to ACD					
strongly favor	■	■	■		
conditionally favor				■	
strongly oppose					
conditionally oppose					
no predictable position					

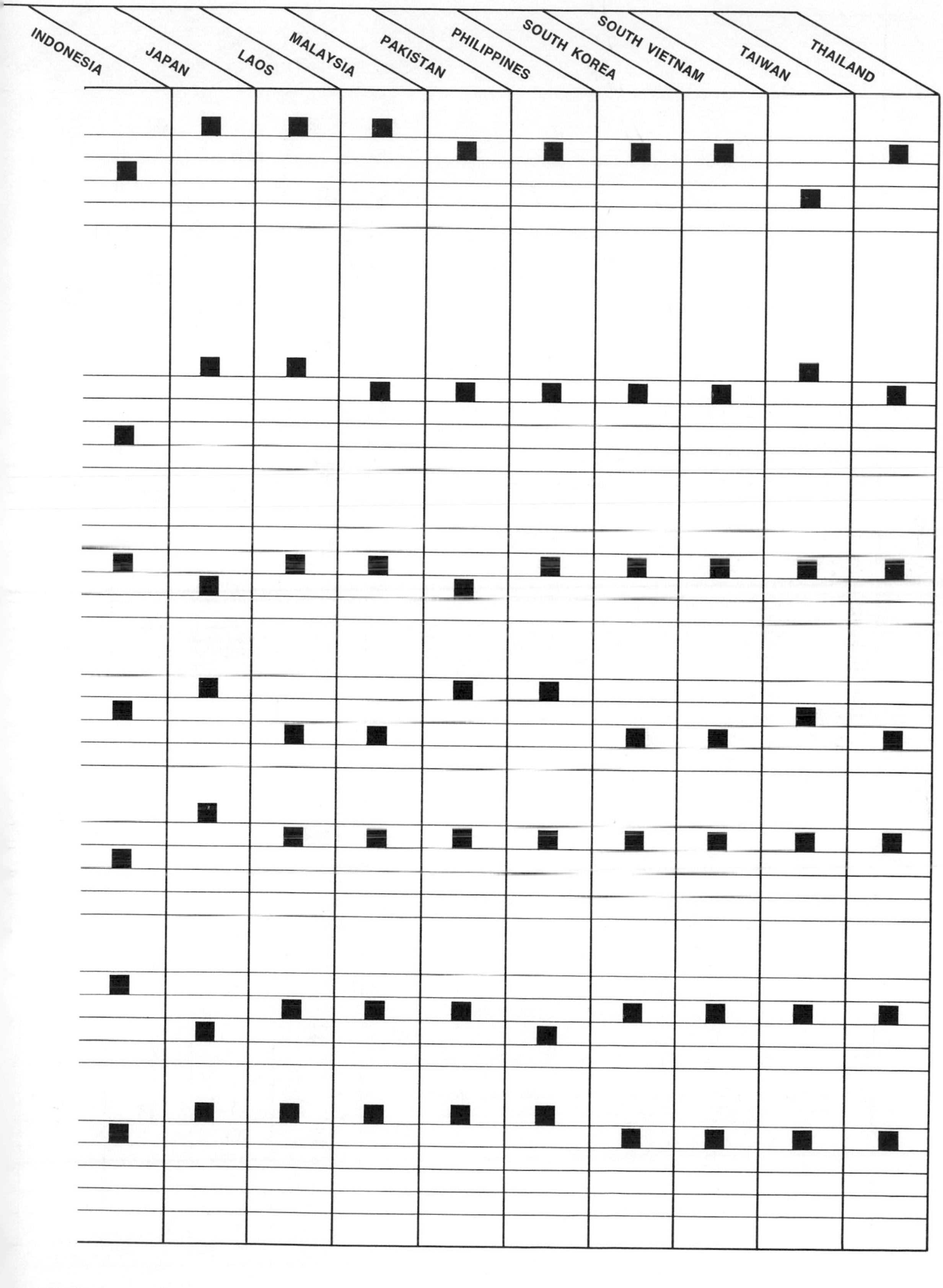

INDONESIA	JAPAN	LAOS	MALAYSIA	PAKISTAN	PHILIPPINES	SOUTH KOREA	SOUTH VIETNAM	TAIWAN	THAILAND

	AUSTRALIA NEW ZEALAND	BURMA	CAMBODIA	CEYLON	INDIA
G. ACD prior to political settlement					
strongly favor			■		
conditionally favor		■			
strongly oppose					
conditionally oppose	■				
no predictable position					
H. ACD simultaneous with political settlement					
strongly favor			■		
conditionally favor		■			
strongly oppose					
conditionally oppose	■				
no predictable position					
II. CONTROL ORGANIZATION AND FIELD STAFF AND INSPECTORATE					
A. Control organization subject to veto					
strongly favor	■				
conditionally favor		■	■		
strongly oppose					
conditionally oppose					
no predictable position					
B. Control organization not subject to veto					
strongly favor			■		
conditionally favor		■			
strongly oppose	■				
conditionally oppose					
no predictable position					
C. Field Staff and Inspectorate to be chosen on a national basis (nationals to serve only in their own country)					
strongly favor					
conditionally favor		■	■		
strongly oppose	■				
conditionally oppose					
no predictable position					
D. Field Staff and Inspectorate to be chosen on a neutral basis (only neutrals to serve)					
strongly favor			■		
conditionally favor		■			
strongly oppose					
conditionally oppose	■				
no predictable position					
E. Field Staff and Inspectorate to be chosen on an international basis					
strongly favor			■		
conditionally favor	■	■			
strongly oppose					
conditionally oppose					
no predictable position					

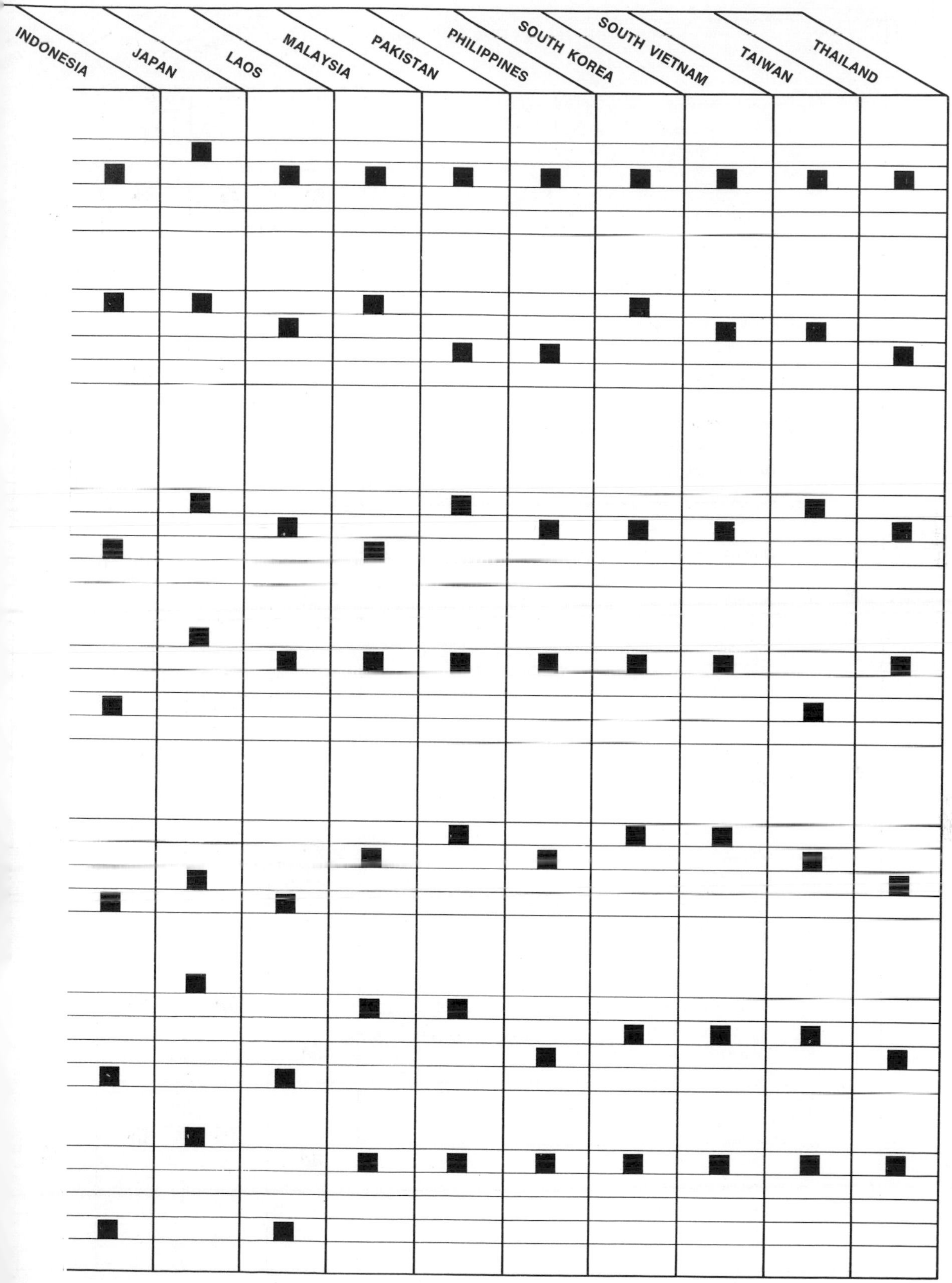

INDONESIA	JAPAN	LAOS	MALAYSIA	PAKISTAN	PHILIPPINES	SOUTH KOREA	SOUTH VIETNAM	TAIWAN	THAILAND

	AUSTRALIA NEW ZEALAND	BURMA	CAMBODIA	CEYLON	INDI
III. METHODS OF INSPECTION AND VERIFICATION					
A. For nuclear weapons only					
1. Long-range scientific methods of control from stations outside one's own country					
strongly favor	■	■	■		
conditionally favor				■	
strongly oppose					
conditionally oppose					
no predictable position					
2. Long-range scientific methods of control stationed inside the country and controlled with inspection by outsiders					
strongly favor		■	■		
conditionally favor	■			■	
strongly oppose					
conditionally oppose					
no predictable position					
3. Long-range scientific methods of contol stationed inside the country but without inspection by outsiders					
strongly favor					
conditionally favor			■	■	
strongly oppose	■				
conditionally oppose		■			
no predictable position					
B. For all types of weapons systems considered					
1. Aerial inspection					
strongly favor			■	■	
conditionally favor	■	■			
strongly oppose					
conditionally oppose					
no predictable position					
2. Occasional or periodic on-site inspection by control teams					
strongly favor					
conditionally favor		■	■	■	
strongly oppose					
conditionally oppose	■				
no predictable position					
3. Continuous on-site inspection by control teams					
strongly favor		■	■		
conditionally favor	■			■	
strongly oppose					
conditionally oppose					
no predictable position					

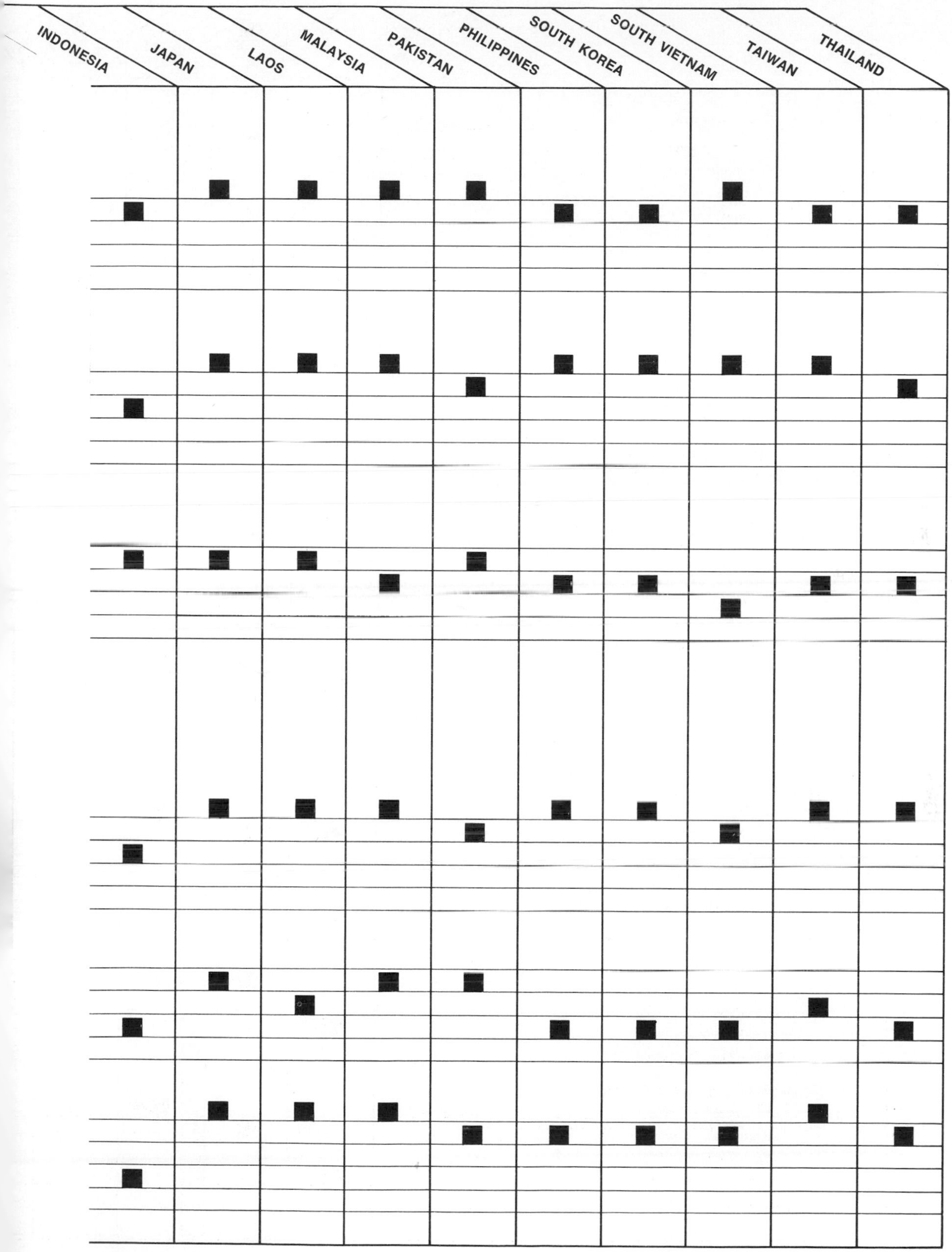

INDONESIA	JAPAN	LAOS	MALAYSIA	PAKISTAN	PHILIPPINES	SOUTH KOREA	SOUTH VIETNAM	TAIWAN	THAILAND
	■	■	■	■			■		
■					■	■		■	■
	■	■	■		■	■	■	■	
				■					■
■									
■	■	■		■					
			■		■	■		■	■
							■		
	■	■	■		■	■		■	■
				■			■		
■									
	■		■	■					
		■						■	
■					■	■	■		■
	■	■	■					■	
				■	■	■	■		■
■									

	AUSTRALIA NEW ZEALAND	BURMA	CAMBODIA	CEYLON	INDIA
4. Limited freedom of access to control teams					
strongly favor					
conditionally favor		■	■		
strongly oppose	■				
conditionally oppose					
no predictable position					
5. Unlimited freedom of access to control teams					
strongly favor		■	■		
conditionally favor	■				
strongly oppose					
conditionally oppose					
no predictable position					
IV. INTERNATIONAL POLICE FORCE					
A. Establishment on a permanent basis					
strongly favor	■		■		
conditionally favor		■			
strongly oppose					
conditionally oppose					
no predictable position					
B. Occasionally established when needed					
strongly favor			■		
conditionally favor	■	■			
strongly oppose					
conditionally oppose					
no predictable position					
C. Composed of international troops					
strongly favor			■		
conditionally favor	■	■			
strongly oppose					
conditionally oppose					
no predictable position					
D. Composed of troops from regional states only					
strongly favor					
conditionally favor		■	■		
strongly oppose					
conditionally oppose	■				
no predictable position					
E. Composed of troops from states only					
strongly favor			■		
conditionally favor		■			
strongly oppose					
conditionally oppose	■				
no predictable position					

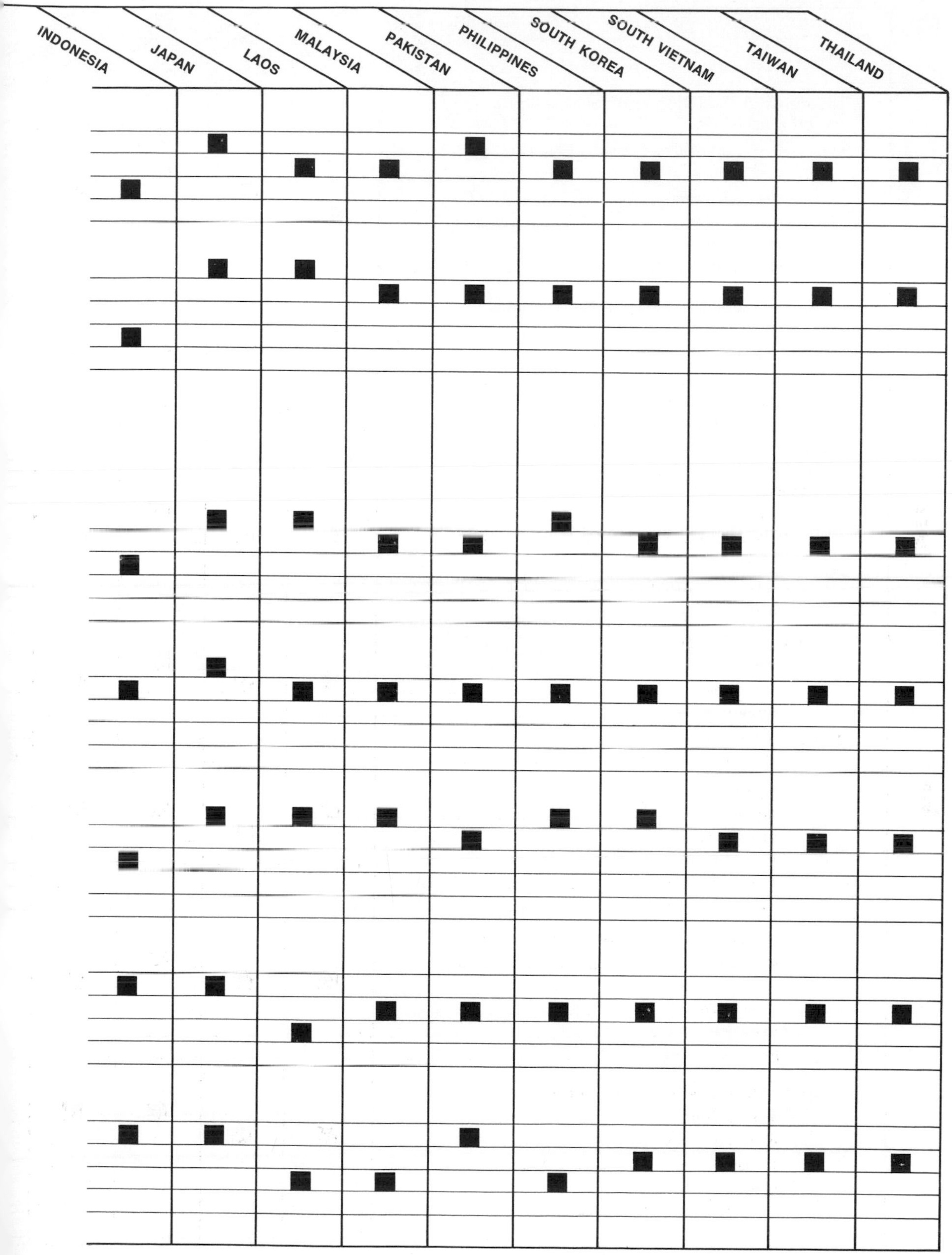

INDONESIA	JAPAN	LAOS	MALAYSIA	PAKISTAN	PHILIPPINES	SOUTH KOREA	SOUTH VIETNAM	TAIWAN	THAILAND

	AUSTRALIA NEW ZEALAND	BURMA	CAMBODIA	CEYLON	INDIA
V. DETERMINATION AND PUNISHMENT OF VIOLATIONS OF ACD AGREEMENTS					
A. Determined by an international authority not subject to veto					
strongly favor			■		
conditionally favor		■			
strongly oppose	■				
conditionally oppose					
no predictable position					
B. Determined by an international authority subject to veto					
strongly favor	■				
conditionally favor		■	■		
strongly oppose					
conditionally oppose					
no predictable position					
C. Sanctions					
1. Political sanctions					
strongly favor			■		
conditionally favor	■	■			
strongly oppose					
conditionally oppose					
no predictable position					
2. Economic sanctions					
strongly favor			■		
conditionally favor	■	■			
strongly oppose					
conditionally oppose					
no predictable position					
3. Military sanctions					
strongly favor	■		■		
conditionally favor		■			
strongly oppose					
conditionally oppose					
no predictable position					
4. Combination of political, economic, and military sanctions					
strongly favor			■		
conditionally favor	■	■			
strongly oppose					
conditionally oppose					
no predictable position					
D. Sanctions to be applied by an international authority					
strongly favor			■		
conditionally favor	■	■			
strongly oppose					
conditionally oppose					
no predictable position					

	INDONESIA	JAPAN	LAOS	MALAYSIA	PAKISTAN	PHILIPPINES	SOUTH KOREA	SOUTH VIETNAM	TAIWAN	THAILAND
		■	■	■						
					■	■	■	■		■
	■									
									■	
		■			■				■	
			■	■		■	■	■		
	■									■
		■								
			■	■	■	■	■	■		■
	■								■	
			■							
		■		■	■	■	■	■		■
	■								■	
		■	■	■		■	■	■		■
					■					
	■								■	
		■	■	■	■	■	■	■		■
	■								■	
		■	■	■		■				
							■	■		■
	■								■	
					■					

E. Sanctions to be applied by regional powers only	AUSTRALIA NEW ZEALAND	BURMA	CAMBODIA	CEYLON	INDIA
strongly favor					
conditionally favor		■	■	■	
strongly oppose					
conditionally oppose	■				
no predictable position					

	INDONESIA	JAPAN	LAOS	MALAYSIA	PAKISTAN	PHILIPPINES	SOUTH KOREA	SOUTH VIETNAM	TAIWAN	THAILAND
	■	■	■			■				
									■	
				■			■	■		■
					■					

APPENDIX III

REGIONAL CONFLICT AND TENSION CHART

(*See* inside back cover)

INDEX

A

ACD, See Arms Control and Disarmament
ACD Matrix, 11-16, 108; Appendix I
Acheson, Dean, 43
Afghanistan, 17, 30, 73; and ACD: 15
Africa, 29, 32, 33, 40, 42
Albania, 33
ANZUS, 25, 109, 118, 128
Armed Forces, 6, 80-81; and ACD: 12, 90-91, 105-08 *passim*, 115-116, 119, 121, 122, 128; Appendix I, Appendix II, see also individual countries and deployment; and utilization for regional development, 114-116, 120, 124, 127-128
Arms Control and Disarmament, definition of, 1; extraregional attitude toward, 48-50; Appendix I; see also previous proposals; factors influencing, 4-10, 76-103 *passim*, 104, 106-110; previous ACD proposals, 2, 11-17, 67, 105; Appendix I; purpose of, 1-2; regional attitude toward, 12-14, 55-74 *passim*, 76-103, 104-122; Appendix I, Appendix II; see also previous ACD proposals; suggested ACD measures, 104-122 *passim*, 124-131 *passim*
Note: see also individual countries and the United Nations, as well as armed forces, chemical, biological, and radiological weapons, control organization, conventional weapons, delivery systems, deployment, heavy offensive weapons, inspection and verification, international police force, military expenditures, nuclear free zones, nuclear weapons, outer space, sanctions, sequence of ACD, and violation of ACD
Arms Control Implications of Communist China's Domestic and Foreign Policies, 105, 118
ASA (Association of Southeast Asia), 68, 116
Asian and Pacific Council, see ASPAC
Asian Development Bank, 116
Asian Payments Union, 116
ASPAC (Asian and Pacific Conference), 116
Association of Southeast Asia, see ASA
Atomic Weapons, see Nuclear Weapons
Australia and New Zealand, 1, 17, 19, 22-26 *passim*, 31, 37, 43, 44, 67, 73-75 *passim*, 77-81 *passim*, 84, 108, 109, 116; Appendix III; and ACD (general): 12, 13, 74, 76-103 *passim*, 104-122 passim; and ACD (specific aspects): Appendix I, Appendix II; armed forces, 90-91 *passim*, 122; chemical, biological, and radiological weapons, 81, 122; control organization, 96-97 *passim*; conventional weapons, 86-90 *passim*, 122; delivery systems, 81, 122; deployment, 90-91 *passim*, 122; heavy offensive weapons, 82-90 *passim*, 122; inspection and verification, 96-99 *passim*; international police force, 99-101 *passim*; military expenditures, 91-92 *passim*, 122; nuclear free zones, 81, 122; nuclear weapons, 81, 122; outer space, 81; previous ACD proposals, 15; sanctions, 82, 101-103 *passim*; sequence of ACD, 92-96 *passim*; violations of ACD, 101-103 *passim*; and Communist China, 17, 74, 78, 79; and the United States, 43, 73, 74

B

Baguio Conference (1950), 17
Bandung Conference (1955), 12, 33, 39, 40, 43
Bengal, 72
Bhutan, 31
Borneo, 44
Brunei, 44
Buddhism, 61, 72, 82, 86-87, 90, 103
Bulganin, Nikolai A., 114

Burma, 1, 17, 19, 20, 22-24 passim, 26, 30, 38, 39, 42, 44, 58, 66-67, 68, 71, 77-81 passim, 107, 114, 117, 128; Appendix III; and ACD (general): 67, 76-103 passim, 104-122 passim; and ACD (specific aspects): Appendix I, Appendix II; armed forces, 90-91 passim, 122; chemical, biological, and radiological weapons, 81, 122; control organization, 96-97 passim; conventional weapons, 86-90 passim, 122; delivery systems, 81, 122; heavy offensive weapons, 82-90 passim, 120, 122; inspection and verification, 96-99 passim; international police force, 99-101 passim, 116; military expenditures, 91-92 passim, 122; nuclear free zones, 81, 122; nuclear weapons, 67, 81, 122; outer space, 81, previous ACD proposals, 15; sanctions, 82, 101-103 passim; sequence of ACD, 92-96 passim; violations of ACD, 101-103 passim; and Communist China, 31, 40, 66-67, 78, 79; and the United Nations, 66, 67; and the United States, 43

C

Cambodia, 1, 17, 19, 22-26 passim, 29, 30, 34, 58, 61, 62, 63-66, 77-81 passim, 84, 108, 109, 117, 123, 130; Appendix III; and ACD (general): 64-65, 76-103 passim, 104-122 passim; and ACD (specific aspects): Appendix I, Appendix II; armed forces, 90-91 passim, 122; chemical, biological, and radiological weapons, 81, 122; control organization, 96-97 passim; conventional weapons, 86-90 passim, 122; delivery systems, 81, 122; deployment, 90-91 passim, 122; heavy offensive weapons, 82-90 passim, 122; inspection and verification, 96-99 passim; international police force, 99-101 passim, 116; military expenditures, 91-92 passim, 122; nuclear free zones, 81, 122; nuclear weapons, 65, 81; 122; outer space, 81; previous ACD proposals, 15; sanctions, 82, 101-103 passim; sequence of ACD, 92-96 passim; violation of ACD, 101-103 passim; and Communist China, 31, 40, 62, 63-64, 65, 78, 79, 109; and the United States, 43, 64, 66, 79, 109

Canada, 16, 34; Appendix I

Celebes, 68, 69

CENTO (Central Treaty Organization), 31

Ceylon, 1, 19, 20, 22, 23, 25, 26, 58, 71, 73, 77-81 passim, 85, 106, 109, 116, 128, 130; Appendix III; and ACD (general): 73, 76-103 passim, 104-122 passim; and ACD (specific aspects): Appendix I, Appendix II; armed forces, 90-91 passim, 122; chemical, biological, and radiological weapons, 81, 122; control organization, 96-97 passim; conventional weapons, 86-90 passim, 122; delivery systems, 81, 122; deployment, 90-91 passim, 122; heavy offensive weapons, 82-90 passim, 122; inspection and verification, 96-99 passim; international police force, 99-101 passim, 116; military expenditures, 91-92 passim, 122; nuclear free zone, 81, 122; nuclear weapons, 81, 122; outer space, 81; previous ACD proposals, 15; sanctions, 82, 101-103 passim; sequence of ACD 92-96 passim; violations of ACD, 101-103 passim; and Communist China, 79

China, see Communist China and Republic of China

Chemical, Biological, and Radiological Weapons, 81, 105, 106, 114, 121, 122, 124; Appendix I, Appendix II; see also individual countries

Chou En-lai, 33, 48, 51, 65

Colombo Plan, 5, 25

Commonwealth, 67, 78; see also United Kingdom

Communist China, 1, 13, 19, 26, 28, 29, 30, 37, 39-41, 42, 43, 46, 50, 51, 59, 77, 82, 83-87 passim, 90, 92, 94, 95, 97, 98 100, 101-103 passim, 107, 109

118, 119, 125; and ACD (general): 12, 46-48, 49, 66, 79, 85, 90, 100, 104-106 passim, 113, 117, 118; and ACD (specific aspects): Appendix I; conventional weapons and manpower, 3; no-first-use proposal, 48; nuclear test ban treaty, 47; nuclear tests, 46, 48, 55, 57; nuclear weapons, 4 20, 46-48, 49, 57, 65, 71, 110, 111, 112; previous ACD proposals, 14, 15; proliferation, 16, 47, 48; and the extraregional powers: France, 44, 57; North Korea, 33, 40, 41, 51, 57; North Vietnam, 34, 35, 40, 42, 65; the Soviet Union, 32-35 passim, 47, 109, 118; see also Sino-Soviet Conflict; the United States, 5, 10, 109; and the regional powers: 10, 16, 17, 31-33, 36, 76-103 passim; Appendix III; Australia, 19, 74, 78, 79; Burma, 31, 40, 62, 63-67 passim, 78, 79; Cambodia, 31, 40, 62, 63-64, 65, 78, 79, 109; Ceylon, 79; India, 16, 25, 31, 40, 41, 70, 71-72, 78, 79, 104, 109, 112, 113, 118; Indonesia, 33, 68, 69, 78, 79; Japan, 17, 40, 41, 53-59 passim, 78, 79, 111; Laos, 31, 62, 63, 78, 79; Malaysia, 17, 67-68, 78, 79; Pakistan, 25, 71, 78-80 passim; Philippines, 69, 78, 79; Republic of China, 31, 32, 43, 51, 58-60 passim, 78, 102; Republic of Korea, 37, 57, 78, 79; South Vietnam, 61, 78, 79; and Thailand, 31, 65, 78, 79

Confrontation, 65, 67, 68, 69, 74, 108; see also Indonesia and Malaysia

Control Organization, 96-97, 119; Appendix I, Appendix II; see also inspection and verification, sanctions, sequence of ACD, violations of ACD and individual countries

Conventional Weapons, 12, 15, 46, 50, 67, 82, 86-90 passim, 105-108 passim, 119-122 passim; Appendix I, Appendix II; see also individual countries

Cuba 47

Czechoslovakia, 49

D

Declaratory and Voluntary Renunciations, 113-114, 124, 126-127, 131

Delivery systems, 81, 105, 106, 114, 121, 122, 124; Appendix I, Appendix II; see also individual countries

Deployment, 90-91 passim, 105-106, 108, 121, 122; Appendix I, Appendix II

Dien Bien Phu, 43

Disarmament, see Arms Control and Disarmament; General and Complete Disarmament

Dulles, John Foster, 43

E

East Asia, 24-25, 53-60; see individual countries

Eastern Europe, 30, 31

Eighteen Nation Disarmament Conference,(ENDC), see United Nations

Eisenhower, Dwight D., 14, 43

England, see United Kingdom

Extraregional Powers, defined, 1; 5, 10, 28-53, 117-119; Appendix III; see individual countries

F

Five Principles of Peaceful Coexistence (Panch Shila), 33, 72

Food and Agriculture Organization, 116

France, 12, 16, 28, 34, 35, 37, 43, 44, 57, 58, 62, 63, 64, 107, 109, 110, 111; Appendix III

G

Gallois, P. M., 111

Gandhi, Indira, 71

Gandhi, Mahatma, 72

Gaulle, Charles de, 44, 64, 64, 111

General and Complete Disarmament, 15, 55, 67, 72

Geneva Conference (1954), 39, 40, 43, 44

Guam, 127

H

Habomai, 54
Hatta, Mohammed, 68
Heavy Offensive Weapons, 66, 82-90 passim, 105, 106, 107, 108, 119, 120, 121, 122; Appendix I, Appendix II; see also individual countries
Hindi, 70
Hinduism, 72, 77, 103
Ho Chi Minh, 34, 42, 49, 63
Ho Chi Minh Trail, 61, 62
Hoa Hao, 61
Hong Kong, 31, 37, 44
Huang K'o-ch'eng, 47
Hukbalahap, 69

I

ICC (International Control Commission), 63, 64, 97
Implementation of ACD, see control organization, inspection and verification, international police force, sanctions, sequence of ACD, violations of ACD
Indian Ocean, 73
India, 1, 17, 19, 22, 23, 25, 26, 32, 38, 42, 44, 58, 66, 70-72, 73, 74, 77-81 passim, 86, 107, 108, 109, 115, 116; Appendix III; and ACD (general): 13, 14, 16, 72, 76-103 passim, 104-122 passim; and ACD (specific aspects): Appendix I, Appendix II; armed forces, 90-91 passim, 122; chemical, biological, and radiological weapons, 81, 122; control organization, 96-97 passim; conventional weapons, 86-90 passim, 122; delivery systems, 81, 122; deployment, 90-91 passim, 122; heavy offensive weapons, 82-90 passim, 122; inspection and verification, 96-99 passim; international police force, 99-101 passim, 116; military expenditures, 91-92 passim, 122; nuclear free zone, 81, 122; nuclear weapons, 14, 16, 72, 81, 110, 112-113, 118, 122, 123, 125-126; outer space, 81, 122; previous ACD proposals, 15; proliferation, 110-113, 118, 124, 125-126, 131; sanctions, 82, 101-103 passim; sequence of ACD, 92-96 passim; violations of ACD, 101-103 passim; and Communist China, 16, 25, 31, 40, 41, 70, 71-72, 78, 79, 104, 109, 112, 113, 118; and Pakistan, 70-71, 72-73, 78, 80, 83-85 passim, 104, 108-109, 113; see also Kashmir; and the Soviet Union, 17, 70, 117, 118; and the United Nations, 71; and the United States, 109, 112
Indochina, 37, 38, 43, 44, 63, 64, 65, 107
Indonesia, 1, 19, 22-26 passim, 30, 37, 38, 42, 45, 58, 66, 68-69, 75, 77-81 passim, 84, 114, 116; Appendix III; and ACD (general): 13, 69, 76-103 passim, 104-122 passim; and ACD (specific aspects): Appendix I, Appendix II; armed forces, 90-91 passim, 122; chemical, biological, and radiological weapons, 81, 122; control organization, 96-97 passim; conventional weapons, 86-90 passim, 122; delivery systems, 81, 122; deployment, 90-91 passim, 122; heavy offensive weapons, 82-90 passim, 122; inspection and verification, 96-99 passim; international police force, 99-101 passim, 116; military expenditures, 91-92 passim, 122; nuclear free zones, 81, 122; nuclear weapons, 69, 81, 122; outer space, 81; previous ACD proposals, 15; sanctions, 82, 101-103 passim; sequence of ACD, 92-96 passim; violations of ACD, 101-103 passim; and Communist China, 33, 68, 69, 78, 79; and Malaysia, 65, 67, 68, 78, 79, 84, 108; see also Confrontation; and Singapore, 69, 108; and the Soviet Union, 69, 118; and the United States, 43, 68, 69, 79
Indus River, 71, 116
Informal Discussions, 116-117, 124, 129-130, 131
Inspection and Verification, 9, 46, 96-99 passim, 119; Appendix I,

Appendix II; see individual countries
International Control Commission, see ICC
International Police Force, 99-101, 115-116, 124, 128, 131
Islam, 72

J

Jammu, 71, 72
Japan, 1, 12, 17, 19, 22-26 passim, 30, 32, 42, 47, 50, 53-56, 58, 66, 68, 69, 77-81 passim, 111, 115-117 passim, 123; Appendix III; and ACD (general): 53-54, 55-56, 76-103 passim, 104-122 passim; and ACD (specific aspects): Appendix I, Appendix II; armed forces, 90-91 passim, 122; chemical, biological, and radiological weapons, 81, 122; control organization, 96-97 passim; conventional weapons, 86-90 passim, 122; delivery systems, 81, 122; deployment, 90-91 passim, 122; heavy offensive weapons, 82-90 passim, 120, 122; inspection and verification, 96-99 passim; international police force, 99-101 passim, 116; military expenditures, 91-92 passim, 122; nuclear free zones, 81, 122; nuclear weapons, 16, 20, 55, 56, 81, 110-113, 118, 124, 125-126; outer space, 81; previous ACD proposals, 15; proliferation, 110-113, 124, 125-126; sanctions, 82, 101-103 passim; sequence of ACD, 92-96 passim; violations of ACD, 101-103 passim; and Communist China, 17, 40, 41, 53-59 passim, 78, 79, 111; and the Soviet Union, 17, 53, 54, 56, 79, 104, 109, 111; and the United States, 53-56 passim, 93, 109, 111
Johnson, Lyndon B., 16, 112
Joint Defense and Mutual Aid Arrangement, 114-116, 119, 120, 124, 127-128, 131
Joint Technical, Scientific, and Economic Exchanges and Programs, 116, 119, 124, 128-129, 131

K

Kashmir, 14, 25, 71, 72-73, 83, 105, 108; see also India and Pakistan
Kerala, 70
Kha, 62
Khan, Mohammed Ayub, 72
Khmer Peoples' Liberation Army, 63
Khmer Serei, 63
Khrushchev, Nikita, 29
Kim Il-song, 41
Korean Armistice, 40, 41, 43, 113
Korean War, 13, 23, 32, 37, 39-43 passim, 56, 57, 72, 94, 113
Kosygin, Aleksei N., 29
Kuomintang, 59
Kuriles, 54
Ky, Nguyen Cao, 61, 62

L

Laos, 1, 19, 22-26 passim, 30, 34, 39, 44, 57, 58, 61, 62-65 passim, 77-81 passim, 105, 116, 117; Appendix III; and ACD (general): 63, 76-103 passim, 104-122 passim; and ACD (specific aspects): Appendix I, Appendix II; armed forces, 90-91 passim, 122; chemical, biological, and radiological weapons, 81, 122; control organization, 96-97 passim; conventional weapons, 86-90 passim, 122; delivery systems, 81, 122; deployment, 90-91 passim, 122; heavy offensive weapons, 82-90 passim, 122; inspection and verification, 96-99 passim; international police force, 99-101 passim; military expenditures, 91-92 passim, 122; nuclear free zone, 81, 122; nuclear weapons, 81, 122; outer space, 81; sanctions, 82, 101-103 passim; sequence of ACD, 92-96 passim; violations of ACD, 101-103 passim; and Communist China, 31, 62, 63, 78, 79; and the United States, 43
Ladakh, 31, 71
Lenin, V.I., 38, 40, 45
Limited War, 3, 4, 50
Liu Shao-ch'i, 32, 49

M

Macao, 31
Madras, 70
Magsaysay, Ramon, 69
Malaya, 38, 39, 44, 65
Malaysia, 1, 17, 19, 22-26 passim, 37, 59, 67-69, 75, 77-81 passim, 116, 117; Appendix III; and ACD (general): 68, 76-103 passim, 104-122 passim; and ACD (specific aspects): Appendix I, Appendix II; armed forces, 90-91 passim, 122; chemical, biological, and radiological weapons, 81, 122; control organization, 96-97 passim; conventional weapons, 86-90 passim, 122; delivery systems, 81, 122; deployment, 90-91 passim, 122; heavy offensive weapons, 82-90 passim, 122; inspection and verification, 96-99 passim; international police force, 99-101 passim; military expenditures, 91-92 passim, 122; nuclear free zones, 81, 122; nuclear weapons, 81, 122; outer space, 81; previous ACD proposals, 15; sanctions, 82, 101-103 passim; sequence of ACD, 92-96 passim; violations of ACD, 101-103 passim; and the Commonwealth, 78; and Communist China, 17, 67-68, 78, 79; and Indonesia, 65, 67, 68, 78, 79, 84, 108; see also Confrontation; and Singapore, 67, 68; and the Soviet Union, 17, 67-68, 78, 79; and the United Kingdom, 44, 109
Malenkov, G. M., 29
Malik, Adam, 68, 116
"Manhattan Affair," 51
Mao Tse-tung, 29, 32, 33
Maphalindo, 68, 116
Maritime Provinces, 31
Matsu, 43
Meo, 62
Midway, 127
Military Alliances, 91; Appendix I, Appendix II; see also deployment and individual countries
Military Expenditures, 91-92, 105, 106, 119, 121, 122; Appendix I, Appendix II; see individual countries
Mon Khmer, 77
Mongolia, 30, 31, 32
Montagnards, 61
Moslems, 77

N

National Liberation Front, 34
National liberation movements, 40 47
Nationalist China, see Republic of China
NATO (North Atlantic Treaty Organization), 49, 67, 112
Nehru, Jawaharal, 33, 72
Nepal, 15, 17, 31
Netherlands, 12, 35, 37, 44-45
New Guinea, 44, 45, 74, 108
New Zealand, see Australia and New Zealand
"No-First-Use" Agreement, 48
Nonproliferation, see Proliferation
North Atlantic Treaty Organization, see NATO
North Korea, 1, 30, 31, 33-35, 41-42, 51, 54, 56, 57, 59, 77, 78, 79, 82-84 passim, 87, 109; Appendix III; and ACD: 34, 48-49, 57; and Communist China, 33, 40, 40, 41, 51, 57; and the Soviet Union, 33, 41; and the United States, 5, 33, 42
North Vietnam, 1, 30, 34, 42, 44, 51, 59-65 passim, 77, 78, 82-84 passim, 87, 109, 117, 118; Appendix III; and ACD: 48, 49; and Communist China, 34, 35, 40, 42, 65; and the Soviet Union, 34, 35, 42, 49; and the United States, 5, 34
Northeast Frontier Agency, 71
Nuclear Blackmail, 34, 49, 111, 112
Nuclear Free Zones, 47-49 passim, 56, 60, 73, 81, 105, 106, 121, 122, 127; Appendix I, Appendix II; see individual countries
Nuclear Test Ban Treaty (1963), 3, 11, 16, 34, 46-49 passim, 55, 57, 59, 65, 66, 69, 123; Appendix I
Nuclear Weapons, 3, 5, 6, 7, 11

12, 15, 16, 20, 81, 90, 105, 106, 110-113, 114, 121, 122, 124; Appendix I, Appendix II; see individual countries, proliferation, nuclear free zones

O

Okinawa, 1, 55, 56
Outer Space, 81-82, 105, 106, 114, 120, 121, 122, 124; Appendix I, Appendix II; see individual countries

P

Pakhtoonistan, 73
Pakistan, 1, 19, 22-26 passim, 58, 72-73, 77-81 passim, 109, 114, 116, 123; Appendix III; and ACD (general): 73, 76-103 passim, 104-122 passim, 108; and ACD (specific aspects): Appendix I, Appendix II; armed forces, 90-91 passim, 122; chemical, biological, and radiological weapons, 81, 122; control organization, 96-97 passim; conventional weapons, 86-90 passim, 122; delivery systems, 81, 122; deployment, 90-91 passim, 122; heavy offensive weapons, 82-90 passim, 122; inspection and verification, 96-99 passim; international police force, 99-101, passim; military expenditures, 91-92 passim, 122; nuclear free zones, 81, 122; nuclear weapons, 81, 112, 122; outer space 81; previous ACD proposals, 15; sanctions, 82, 101-103 passim; sequence of ACD, 92-96 passim; violations of ACD, 101-103 passim; and Communist China, 25, 71, 78-80 passim; and India, 70-71, 72-73, 78, 80, 83-85 passim, 104, 108-109, 113; see also Kashmir ; and the Soviet Union, 73, 79, 80, 109; and the United Nations, 71, 73; and the United States, 73, 109
Panch Shila, see Five Principles of Peaceful Coexistence
Partial Nuclear Test-Ban Treaty, see Nuclear Test Ban Treaty
People's Republic of China, see Communist China
Philippines, 1, 19, 22-24 passim, 38, 39, 59, 60, 61, 69, 77-81 passim, 109, 115, 116, 117; Appendix III; and ACD (general): 13, 70, 76-103 passim, 104-122 passim; and ACD (specific aspects): Appendix I, Appendix II; armed forces, 90-91 passim, 122; chemical, biological, and radiological weapons, 81, 122; control organization, 96-97 passim; conventional weapons, 86-90 passim, 122; delivery systems, 81, 122; deployment, 90-91 passim, 122; heavy offensive weapons, 82-90 passim, 122; inspection and verification, 96-99 passim; international police force, 99-101 passim; military expenditures, 91-92 passim, 122; nuclear free zones 81, 122; nuclear weapons, 81, 122; previous ACD proposals, 15; sanctions, 82, 101-103 passim; sequence of ACD, 92-96 passim; violations of ACD, 101-103 passim; and Communist China, 69, 78, 79; and the United Nations, 70; and the United States, 43, 69, 70, 85, 86
Phu Quoc, 61
Proliferation, 16, 47, 48, 55, 57, 59, 67, 72, 81, 110-113, 118, 124, 125-126; see also nuclear weapons and individual countries
Proposals, see Arms Control and Disarmament: previous proposals, suggested proposals, as well as individual countries
Punjabis, 72

Q

Quemoy, 43, 59

R

Rann of Kutch, 108

Regional Attitudinal Matrix, 81, 76-103 passim, 119, 130; Appendix II.

Regional Cooperation, 6, 104, 107, 114-116, 119, 120, 124, 127-130; see also informal discussions, joint defense and mutual aid arrangements, joint technical, scientific, and economic exchanges and programs, and regional police force

Regional Police Force, 115-116, 124, 128, 131

Regional Powers, defined, 1; 18-27, 53-75; Appendix III; and ACD: 12-16, 76-103, 104-122; Appendix I, II; see individual countries

Regional Tension Chart, 74; Appendix III

Republic of China, 19, 20, 22, 23, 26, 32, 44, 54, 55, 58-60, 66, 69, 77-81 passim, 81, 85, 107, 108, 114, 115, 116; Appendix III; and ACD (general): 12, 13, 58, 59-60, 76-103 passim, 104-122 passim; and ACD (specific aspects): Appendix I, Appendix II; armed forces, 60, 90-91 passim, 122; chemical, biological, and radiological weapons, 81, 122; control organization, 96-97 passim; conventional weapons, 60, 86-90 passim, 122; delivery systems, 81, 122; deployment, 90-91 passim, 122; heavy offensive weapons, 82-90 passim, 122; inspection and verification, 96-99 passim; international police force, 99-101 passim; military expenditures, 91-92 passim, 122; nuclear free zone 81, 122; nuclear weapons, 59, 60, 81, 122; outer space, 81; sanctions, 82, 101-103 passim; sequence of ACD, 92-96 passim; violations of ACD, 101-103 passim; and Communist China, 31, 32, 43, 51, 58-60 passim, 78, 102; and the Soviet Union, 59; and the United States, 43, 59, 60, 109

Republic of South Korea, 1, 19-23 passim, 26, 37, 41, 42, 44, 54, 56-58, 60, 77-81 passim, 111, 114, 115, 116, 117; Appendix III; and ACD (general): 57-58, 79, 76-103 passim, 104-122 passim; and ACD (specific aspects): Appendix I, Appendix II; armed forces, 90-91 passim, 122; chemical, biological, and radiological weapons, 81, 122; control organization, 96-97 passim; conventional weapons, 86-90 passim, 122; delivery systems, 81, 122; deployment, 90-91 passim, 122; heavy offensive weapons, 82-90 passim, 122; inspection and verification, 96-99 passim; international police force, 99-101 passim; military expenditures, 91-92 passim, 122; nuclear free zones 81, 122; nuclear weapons, 81, 122; outer space 81; sanctions 82, 101-103 passim; sequence of ACD, 92-96 passim; violations of ACD, 101-103 passim; and Communist China, 37, 57, 78, 79; and the Soviet Union, 56, 57, 79, 109; and the United Nations, 58; and the United States, 41, 43, 57, 109

Rhee, Syngman, 56

Rice Institute of the Philippines, 116

Russia, see Soviet Union

Russian Turkestan, 31

Ryukyu Islands, 31

S

Sabah, 67, 69

Sanctions, 82, 101-103; Appendix I, Appendix II; see individual countries

Sangkum Reastr Niyum (People's Socialist Community), 63

Sato Eisaku, 54

Sea of Okhotsk, 54

SEACDT (Southeast Asia Collective Defense Treaty), 43

SEATO (Southeast Asia Treaty Organization), 5, 31, 37, 43-45 passim, 65, 70, 104, 109, 117

Sequence of ACD, 92-96; Appendix

I, Appendix II; see individual countries
Shastri, Lal Bahadur, 71
Shikotan, 54
Siberia, 30, 31
Sihanouk, Norodom, 61-65 passim
Sikkim, 31
Singapore, 1, 37, 38, 44, 67, 68, 75, 108, 109, 116; see also Malaysia
Sinkiang, 31
Sino-Indian Border Dispute, 25, 70, 71; see also India and Communist China
Sino-Soviet Conflict, 5, 32, 33, 34, 35, 42, 47, 109; see also Communist China and the Soviet Union
South Asia, 24, 25, 26, 30, 53, 70-73, 77; see also individual countries
South Korea, see Republic of Korea
South Vietnam, 1, 19-26 passim, 34, 44, 59, 60-62, 63-65 passim, 77-81 passim, 84, 86, 107-109 passim, 114, 116, 123; Appendix III; and ACD (general): 62, 76-103 passim, 104-122 passim; and ACD (specific aspects): Appendix I, Appendix II; armed forces, 90-91 passim, 122; chemical, biological, and radiological weapons, 81, 122; control organization, 96-97 passim; conventional weapons, 86-90 passim, 122; delivery systems, 81, 122; deployment, 90-91 passim, 122; heavy offensive weapons, 82-90 passim, 122; inspection and unification, 96-99 passim; international police force, 99-101, passim; military expenditures, 91-92 passim, 122; nuclear free zones, 81, 122; nuclear weapons, 81, 122; outer space, 81; sanctions, 82, 101-103 passim; sequence of ACD, 92-96 passim; violations of ACD, 101-103 passim; and Communist China, 61, 78, 79; and the Soviet Union, 61; and the United Nations, 64; and the United States, 43, 44, 61-62
Southeast Asia, 24, 25-26, 30, 31, 36-39 passim, 43-45 passim, 53, 60-70, 74; see also individual countries
Southwest Pacific, 25, 26, 53, 74; see individual countries
Soviet Union, 1, 17, 19, 28-32 passim, 37-40 passim; 43, 44, 47, 50, 51, 68, 98, 111-113 passim, 119; Appendix III; and ACD (general): 2, 4, 12, 45-46, 117-118; and ACD (specific aspects): Appendix I; control organization, 12; conventional weapons, 46; nuclear test ban treaty, 46, 47; nuclear weapons 13, 14, 46, 47; previous ACD proposals, 11-16 passim, 67; and proliferation 110-113, 118, 124, 125-126; and the extraregional powers, Communist China, 32-35 passim, 42, 47, 109, 118; See also Sino-Soviet Conflict ; North Korea 33, 41; North Vietnam, 34, 35, 42, 49; the United States, 2, 3, 5, 10, 11, 109, 111, 120; and the regional powers, 36, 38; Appendix III, India, 17, 70, 117, 118; Indonesia, 69, 118; Japan, 53, 54, 56, 79, 104, 109, 111; Malaysia, 68, 69; Pakistan, 73, 79, 80, 109; Republic of China, 59; Republic of Korea, 56, 57, 79, 109; South Vietnam, 61; Thailand, 30, 66
Spain, 28
Suggested ACD measures, 115, 110-131 passim
Stalin, Josef, 29, 38, 118
Sukarno, 45, 67-69 passim
Sweden, 58

T

Taiwan, see Republic of China
Taiwan Strait, 59, 113
Tamil, 70, 71
Tashkent Agreement, 71, 78, 109; see also India and Pakistan
Test Groupings, 77-81, 82-103 passim

Thailand, 1, 12, 19, 24-26 passim, 38, 44, 59, 60, 63-68 passim, 77-81 passim, 84, 86, 108, 109, 114-117 passim, 128; Appendix III; and ACD (general): 66, 76-103 passim, 104-122, passim, and ACD (specific aspects): Appendix I; Appendix II; armed forces, 90-91 passim, 122; chemical, biological, and radiological weapons, 81, 122; control organization, 96-97 passim; conventional weapons, 66, 86-90 passim, 122; delivery systems, 81, 122; deployment, 90-91 passim, 122; heavy offensive weapons, 66, 82-90 passim, 122; inspection and verification, 96-99 passim; international police force, 99-101 passim; military expenditures, 91-92 passim, 122; outer space, 81; nuclear free zones, 81, 122; nuclear weapons, 66, 81, 122; previous ACD proposals, 15; sanctions, 82, 101-103 passim; sequence of ACD, 92-96 passim; violations of ACD, 101-103 passim; and Communist China, 31, 65, 78, 79; and the Soviet Union, 30, 66; and the United Nations, 66; and the United States, 43, 65

Thanom Kittikhachorn, 75

Thanat Khoman, 116

Tibet, 31, 41

Trade, 7, 18, 21, 22, 23, 24, 37, 42, 44, 58, 59

Trade and Aid, 39

"Two Chinas," 54, 59

Truman, Harry S., 43

U

United Kingdom, 12, 25, 35, 37, 44, 109

United Nations, 9, 14, 44, 56-58 passim, 64, 66, 67, 71, 73, 107, 112, 128; and ACD: 5, 14, 16, 45, 55, 57, 58, 64, 66, 67, 116, 117; and the Eighteen Nation Disarmament Conference (ENDC): 14, 16, 58, 67, 110, 112

United States, 1, 2, 17, 26, 28, 29, 47, 50, 51, 80, 84, 91, 105, 107-109 passim, 113, 117, 120; Appendix III; and ACD (general): 2, 3, 9-10, 13, 46, 49-50, 57, 60, 105, 116, 124-131; and ACD (specific aspects): Appendix I; control organization, 12; conventional weapons, 50; inspection and verification, 46, 50; "no-first-use" agreement, 48; nuclear weapons, 50, 56; previous proposals, 11-16 passim; proliferation, 110-113, 118, 124, 125-126; and suggested ACD measures, 115, 117, 120, 124-131; and the extraregional powers: 5; Communist China, 5, 10, 109; North Korea, 5, 33, 42; North Vietnam, 5, 34; the Soviet Union, 2, 3, 5, 10, 11, 109, 111, 120; and the regional powers: 5, 23, 25, 30, 35-37, 42-44; Appendix III; Australia and New Zealand, 43, 73, 74; Burma, 43; Cambodia, 43, 64, 66, 79, 109; India, 109, 112; Indonesia, 43, 68, 69, 79; Japan, 53-56 passim, 93, 109, 111; Laos, 43, Pakistan, 73, 109; Philippines, 43, 69, 70, 85, 86; Republic of China, 43, 59, 60, 109; Republic of Korea, 41, 43, 57, 109; South Vietnam, 43, 44, 61-62; Thailand, 43, 65

V

Viet Cong, 60-63 passim, 123

Viet Minh, 43, 107

Vietnam, 31, 32, 39, 43, 44, 50, 54, 57, 63, 66; see also North Vietnam and South Vietnam

Violations of ACD, 101-103, 119; Appendix I; Appendix II

Voluntary Declarations, 113-114, 119, 124, 126-127, 131

W

Wake Island, 127

"Wars of national liberation," 38, 63, 66

Warsaw Meetings, 43, 48
Warsaw Treaty Organization, 49, 67
West Germany, 34
Western Europe, 30, 51
Western New Guinea, see New Guinea
World Congress for General Disarmament and Peace, 48

Y

Yalu River, 57
Yao, 62